The Rise of the Seleukid Empire (323–223 BC)

The Rise of the Seleukid Empire (323–223 BC)

Seleukos I to Seleukos III

John D. Grainger

Pen & Sword
MILITARY

First published in Great Britain in 2014
and reprinted in this format in 2016 by
PEN & SWORD HISTORY
An imprint of
Pen & Sword Books Ltd
47 Church Street
Barnsley, South Yorkshire
S70 2AS

ISBN 978 1 78303 053 8

A CIP catalogue record for this book is
available from the British Library

Typeset in Ehrhardt by
Mac Style, Bridlington, East Yorkshire

Printed and bound in England
By CPI Group (UK) Ltd, Croydon, CR0 4YY

Pen & Sword Books Ltd incorporates the Imprints of Aviation, Atlas,
Family History, Fiction, Maritime, Military, Discovery, Politics, History,
Archaeology, Select, Wharncliffe Local History, Wharncliffe True Crime,
Military Classics, Wharncliffe Transport, Leo Cooper, The Praetorian Press,
Remember When, Seaforth Publishing and Frontline Publishing.

For a complete list of Pen & Sword titles please contact
PEN & SWORD BOOKS LIMITED
47 Church Street, Barnsley, South Yorkshire, S70 2AS, England
E-mail: enquiries@pen-and-sword.co.uk
Website: www.pen-and-sword.co.uk

Contents

List of Maps and Tables

Maps

1. The Growth of Seleukos' Kingdom.
2. Syria and Mesopotamia.
3. Asia Minor c.275.

Tables

A. The Seleukid Dynasty.
B. The Family of Akhaios.

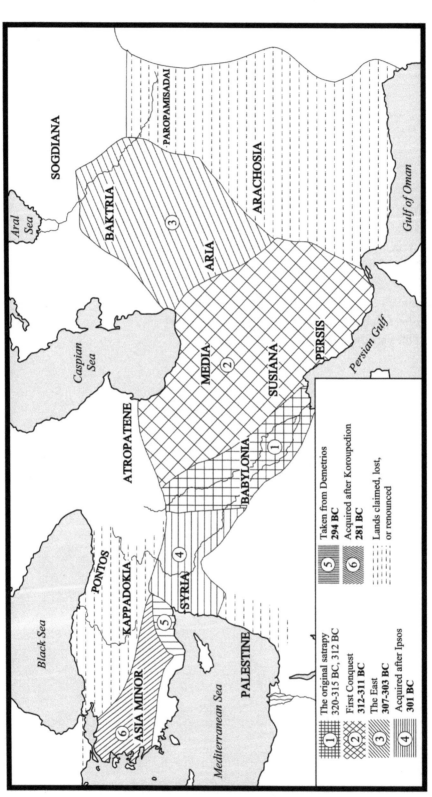

Map 1: The Growth of Seleukos' Kingdom.

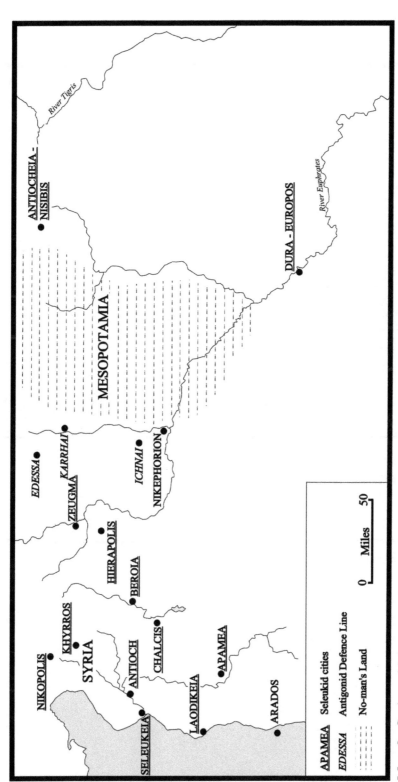

Map 2: Syria and Mesopotamia.

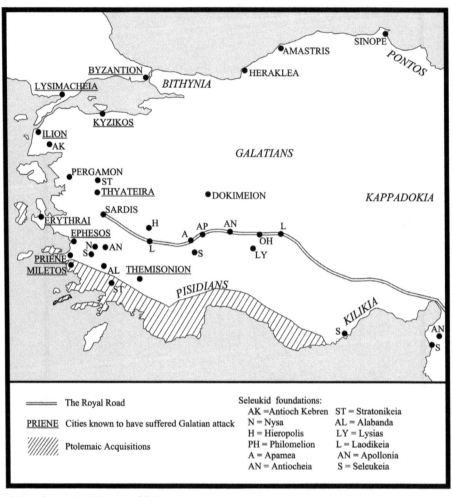

Map 3: Asia Minor c.275.

The Royal Road

PRIENE Cities known to have suffered Galatian attack

Ptolemaic Acquisitions

Seleukid foundations:
AK = Antioch Kebren   ST = Stratonikeia
N = Nysa   AL = Alabanda
H = Hieropolis   LY = Lysias
PH = Philomelion   L = Laodikeia
A = Apamea   AN = Apollonia
AN = Antiocheia   S = Seleukeia

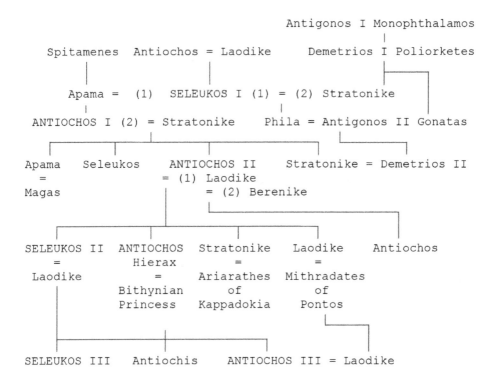

Seleukid Kings are in Capitals.

Table A: The Seleukid Dynasty

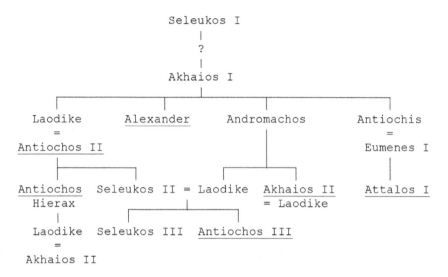

Kings and Governors in Asia Minor Underlined.

Table B: The family of Akhaios

Introduction

The Seleukid kingdom, actually an empire, was the largest state in the ancient world for a century and a half. In that time it had more than its fair share of vicissitudes. It was built up from fragments of the empire of Alexander the Great by one man over a period of thirty years. In the next two centuries (for it lasted two generations beyond its reduction to minor power status), it collapsed twice. From the first collapse it recovered, though detached sections remained independent; the second collapse reduced it to little more than Syria. It was in that final agonizing stage that Rome met it, with the consequence that ever after the kings have been referred to as 'Syrian'. Among the Romans this was a derogatory term, and this has helped reduce the reputation of the kings and that kingdom.

Another reason for the comparative neglect of the kingdom is the general inadequacy of the historical sources, which is a recurrent refrain in this account. This is partly the result of the geography of the state, since beyond the eastern boundary of the later Roman Empire the ancient historians showed little interest, and the alternatives to their written accounts – archaeology and inscriptions – have not been very productive. Among those written accounts there is not one which takes the kingdom, or any of the kings, as a subject. The story must therefore be pieced together from fragments and later allusions.

The geographical range of the kings, however, was much greater than simply Syria, even if Syria was a crucial part of the kingdom. At its greatest the empire abutted on India in the east and reached into the southeastern part of Europe in the west. It existed because, as its name implies, it was ruled by kings descended from the founder, Seleukos I Nikator, and its collapses coincided with genetic failures of the royal family. The male representatives of the dynasty were twice reduced to one man only. In other words, the central element in the empire was the royal family, everything operated through and around the kings, and when the dynasty finally failed, so did the empire. Ancient accounts of the kingdom are non-existent, and perhaps never did exist. Modern accounts are almost as few. Two comprehensive treatments, one in French and one in English, date from the first part of the twentieth century, and a revisionist examination from 1993.[1] The early ones are now out of date, and the revisionist one is not a straightforward history. Otherwise the kingdom is treated in a discontinuous fashion by all the general histories of the Hellenistic period, of which only two are in any way detailed.[2]

This is the first in a set of three books, each dealing with a section of the empire's history. The first will cover the origin of the kingdom until its first serious breakdown; the second, largely because the sources are much better than for the other parts, deals only with the reign of Antiochos III (222–187 BC), who, after the founder, was the most capable and longest ruling of the kings; the third volume covers the empire's last century, as it fell into collapse, fragmentation, and futility.

The legacy of its existence was, however, by no means a matter of futility. When Seleukos built his kingdom it was poor, even the richest areas were failing, having been subject to the neglect of previous rulers for several centuries and then seriously damaged by twenty years of the military campaigns by Alexander and his combative successors, a practice which involved looting, heavy taxation, and destruction. This changed during the rule of these kings so that when Rome took over the last Syrian fragment it found it had acquired perhaps the most enterprising, urbanized region in the Mediterranean area. This was the true legacy of the Seleukid kingdom, a set of wealthy and enterprising cities, and a vigorous peasantry. They remained rich and enterprising until destroyed in the Crusader Wars a thousand years later.

Further, the kingdom, as it declined, gave birth to a long series of other states, from Baktria and the Greek kingdoms in India to the Pergamene Attalid kingdom in Asia Minor and the curious Judaean kingdom of the Maccabees. All of these inherited the ethos and the government system of the Seleukids, whose inheritance, therefore, continued to operate throughout the Middle East and Central Asia as long as it did in Syria. These fragments of the empire will also be part of the story.

Chapter One

The Collapse of Alexander's Empire

The empire conquered with such speed by Alexander the Great in his campaigns against the empire of the Akhaimenid Great King, crumbled into fragments almost as soon as he was dead. In part this was due to his premature death at the age of 32, before he had time to devise a proper administrative system for his conquests. But it seems unlikely that he would have bothered to do that even if he had lived. As he lay dying he was still planning an expedition to sail round Arabia to get to Egypt. He must have known that a prolonged absence on such an expedition would produce rebellions and corruption and oppression in the empire, for this is what had already happened while he was marching through the desert from India.

Such administration as existed was a relic of the system of the Akhaimenids, with aristocratic Macedonians largely, but not completely, replacing aristocratic Persians as satraps, the governors of huge provinces. These men had their own armed forces, since there was a good deal of local opposition to the Macedonians, not to mention continuing banditry in the mountainous regions. This meant that the satraps were largely independent and could, and often did, refuse to pay any attention to instructions from the king. On his return from India, Alexander had dealt with some of the worst cases by execution, but this would not be much of a threat when he was off a-voyaging and a-conquering elsewhere. (And after reaching Egypt he planned expeditions throughout the Mediterranean, which would take several years at the minimum.)[1]

This was no way to run an empire, as was rapidly shown when he, the one man who had the charisma and authority to extract obedience from the satraps, died. Two main results followed; there were serious rebellions in Baktria and in Greece, and the military men in Babylon began quarrelling over their new positions and powers almost at once. The two problems partly neutralized each other, for the rebellions were sufficiently serious to compel the men in Babylon to mute their rivalries for a time. Nevertheless, more than one of them struck out for himself almost as soon as Alexander had died.

The problem of the succession to Alexander as king was also a delaying factor, and it aggravated the situation in Babylon as well. Alexander's half-brother Philip Arrhidaios was judged mentally unfit to rule, and one of his widows, Roxane, was pregnant. Whatever child she produced there could obviously be no effective king for at least the next twenty years, so a regency was required. At first Perdikkas, the senior commander in Babylon, took the position, claiming to have been in effect appointed by Alexander when he was dying, but he had competitors; in Macedon an even more senior man, Antipater, had ruled the home kingdom while Alexander was on campaign, and in Kilikia, marching slowly towards Macedon with an army of veteran soldiers who were to be discharged, there was Krateros, who was also supposed to take over from Antipater in Macedon, a prospective confrontation he apparently did not relish. The reaction of these men to what amounted to Perdikkas' *coup* in Babylon would not be known for some time.

Seleukos son of Antiochos was one of the contenders among the Macedonian commanders at Babylon. He had emerged in the latter part of Alexander's career of conquest as a senior commander, though with little in the way of personal distinction to mark him out from the rest. He was one of a group of Alexander's contemporaries who were clearly being promoted by the king to free him from the influence and caution of the older men he had inherited from his father – such as Antipater. In the crisis at Babylon Seleukos supported Perdikkas, who was soon challenged by the commander of the infantry, Meleager. This pushed Perdikkas into accepting both Philip and Roxane's child, if it was a boy, to share the kingship. Meleager and his followers – 'mutineers' to those who continued in charge – were soon killed, but the joint kingship continued. Perdikkas organized a new distribution of offices, in which Seleukos became his second-in-command.[2]

It is notorious that more than one man decided at this point that it would be more profitable to secure control of a rich province than to continue as a subordinate in the imperial administration. Ptolemy, by choosing to go to Egypt, is the best known, but others did the same, notably Peithon in Media, who defeated the Greek rebellion there. Neither Antipater nor Antigonos (in Asia Minor) could be moved at Perdikkas' word, so they remained where they were. Krateros, still in Kilikia, was made joint regent with Perdikkas, but since Perdikkas kept control of the kings' persons, Krateros' position was largely honorary, though he had the loyalty of the troops he commanded.

Perdikkas was soon suspected by his fellows of aiming to seize the kingship, a suspicion fuelled by his apparent intention of marrying Alexander's sister

Kleopatra. This brought all the rest out against him. The Greek wars – in Greece and Baktria – were won, but Perdikkas himself had done little in those struggles. He turned to deal with Ptolemy who had proved unexpectedly active in Egypt, eliminating the former administration in his own favour, annexing Cyrenaica, and seizing control of the great catafalque carrying Alexander's body which was moving infinitely slowly towards Macedon.[3] He took it instead to Egypt where eventually it was installed, supposedly preserved, in a tomb in Alexandria. This was a direct challenge to Perdikkas' authority, and he came south through Syria with the imperial army to deal with Ptolemy.

This was a very unpopular move. It was not that Ptolemy himself was popular among his fellows, but this was a fight between elements of Alexander's own army, Macedonians against Macedonians, and none of the soldiers wanted that. Ptolemy successfully played on their feelings, which no doubt he shared, and when Perdikkas organized a crossing of the river which failed with substantial casualties, and more men were killed by crocodiles, Perdikkas' officers turned on him. One of those who literally wielded the knife was Seleukos.[4]

This stopped the invasion of Egypt; Ptolemy quickly brought supplies of food across the river for the invaders, and the army, grumbling at a lack of pay, marched back into Syria. At a meeting of army and commanders at a Persian resort called Triparadeisos in middle Syria, Seleukos emerged as one of the key players. Antipater arrived from Macedon, and was immediately chosen as the new regent. When trouble over the lack of pay developed it was Seleukos, along with Antigonos, the satrap of Phrygia, who calmed everything down.[5] This was the first and last time these two men co-operated.

Antipater distributed posts again. Several of the major commanders, including Krateros, had been killed in the recent fighting, and others had earned rewards. There was still a party of former supporters of Perdikkas, led by Alexander's Greek secretary Eumenes, to be suppressed; since they were mainly in Asia Minor, Antigonos was given the task of doing this, with a substantial part of the army. Ptolemy could not be shifted from Egypt, and anyway Antipater, 80 years old, probably did not have the will or the energy to tackle him. Seleukos had now appreciated that power in the future lay not in being part of the imperial government, which was in the feeble hands of Antipater, if it existed at all, but in controlling a province. He was made satrap of Babylonia, quite probably his own choice. After Egypt, this was the richest province of all.[6]

This war had winnowed out the competing generals down to half a dozen of real importance. Apart from Ptolemy, Antigonos, and Seleukos, there were Peithon in Media, Peukestas in Persis, and Eumenes. By now Eumenes was outlawed, but he was both talented and ingenious. He was for the present in interior Asia Minor. Antipater lived another year, and when he died his son Kassander seized control of Macedon itself. So from 319 there were several men who were in effect independent lords of major parts of the empire, and several more ruled smaller sections. There was no one man with empire-wide authority. It looked as though the empire was in the process of disintegration. Its reconstitution was a standing challenge and temptation to all these men, and was the main theme of the events of the next half-century.

Antigonos' task of eliminating Eumenes turned out to be very difficult. Eumenes proved to be adept at persuading Alexander's old soldiers (Macedonians and Greeks) to support him, though it was never easy. (He set up a throne in the royal tent, and had held Councils of War there, with Alexander's spirit presiding from the empty throne.)[7] Antigonos in turn proved to be an outstanding military commander. He had shown this in a difficult series of campaigns inside Asia Minor while Alexander was conquering in the east, but it seems that few had really noticed. One who had was Antipater. This made him suspicious of Antigonos' intentions, and he had placed Kassander at Antigonos' elbow to assist and watch him. Antigonos was a man of the same generation as Antipater, but he had not been part of the great adventure as far as India; he was therefore something of a mystery to those who had campaigned with Alexander; he was careful to keep his ambition within bounds for several years, partly because he had only a small armed force under his control.[8]

Antigonos used the campaign against Eumenes to build up his armed strength, and to eliminate or recruit possible competitors. In the process his ambition expanded. The conflict, starting in Kappadokia, moved gradually south and east until the final battles were fought in Iran. The satraps of Kilikia, Syria, Mesopotamia, Babylonia, and Media, and the eastern regions, were successively faced with the need to make the choice between Eumenes and Antigonos. For most of them the choice was not actually difficult. Eumenes had been condemned as a rebel at the time of the Triparadeisos meeting, and Antigonos had been tasked with suppressing him by the Macedonian assembly of men under arms, the nearest thing to a legal legislative body there was by that time. So when Eumenes and his army – consisting of a substantial part of the old army of Alexander – arrived on their doorstep each of the satraps had to make the decision whom to support. In theory Eumenes' condemnation should have been decisive; in fact plenty of other considerations entered into the decision. Opposing Eumenes was dangerous. He had a substantial army, one greater than any of the forces commanded by any of the satraps. Defying him might well end a satrap's life or at least his career.

The Syrian satrap, Laomedon of Mitylene, had already been removed by Ptolemy, and it seems that no replacement had been appointed; no doubt Ptolemy made himself the new governor.[9] The land had been campaigned through at least twice since Alexander's brutal conquest, and Ptolemy was occupying much of it by the time Eumenes arrived. Ptolemy did not fight him, but neither did he join him. He was effectively declaring that the contest was none of his concern, and so was indicating his independence; this was the first concrete indication that the empire of Alexander might not survive intact. When Antigonos came into Syria in pursuit Eumenes moved off to the east. The satrap of Mesopotamia, Amphimachos, joined Eumenes, but in a sparsely populated region with few soldiers he probably had no choice. Eumenes moved further east and spent the winter in northern Babylonia. Antigonos, having established his own control of Kilikia and northern Syria, moved eastwards also, but then camped in Mesopotamia for the winter (of 317/316).[10]

The problem of the approaching armies had brought Seleukos in Babylonia and Peithon in Media together. Eumenes negotiated with both of them during the winter, but news arrived that the dowager queen Olympias, allied with Eumenes and with Polyperchon – the official regent, but politically powerless – had returned to Macedon. She there killed King Philip and his wife (his half sister Eurydike) and then murdered a hundred of their Macedonian supporters.[11] Although Eumenes had nothing to do with this atrocity he was inevitably tarred by it, and this perhaps tipped the balance in the negotiations in Babylonia, for neither Seleukos nor Peithon could join Eumenes after that. In the spring Eumenes, who was militarily stronger than both of them together, marched through Babylonia and into Susiana.

Seleukos' position in the negotiations had been a rather subtle one. Eumenes was campaigning as a champion of the kings (Philip III and Alexander IV), and had authority from Polyperchon to do so. This argument often worked, as it would in Iran in the next months. It clearly worked with his own army, whose core was the regiment of Argyraspides, the Silver Shields, commanded by Antigenes. These were royalists to a man and accepted, no doubt with a cynical grin, the play-acting of the royal tent and the empty throne. But the equally royalist meeting at Triparadeisos had condemned Eumenes; Seleukos had been at that meeting, as had Peithon, so when he was asked to give his support to Eumenes, Seleukos replied that he was as much a royalist as Eumenes, but that he could not accept orders from him.[12]

Seleukos could take his stand on the origin of his authority as satrap, for he had been appointed to the post by the conclave and assembly at Triparadeisos, where Eumenes had been condemned. Eumenes might argue that he had been forgiven – his authority from Polyperchon implied as much – but Seleukos' post was clearly earlier and more authoritative in its origin than anything Eumenes could demonstrate. Peithon could go even better, for his authority as satrap of Media antedated even the Triparadeisos meeting, not that this did him any good, for he had attempted to enforce his authority over other satraps in Iran only to be defeated by them. He held onto Media, but by joining Seleukos, he aligned his enemies with Seleukos' enemy, that is Eumenes. The confederate eastern satraps kept their army in being after defeating Peithon, and moved into Susiana, Antigenes' satrapy. Seleukos and Peithon may be allied, but they were weak militarily, yet they had to oppose Eumenes.[13] So the only way for Eumenes to get through Babylonia to Antigenes' satrapy, as Antigonos approached from the west, was by force.

Seleukos had to try to stop him, for Eumenes had no authority to move into Babylonia. The invading army was unable to get across the Tigris. Eumenes gathered boats, but Seleukos arrived at the crossing place with two triremes, which had originally been built for Alexander's intended Arabian campaign. Speaking from one of them, he tried, for a second time, to persuade Antigenes and the Silver Shields to depose Eumenes, but again failed. He then sailed upstream along a canal and broke a sluice to let the water out to flood Eumenes' camp. But by doing so Seleukos (as he must have realized) left the crossing unguarded, except for some cavalry. Eumenes now got his army across, using the boats he had collected. He had to go back for the baggage and the camp followers, which were more difficult to shift, and then began his own excavation to divert the waters.

There was a certain amount of fighting, but once Eumenes had secured the crossing with his boats, Seleukos was unable to stop him marching on. Some casualties had been incurred, but neither side lost many men. Seleukos had sent messengers to Antigonos, who was following on but clearly was not going to arrive soon. Seleukos offered Eumenes a truce, but Eumenes marched his army onwards without any further hindrance, into Susiana.

He was even able to march in three separate columns to facilitate gathering food. Seleukos was not strong enough to interfere.[14]

Eumenes managed to persuade the assembled eastern satraps to join him. He sent letters asserting his authority, derived from Polyperchon, but it was perhaps the fact that he and they were both opposed to Peithon which was the more persuasive argument. Refuelled by the treasure held at Antigenes' capital of Susa, and resupplied by the looted resources of Babylonia, Eumenes now commanded a very large army. But he had forced Seleukos and Peithon into supporting Antigonos, who soon arrived.

Antigonos followed in Eumenes' tracks into Susiana, by which time Eumenes had moved on into central Iran. Antigonos continued, leaving Seleukos to govern Susiana and to lay siege to Susa. Diodoros explains this as Antigonos appointing Seleukos as satrap in place of Antigenes, and ordering him to conduct the siege, but this is rather anticipating Antigonos' later conduct. Seleukos would have said that he was assisting the legitimate commander in his appointed task. He certainly added some of his own troops to Antigonos' army, and more were with him in Susiana. He did not, however, press on with the siege of Susa very vigorously, which gave him an excuse not to join Antigonos in the campaign against Eumenes.[15]

Seleukos' position with regard to Antigonos was exactly what it had been with regard to Eumenes. He based his authority as satrap in Babylonia on his appointment at Triparadeisos, and this was exactly the same as Antigonos' basis of authority. Antigonos, however, also claimed to hold a position as 'general over Asia', an appointment of Antipater's, and this was the basis for his command of the forces hunting Eumenes. There was clearly a contradiction involved. Presumably once Eumenes was removed, Antigonos' position as *strategos* should lapse, but it is clear that Antigonos had no intention of allowing this. During his anti-Eumenes campaign, therefore, it seems that Antigonos had decided that his over-arching position would become the foundation for a permanent position of supreme authority. Seleukos' behaviour in separating himself from Antigonos' campaign in Iran suggests that he already assumed that Antigonos was aiming for the empire.

Antigonos' new ambition became clear in the aftermath of the defeat of Eumenes. Having defeated the joint armies of the rebel and his supporters and allies, Antigonos enforced his authority on them all. Eumenes was executed, which was only to be expected, and for which Antigonos could claim full authority. Antigenes, who had stayed with Eumenes all through, was also executed, as were two or three others who had been conspicuously loyal to

Eumenes. On the other hand Xenophilos, who had guarded the treasure at Susa on Eumenes' behalf and who surrendered to Seleukos, probably once the news of Eumenes' defeat arrived, was sent to Antigonos (perhaps with Seleukos' safe-conduct), and was welcomed into Antigonos' circle; yet he had been conspicuously loyal, or perhaps obedient, to Eumenes.[16]

Soon Peithon, who had been Antigonos' ally in the fighting (much of which had taken place in his Median satrapy), was accused of plotting to undermine the loyalty of some of Antigonos' forces, though perhaps he simply wanted to recover control of his own men. He was enticed to headquarters, given a drumhead trial, and executed.[17] And yet two of the satraps who had opposed Antigonos, Tlepolemos of Karmania and Stasanor of Baktria, who also maintained their hostility even after Eumenes' death, were left alone, as was Oxyartes (Roxane's father) in the Paropamisadai, on the borders of India. Sibyrtios, the satrap of Arachosia, which, like the Paropamisadai, faced a newly independent India (the satraps left by Alexander had withdrawn or fled), was also left in place. He had quarrelled with Eumenes, so that he could be regarded as now on Antigonos' side, if with a stretch of the imagination. He was given a portion of the Silver Shields and told to use them up. Whether he did so is not known. It was clear in all this that Antigonos was simply not interested in the east, partly because he knew nothing of the region – he had not been part of Alexander's great expedition – and partly because none of the satraps had any real power. Their hostility he could ignore; and his dispositions were designed to prevent any further joint action they might contemplate.

In the main Iranian satrapies Antigonos was more decisive. Peithon of Media being dead, he had to be replaced. A Persian, Orontobates, was chosen. In addition, a Thessalian, Hippostratos, was made general of the Upper Satrapies. The 'Upper Satrapies' is a pleasantly vague term which might mean Media (as it later seems to have become), but was also applied to those satrapies to the east of Media – Parthia, Baktria, Arachosia, Persis. On the other hand, Hippostratos did not have a very large force – it is quoted as being 3,500 infantry, with the figure for cavalry missing from Diodoros' manuscript. This would perhaps be enough to threaten any of the individual satraps of the east, but not enough for Hippostratos to set off on a career of conquest.

As it happens, this arrangement collapsed almost at once. Partisans of the dead Peithon led by two Macedonians, Meleager and Menoitas, gathered a force and attacked the camp of Orontobates and Hippostratos, which was apparently carelessly guarded. Considerable casualties occurred, including Meleager; neither Orontobates nor Hippostratos is heard of again, so either they also died in the fighting, or were swiftly removed by Antigonos for their evident incompetence. The next satrap we hear of in Media is Nikanor, four years later, whose authority included the satrapy and the Upper Satrapies' generalship, a combination which became common later. He also commanded a much larger force than Hippostratos had. Antigonos had been compelled to rethink his intentions.[18] At Ekbatana, the Median capital, Antigonos collected a substantial treasure, originally part of the Akhaimenid hoard, then marched to Persepolis, the old Akhaimenid imperial capital, and collected another treasure. He was greeted and feasted there by the satrap Peukestas, whom he had probably already decided to remove from his post. Peukestas had been made satrap of Persis by Alexander himself, and had retained the position in the redistributions at Babylon and Triparadeisos; he was very popular locally; he had been the commander of the satraps' armies when they defeated Peithon; he had joined Eumenes and fought as a senior commander in his army. All these were very good reasons for Antigonos to suspect him. He promised him an even better situation and then removed him from the Persian satrapy, whereupon a Persian, whose name is given as Thespios, protested. Antigonos killed Thespios for his presumption; Peukestas' replacement was Asklepiodoros.[19]

Taking his accumulated load of treasure, Antigonos headed westwards towards Susa, and was met by Xenophilos on the way, who handed over the bigger treasure of Susa. Antigonos now had a hoard of 25,000 talents.[20] He also commanded a huge army. At the final battle with Eumenes each had commanded about 40,000 men; part of Eumenes' forces were returned to the eastern satrapies with their satraps in the settlement of affairs, some died, some fled, but some had been recruited into Antigonos' army. He must have had at least 50,000 men under his command on the march towards Babylon, his next staging post after Susa. At Susa he appointed a new satrap, a local man called Aspeisas, to the post.[21]

Seleukos had returned to Babylon well before Antigonos reached Susa. His policy toward Eumenes had been correct, insofar as the confused situation allowed, refusing assistance to the rebel but trying to protect his satrapy from too much damage. That he had hardly been successful was not material. Similarly he had been correct in his dealings with Antigonos, lending him troops, providing supplies, and supporting him in Susiana, thereby clearly recognizing his authority as 'general over Asia' in the contest with Eumenes. This had been all very well until Antigonos' victory, but then, with the defeat of Eumenes, Antigonos' activities and intentions had changed. By his execution of Macedonian commanders and satraps, and his arbitrary appointment of replacements, he had indicated that his aims and policies were now imperial. The killing of satraps in the war was one thing – his opponents, by joining with Eumenes, were certainly rebels – but killing or deposing them after the fighting was over indicated that Antigonos was arrogating to himself an authority others could not support. He might have had a good reason for killing Peithon, but Peukestas was the real test case, for he had been appointed by Alexander and re-appointed at the Babylon and Triparadeisos meetings. These deposed satraps had had to accept their treatment, and most were clearly reconciled to their demotion, but that did not mean that Antigonos had right on his side. The distribution of governing posts had been a collective decision of the chiefs of the army at the meetings at Babylon and Triparadeisos, and legally, if such a term could be used in the circumstances, the replacements, the depositions, the confirmations, should have been the responsibility of a new meeting.

Such a meeting was by now impracticable, but it was the nearest the Macedonians had for an imperial government until the king was of an age to rule. Until a new meeting the satraps themselves were the imperial governors. Antigonos had no right to appoint any of them, still less to kill or depose any of them. Yet he had done all these things. As he approached Babylon with his huge army and the enormous wealth he had collected, Seleukos was no doubt apprehensive.

The army was greeted with supplies and the chiefs with a feast. By this time it was several months since the death of Peithon, which was the event which really revealed Antigonos' new ambitions. Seleukos, suspicious from the first, had had long enough to understand the implications, but like every other satrap, he could not openly defy Antigonos in the face of his great army, though he could continue to rule his satrapy. It is evident that the two men were wary of each other from the time Antigonos arrived, with Antigonos watching to see that Seleukos was properly submissive, and Seleukos alert to discover Antigonos' actual intentions and to resist encroachments on his satrapal authority.

The crisis emerged into the open when Seleukos punished 'one of the governors (*hegemon*)' while Antigonos was present. Presumably Seleukos was the erring man's superior, that is, the man was the governor of a section to Babylonia, and had presumably been appointed by Seleukos; being on his best behaviour, Seleukos was highly unlikely to presume to exercise authority outside his own sphere. But Antigonos objected that he should have been consulted over the punishment, basing himself on his authority as 'general over Asia'. That is, he was deliberately claiming a superior legal authority over Seleukos. And to reinforce the point he demanded that Seleukos render an account of the revenues he had collected from his satrapy, and of his possessions. Anyone who has been subject to an audit knows full well that accountants are very ingenious in discovering items which they can claim to be wrong, exaggerated, or otherwise putting one at fault; Antigonos' auditors would have no difficulty in convicting Seleukos of something or other; but that, of course, was not the issue.

The two men had a public row, one which continued over several days, no doubt as Seleukos failed to produce his accounts, and Antigonos ever more vehemently insisted. Antigonos, of course, was in almost as difficult a situation as Seleukos. It was well known that they had co-operated at Triparadeisos, and that Seleukos had supported the expedition against Eumenes, both in Babylonia and in Susiana. Killing Seleukos, as he had Peithon, was not a real option for Antigonos, and deposing him, as he had Peukestas, was not going to happen since Seleukos was adamant that he had the legal authority to rule the satrapy, and that Antigonos did not have the right to impose himself as his superior as he had claimed. Seleukos therefore would not go quietly. But as the two men argued, Seleukos realized that the fate of Peithon was indeed a possibility – Antigonos did not need to do the killing personally, he had plenty of thugs under his command who would do the job.

Seleukos fled. His flight was clearly arranged in advance, for he went off with a troop of fifty horsemen, who must have been organized and selected before he left. (His family is not mentioned, but it is highly likely he took his wife and children with him; Antigonos was not to be trusted.) Antigonos is said to have been pleased at first, for Seleukos could be branded a deserter. On second thoughts, by an interpretation proposed, it is claimed, by some Chaldaean astrologers, he changed his mind and sent men in pursuit. (It hardly needed astrology to point out the dangers of Seleukos making loud and public accusations when he was free to do so.) The pursuers failed to capture the fleeing party. Indeed, Seleukos received help from the satrap of Mesopotamia, Blitor, a man presumably left in charge by Antigonos after Eumenes had carried off Amphimachos with him. Blitor therefore got the blame.

Seleukos clearly moved fast, and no doubt carefully concealed from Blitor just what had happened at Babylon. The dispute, after all, had been largely private, conducted between the two men inside the palace. Rumours will have spread among the palace servants and the soldiers, but clearly they had not reached Mesopotamia. Seleukos also had a destination in mind from the beginning. In fact there were only two places he could go. One was Macedon, where Kassander had gained power, but to reach it he would need to ride all the way through Antigonos' territory as far as the Aegean, and not all Antigonos' men would be quite so easily gulled as Blitor. The other possibility was to go to Egypt, where Ptolemy had entrenched himself as effectively independent, and had seized control of much of Syria. It was to the closer Egypt, therefore, by way of Syria, that Seleukos went.[22]

Chapter Two

Ptolemy's Commander

Seleukos, the man who had been driven from his Babylonian satrapy by
Antigonos in 315 – or had deserted his post, as Antigonos would have
said – had been born in Macedon about the same time as Alexander
the Great, in the mid-350s. (This near-coincidence was later developed
into an actual coincidence by his flatterers.)[1] His father was Antiochos, his
mother Laodike, which names, along with his own, recur constantly among
his descendants. His father was a locally prominent man, described in one
source as one of Philip II's generals, who was well enough connected that he
could get his son in post as a page at the royal court under Philip II.[2] This
was the key to his later advance under Alexander, for it was from among their
friends and schoolmates and acquaintances that Macedonian kings selected
their councillors, their commanders, and their envoys – all interchangeable
categories, with no noticeable specialization.

Seleukos' fellow pages included Ptolemy, Lysimachos, and many others,
though neither Kassander nor his later enemy Demetrios son of Antigonos
were in that group, being born too late; Antigonos himself was one of Philip's
generation. Seleukos and the others campaigned with Alexander all through
Asia to India, fought in the great battles at Issos and Gaugamela, in the
hideous campaigns in Central Asia and India, and the survivors emerged to
witness the king's useless, near self-inflicted, death at Babylon in June 323.
This was surely a moment which induced in some of them a reflection that
if the king, with the very best medical attention, could die still so young,
then mortality stalked all of them. As it happened, Seleukos, Ptolemy and
Lysimachos all lived into their eighties, as did Antigonos, and even then
three of these men died in battle or were murdered; it was Kassander and
Demetrios who died at much younger ages, the first of disease, the second
perhaps of drink. That is, those who survived the great campaigns, and the
Babylonian climate, were tough.

Until his well-planned and later publicized escape from Antigonos'
clutches, one of the most notable things about Seleukos, apart from his
political actions, had been that he had retained his Persian wife. Alexander

had compelled his commanders to participate in a bizarre mass marriage ceremony at Susa in 324, in which each man was married to a selected Persian lady of noble birth. Neither the bridegroom nor the bride had any choice in the matter, but the real feelings, of the men at least, on this were shown as soon as Alexander had died, when one and all cast off their new wives – except, it is said, Seleukos. How far this mass repudiation really was universal is not known, but Seleukos became well known as the one man who did not do so.

His wife was Apama, who was a daughter of Spitamenes, Alexander's most determined enemy in his central Asian war. In view of his later achievements maintaining this marriage might be seen as constructive foresight, but in 323, when all around him were casting off their wives and blaming it on Alexander, he cannot have anticipated the marriage being as useful to him as it may have turned out to be. So we must assume affection, or perhaps a feeling on Seleukos' part of obligation.

There were at least two sons born of the marriage, Antiochos (named for his grandfather), who was adult enough to command part of his father's army in 301 and so was born soon after the marriage, and Akhaios. The existence of this second son is problematic, but the arguments of those in favour seem to be just a little better than those against. A very late and very unreliable source claims they also had two daughters, but there is no other evidence of this, nor any trace of their marriages.[3] Such daughters were valuable as political pieces, and a record of them might therefore be expected. It is reasonable, given the circumstances, to assume that Apama and the children (however many there were) were in the party which fled from Babylon in 315. They all ended up as Ptolemy's guests in Egypt.

Seleukos' arrival in Egypt brought the news of Antigonos' activities in Iran to Ptolemy for the first time. News moved slowly, and Antigonos will not have wanted his successes and his brutalities to spread to potential enemies too quickly, and from Iran he had surely identified Ptolemy as one of his more difficult potential opponents. Seleukos, for example, did not fully realize until almost too late that Antigonos was determined to dominate or remove him, and he had been close to the action in the east during the previous year. If Seleukos did not understand the change in Antigonos' intentions until they came face-to-face, none of the western satraps can have realized the development of his ambitions, nor will Antigonos have bothered to enlighten them.

Seleukos' story, as related to Ptolemy, comprised a set of frightening facts: the size of Antigonos' army, the huge quantity of treasure he had collected, but above all he laid emphasis on the fates of Peithon and Peukestas and the other satraps who had been killed or deposed, all of them men who were known to and were friends of Ptolemy. He pointed out that Peithon and Peukestas had been allies of Antigonos, and so his treatment of them was particularly treacherous. Seleukos added that it seemed clear that Antigonos' ambition was to become ruler of 'the entire kingdom of the Macedonians' – that is, both the original kingdom (by now under Kassander's control), and the several parts of the old Akhaimenid Empire which, under Alexander's leadership, these satraps had conquered; Ptolemy's Egypt was obviously included.[4]

Ptolemy had so far maintained a tight grip on Egypt and had extended his power into both Cyrenaica and the southern half of Syria. He had been as cavalier over the satraps he had encountered as Antigonos, if not quite so brutal. The man who had come to control Egypt in Alexander's time, Kleomenes, did not long survive Ptolemy's arrival, and Laomedon of Mitylene, who had been satrap of Syria, he had taken captive, though he had then escaped. Neither of these men was of much moment. Kleomenes had become notorious for amassing great personal wealth and had himself usurped authority in Egypt, where Alexander had appointed several men just so that one should not control such a rich region; Laomedon, another Greek, was never a serious political player, and had been wholly ineffectual – but then he had little military strength at his command. And when he escaped he joined Eumenes' supporters. So Ptolemy escaped condemnation, though had anyone chosen to say so, he was vulnerable to many of the same charges as Seleukos laid against Antigonos.[5]

He was also vulnerable in his chosen territory of Egypt. There was little to prevent Antigonos acquiring Syria, for Ptolemy's army was nowhere near large enough to prevail in a serious contest. But if Syria was lost, Egypt was vulnerable. Three times in the previous thirty years an army had succeeded in invading Egypt by way of Syria – by Artaxerxes III in 343, by Alexander in 331, and by Perdikkas in 321. Only the last had failed, and then only just. Ptolemy's move into Syria showed he had learned from this history, using it as a defensive shield for Egypt, his citadel. Similarly, he had established alliances with the Greek kings of the cities of Cyprus, and from the ports of the island, and the Phoenician cities of the Syrian coast, he could dominate the eastern Mediterranean seaways with his ships. But, in the face of

Antigonos' overwhelming army numbers, none of this would be of much avail.

The situation called for an alliance of all those who were threatened. Seleukos sent some of his friends – the word (*philoi*) was coming to be a title given to the men in a ruler's entourage – to explain Antigonos' plans and power to Kassander in Macedon and Lysimachos in Thrace as he himself had to Ptolemy, no doubt emphasizing the threat they posed to all of them.[6] Ptolemy will have provided the ships for these journeys, thereby clearly associating himself with Seleukos' message.[7]

Once he realized where Seleukos had gone, Antigonos sent out his own missions to the three men, urging a maintenance of their friendship, which may well have appealed to Kassander especially, who owed him for his start in securing Macedon. However, Antigonos also installed a new satrap in Babylon, Peithon son of Agenor, who had been one of Alexander's satraps in India until driven out.[8] Then he took over yet another huge treasure which was stored at Kyinda in Kilikia – another 10,000 talents. It was calculated, though we do not know by whom, that he also had a potential tax revenue of 11,000 talents annually on top of his treasure.[9] Of course, these actions only worked to confirm Seleukos' story. The closer he approached to the west with his great army the more formidable and dangerous Antigonos seemed to be to everyone else.

The result of Seleukos' seaborne diplomacy was a joint approach by the four men to Antigonos. Envoys from Ptolemy, Lysimachos, and Kassander met Antigonos and his council of Friends when he arrived in North Syria. The size of his forces and the quantity of baggage they had carried had meant a slow march, so Seleukos' envoys to Kassander and Lysimachos had plenty of time to put forth his message, and the answers of both were co-ordinated with Ptolemy. Antigonos marched as far as Mallos in Kilikia, from where he was able to seize control of the treasure of Kyinda, but he then returned to Syria, where he met the envoys of the three. He must have expected to be challenged, and as Ptolemy was in the best strategic position to interfere with his control of the lands to the east he had probably shifted back to establish his main forces in Syria – an early indication of the strategic importance of North Syria in the new political conditions. For once we have a near-precise date around which to reconstruct events: Diodoros notes that having reached Kilikia, soon after the setting of Orion (November 315) he distributed his army into winter quarters, presumably over several parts of Kilikia and Syria.[10] Given the presumed hostility of Ptolemy in Egypt,

Lysimachos in Thrace, and Kassander in Macedon, Syria was the best place from which to watch events.

The envoys presented the terms on which they would maintain the peace, no doubt taking up the proposition of Antigonos himself that they remain friends. (Seleukos, not being in the category of a friend of Antigonos, was represented at the meeting by the others.) They proposed that, as Antigonos had been campaigning on behalf of the king as 'general over Asia', and as the three were also supporters and subjects of the king as his satraps, Antigonos' conquests should be divided, and his accumulated treasure distributed among them. The precise territorial demands were for Hellespontine Phrygia to Lysimachos, giving him control of both sides of the Straits and the Sea of Marmara; Kassander to be allotted Kappadokia and Lykia, which with Macedon and his domination of Greece would interpose his lands between those of Antigonos in Phrygia and the east; 'all Syria' to Ptolemy, meaning North Syria, in addition to that part he already controlled; Seleukos to return to Babylonia. Antigonos would thus be left with a series of unconnected regions; Iran, Kilikia, Phrygia.[11]

This proposed redistribution made good sense as an attempt to rein in Antigonos. By slicing up the lands he had seized and placing their own lands between his several sections, Antigonos could be reduced to his basic situation, satrap of Phrygia, the office which he held from the time of the Triparadeisos meeting. The unspoken assumption was that other men would be appointed as satraps of the several sections, both of Antigonos' territories and those of Kassander – and these would clearly be independent. On the other hand, Ptolemy and Lysimachos would be able to exercise more direct control over their added lands. The situation in the Far East was ignored, and it may be presumed that the three were prepared to accept Antigonos' replacements in Iran and the eastern satrapies. Since those men – Nikanor (if he was satrap of Media already), Asklepiodoros in Persia, and Aspeisas in Susiana – were his men it is obvious that Antigonos would still have influence there. No mention was made of the easterners in Baktria and eastern Iran, who must have been largely discounted. The division of the treasure could be justified because they had all taken part in the war and so all deserved to be compensated for their trouble. The treasure was originally collected by the Akhaimenids, and so was now Macedonian.

These terms were not accepted. They were, of course, a test. If Antigonos rejected them, as he did, this would indicate that Seleukos' allegations of overweening ambition could be taken as proved. If he accepted at least the possibility of a redistribution of the spoils, the details could be settled in a new meeting on the lines of Triparadeisos, preceded no doubt by private negotiations. This would mean that the empire could be held together for at least a little longer and the possibility of a collective government by the satraps might be developed. Antigonos would, no doubt, dispute the three's justification and quibble about their suggestions, but at least they would be negotiating. This might have resulted in a new war, but by issuing an angry and immediate rejection of any possible terms, Antigonos made his ambitions all too clear, and a new war was inevitable.[12]

This meeting took place, if the sequence in Diodoros can be accepted, in November or December of 315. The news of Antigonos' rejection will therefore have reached the three satraps in their separate satrapies about the beginning of 314. This being the winter, no military moves were likely for two or three months, and so plans could be made. At some point between 317, when he had a substantial fleet, and the return of his forces to north Syria, when he had few ships, Antigonos' navy had disappeared. This was Ptolemy's doing. Antigonos' presence in North Syria in 317 was presumably accompanied by his ships, which sailed to those parts of Phoenicia from which Ptolemy had withdrawn before Eumenes. Antigonos' immediate arrival on Eumenes' heels was followed by his march in pursuit to the east. Then Ptolemy returned to Syria. By seizing the ports he also seized the ships, though since he and Antigonos were at the time on the same side this would not cause alarm. But in late 315 their growing antagonism transformed Phoenicia, controlled by Ptolemy, into enemy territory as far as Antigonos was concerned, and the ships remained in Ptolemy's hands. In the spring of 314 Antigonos moved south from his winter quarters in North Syria and Kilikia into southern Syria, an overt act of war against Ptolemy, who prudently withdrew before his advance, and took the ships with him. Meanwhile Kassander had followed up his demand for Kappadokia by sending a force into the Black Sea which began a siege of the city of Amisos. If that city was taken this would open up the route south along the valley of the Halys River into Kappadokia.[13]

Antigonos, having occupied the ports of Syria, except for Tyre, where Ptolemy left a defiant garrison, ordered the construction of a new fleet in Phoenicia and Kilikia, and sent two envoys to Rhodes to place an order for more ships to be built. He gave another envoy, Artemidoros of Miletos, a thousand talents, and sent him into the Peloponnese in search of allies against Kassander. He sent an army north under his nephew Polemaios first to evict Kassander's forces from Amisos and then to move west to guard the Hellespont. (It does not seem that Lysimachos made any attempt to seize Hellespontine Phrygia, the slice of Asia Minor he had asked for, but Polemaios' army would stop him if he or Kassander mounted an invasion.) Polemaios duly relieved Amisos, and on his march west he found that the city of Astakos was being besieged by the Bithynian chief, Zipoetes; he relieved this siege also, and then made alliances with both the city and the chief. With no danger threatening from Thrace or Macedon, he moved on south into Ionia, where he found that Seleukos was besieging the city of Erythrai; he relieved this siege also.[14]

Seleukos was the man who could best keep Antigonos' enemies in contact with one another. From Egypt he went off in the spring of 314 with a hundred of Ptolemy's ships, sailing north along the Phoenician coast, where Antigonos was beginning the construction of his new ships. No doubt this was deliberate, since Ptolemy's ships had probably been Antigonos' originally. It may also be that Seleukos took the opportunity to send supplies into Tyre, which Antigonos had laid under siege, and certainly he sailed insolently close to Antigonos' camp, provoking annoyance and depression amongst the men.[15] Antigonos had sent another of his envoys, Agesilaos, into Cyprus, where Nikokreon, the king of Salamis, the largest city of the island, was Ptolemy's ally; Agesilaos was, however, able to collect alliances from several of the other kings in the island.[16] Antigonos, having secured much of Phoenicia, now moved south, where Ptolemy still held Palestine. He captured Joppa and Gaza, probably the only fortified places in the country, thus posing an immediate menace to Egypt, but then turned back to deal with the one place which still defied him, Tyre, held by Ptolemy's garrison.[17]

Seleukos sailed on into the Aegean. He had presumably called at Cyprus but as yet it was probably not obvious that much of the island had shifted towards Antigonos. Nor was it yet known just what effect Aristodemos might have in Greece, if indeed his mission was known to anyone yet. It is known that Seleukos was laying siege to Erythrai in Ionia when Polemaios arrived from Amisos and the Hellespont, but there is no record of his activities in the region otherwise. One might guess that he had contacted both Kassander and Lysimachos though neither was apparently able to help him. Kassander was obviously concerned by the new situation developing in the Peloponnese.

Artemidoros had quickly recruited an army of mercenaries and made an alliance with Polyperchon, still recognized by some as the official regent of the king (Alexander IV, held by Kassander in Macedon). The terms of the alliance included the transfer of the regency to Antigonos, who thereupon appointed Polyperchon his *strategos* in the Peloponnese. It was, of course, a purely formal deal, but could be important in propaganda terms, giving Antigonos a quasi-legal authority which would reassure some of the doubtful Macedonians. It was in a way a reply to the demands of the three satraps; now Antigonos really did have some sort of legal right to depose and install satraps.[18] (Antipater had appointed Polyperchon, as he had Antigonos as 'general over Asia'; it could be argued that the transfer of the regency was perfectly correct.)

Polyperchon's son Alexander was his envoy to Antigonos in ratifying the agreement produced by Artemidoros. The meeting took place in the camp before Tyre, probably about midsummer, though July or August would be more acceptable. Alexander was given 500 talents to finance actions in Greece. Kassander was roundly denounced for killing Olympias (though it is doubtful if anyone was really sorry, and the sentence had been pronounced by an army assembly in due form), and for holding Roxane and King Alexander prisoner. Their transfer to his custody was one of Antigonos' first demands as regent, though it is certain that the boy would have been an embarrassment as he grew up. The meeting was a public gathering of his friends and his soldiers, in a style very similar to those at Babylon and Triparadeisos (or of Kassander in Macedon). In form it was organized as an updating of the measures adopted at Triparadeisos, including a ratification of Antigonos' actions since then, and so it was a means of blocking references back to those meetings by, above all, Seleukos. It is doubtful if anyone really accepted it as a true successor to those earlier meetings, since it was so obviously dominated by Antigonos, but Antigonos was certainly going through the right motions.[19]

Antigonos was using the traditional institutions of the Macedonian kingdom – army assembly, regency – to clothe his power in acceptable political garments. The meeting accepted a rather more startling proposition put to it by Antigonos: 'It was also stated that all the Greeks were free, not subject to foreign garrisons, and autonomous', in Diodoros' summary.[20] This unexpected proclamation, which was widely publicized, actually went against the grain of the relations between Macedonians and Greeks over the last couple of decades. Philip's League of Corinth and Alexander's dictatorial pronouncements on the restoration of Greek exiles had been followed by Antipater's defeat of the Spartans and his success in suppressing the Greek 'rebellion', the Lamian war, in 323–322. In all these the Macedonians were victorious and the probable future would have seemed to indicate a continuation and deepening of Macedonian control. But several factors had now intervened. Kassander was clearly the man who, from his position in Macedon, was most closely involved with the Greeks, and he was, just as his father had been, keen to exert control over them. Antigonos' nephew Polemaios, during his campaign to Asia Minor, had relieved the sieges of several Greek cities – Amisos, Chalkedon, Astakos, and Erythrai, and had made an alliance with the tyrant Dionysios of Herakleia Pontike (marrying his daughter as well). Antigonos had in fact sent instructions to Polemaios to save Erythrai.

It is in these two elements, the antagonism to Kassander and his anxiety to save the Ionian cities, which we may detect the origin of the new policy which Antigonos was now proclaiming. By announcing, in his capacity as regent, that the Greeks were to be free and autonomous, he was reaping several advantages – he was exercising his legislative powers as regent, in the same way as Antipater and Perdikkas before him; he distinguished himself from Kassander quite decisively, and reversed the policy proclaimed by the previous regent Antipater; he attracted to himself the wary friendship of several hundred cities in Greece and Asia; he undermined Ptolemy's control of the Cyrenaican Greek cities and Kassander's power in Greece itself; he opened up access to the cities for his military recruiters; and by insisting that the cities should not be garrisoned he saved himself the need to spread his soldiers in many small packets so as to control them. At the same time, though this was not mentioned, he could expect the cities to contribute to his war chest, more or less voluntarily, in return for his help and his policy of protecting them from his, and therefore, their, enemies. He was also, though this was scarcely intended, setting the agenda for the relationship between the kings and the Greek cities for the next two centuries, and even longer, since the Romans, when they arrived in the eastern Mediterranean, adopted the same approach.

It was a propaganda masterstroke, but it also set up hostages for his (and every other ruler's) future conduct. He was the one who interpreted the relationship; any city – Rhodes and Athens in the future in particular – which took such a policy seriously, was liable to find that Antigonos was rigorous in his expectations. But he did certainly wrong-foot Ptolemy and Kassander in the short term. Ptolemy was compelled very soon afterwards (late in 313) to issue his own similar proclamation, though few took it very seriously, and none ever had any confidence in his intentions.[21] Neither Kassander nor Lysimachos paid much attention, and they certainly did not emulate Antigonos in their policy towards Greek cities. On the other hand, it may have had a considerable effect on Seleukos, though at this moment he could scarcely do much about it.

Ptolemy was informed of the intrigues mounted by Antigonos' envoy Agesilaos in Cyprus, and a meeting was arranged between Seleukos, with his part of Ptolemy's fleet, direct from Polemaios' rebuff of him at Erythrai, Ptolemy's brother Menelaos, an Athenian mercenary, Myrmidon, who commanded a force of 10,000 soldiers, and Polykleitos, who commanded another part of Ptolemy's fleet. The meeting, presumably informed of Ptolemy's requirements by Menelaos, who was in overall command, had to work out how to counter Antigonos' various moves. Polykleitos took fifty ships to the Peloponnese to fight against the activities of Aristodemos and Polyperchon; Seleukos and Menelaos, with most of the ships, operated in Cyprus alongside Nikokreon of Salamis to suppress the allies collected for Antigonos by Agesilaos. Meanwhile Polemaios and his Antigonid army were in Karia, where the satrap Asandros was defying Antigonos' authority; Myrmidon and his mercenary army were sent to help Asandros.[22]

In Cyprus Seleukos and Menelaos won back Lapethos and Keryneia and persuaded the kings of Marion and Amathos to join, or rejoin, Ptolemy's alliance; the Phoenician city of Kition, however, defied them and was put under siege.[23] Polykleitos ambushed an Antigonid detachment in Kilikia and captured the whole force.[24] Seleukos is next heard of in the Aegean once more, where the war now centred on the contest between Asandros, the satrap of Karia, and Polemaios. At Tyre Antigonos finally captured the ruins left by Alexander's siege in mid-314.[25] He sent an envoy to Ptolemy to negotiate the ransom of his general and the officers captured by Polykleitos, and used this contact as a means of setting up a meeting between them, which took place at Ekregma, in the no-man's-land between Gaza, Antigonos' southern boundary, and Pelusion, Ptolemy's eastern. This is an otherwise anonymous location where there was an inlet ('ekregma') of some sort on the coast. Whatever Ptolemy demanded in exchange for peace – presumably the terms of two years before – Antigonos could not accept.[26]

Antigonos had now bottled up Ptolemy in Egypt, and with his new and superior fleet dominated the seas, including the Aegean. There he had promoted a league of the Kyklades islands, another scheme to extend his power.[27] The weight of his attack now shifted against the other allies. He got through the Taurus passes in winter – so probably December 313 or January 312 – and took up winter quarters around Kelainai, his old satrapal capital in Phrygia. But in January or February a preliminary agreement with Asandros in Karia broke down, and Antigonos brought out his forces for a swift campaign which conquered Karia in a month, despite assistance to Asandros from Ptolemy and Seleukos (the latter apparently still in the Aegean area), and Kassander, who had sent his brother Prepelaos with a force to assist.[28] This seems to have persuaded Antigonos to take the offensive against the Europeans, into the Black Sea, and across to Euboia, and in the islands. In the face of this Kassander (probably with Lysimachos' agreement) met Antigonos for a peace conference at the Hellespont.[29]

Ptolemy had had to put down a rebellion at Cyrene, which had probably taken his proclamation of freedom and autonomy too seriously. In both Cyprus and Cyrene therefore he had recovered his original position, but in the island there was still trouble. Pygmalion, the king of Kition – the only Phoenician city in Cyprus – had contacted Antigonos, as had King Stasoikos of Marion, who had been allied with Ptolemy earlier. In reply to this 'desertion', Marion was sacked and its people moved to Paphos; Pygmalion was arrested. Nikokreon of Salamis was appointed viceroy for the whole island, and then Ptolemy raided along the adjacent coasts of North Syria and Kilikia. He landed and sacked Mallos and got away to the ships before a force commanded by Antigonos' son Demetrios could reach him.[30]

This force was commanded, in outward form at least, by Demetrios, who was aged at that point about 21 or 22.[31] He was precocious, already married (his wife Phila, Antipater's daughter, was some years older), but he was also impulsive; in attempting to reach Ptolemy he had ridden out all his horses, and rather uselessly arrived well ahead of his men. It may have been the realization of Demetrios' character that persuaded Ptolemy to risk a serious battle in an attempt to recover the southern Syria. In this he was encouraged by Seleukos, now back in Egypt. Seleukos must have been worried by the meetings of Ptolemy and Kassandros with Antigonos as signs that his supporters were willing to consider making peace, for if he was ever to be more than one of Ptolemy's commanders, he would need to regain an independent command.

The impulsive Demetrios was surrounded by a committee of generals of the vintage of Ptolemy and Seleukos, appointed by his father as a restraint: Nearchos of Crete, who had piloted the fleet from India to Babylonia for Alexander; Andronikos of Olynthos, who had been at the siege of Tyre;

Philip, probably a Macedonian, who had served with Eumenes and then joined Antigonos; and, most crucially for Seleukos, Peithon son of Agenor, former satrap in India and Antigonos' choice as Seleukos' replacement as satrap of Babylonia. If Peithon was in Syria, his control of Babylonia was sensibly reduced, and the governing authority there would rest with the local commanders; no-one was apparently in overall control in the satrapy.

Demetrios and his committee of generals was a less than harmonious combination; the generals were professionals and professionally cautious; Demetrios was dashing and a risk-taker. (In a sense this division was mirrored in the partnership of the cautious Ptolemy and Seleukos, who was much more of an adventurous type, but these two worked much better together, at least for this occasion, than their opponents. The command lay decisively with one man, Ptolemy, whose army was doing the fighting.) Demetrios had a substantial army under command, though some of his soldiers were also spread throughout Syria in garrison duties. Reinforcements were no nearer than Asia Minor. So this was clearly a major opportunity for Ptolemy to strike a serious blow at his enemy.[32] And Seleukos had a plan of his own for exploiting a battle victory. (He is to be credited with the plan because of his ingenuity and cunning, qualities he repeatedly displayed in both military and political affairs throughout his life; Ptolemy never did, but then he had his kingdom from 323 onwards, so he did not need to be daring.) Ptolemy gathered an army of 15,000 heavy and light infantry, partly Macedonian and Greek and partly Egyptian, and about 6,000 cavalry. He had no elephants, whereas Demetrios was well supplied with 43 of these fearsome beasts. In cavalry he and Demetrios were about equal, but Demetrios had a smaller number of infantry, only about 11,000 men.

Demetrios' forces had gone into winter quarters after the fighting on the Syrian and Kilikian coasts; Ptolemy, however, decided, possibly persuaded by Seleukos whose brain was more attuned to deception and trickery than Ptolemy's, to move in 'winter'. About the end of December (312), his forces marched along the Sinai road, on the age-old invasion route close to the Mediterranean coast. He had not made any serious attempt to keep his move secret, for one of the aims of the campaign was to bring Demetrios' army to a battle as soon and as far south as possible. Demetrios therefore was able to concentrate his army at Gaza even as Ptolemy approached. The battlefield was Demetrios' choice; he was in position before Ptolemy arrived, but in a wider sense he had been put there by Ptolemy.

One result of this was that Ptolemy could discern the basic battle plan which Demetrios, endorsed by his helpers, above all Peithon, intended to use. Two-thirds of his elephants and most of his cavalry were placed on the Antigonid left; the hoplite phalanx was therefore only lightly protected on its right by a small cavalry force. Clearly the battle plan was for the elephants and the cavalry to attack with the intention of driving off any cavalry on Ptolemy's right and then turning on the phalanx. Ptolemy and Seleukos had begun with a more or less equal distribution of cavalry on either wing, but when they saw the enemy dispositions they also concentrated their cavalry on the right (facing Demetrios' left). Ptolemy had no elephants and it is clear that Peithon, a veteran of Indian warfare and of governing in India, believed they were the battle winner. But Ptolemy and Seleukos also knew elephant warfare from their time in India, and had developed a plan of their own to cope with them. If this worked, of course, Demetrios and Peithon were probably beaten. They were putting very much reliance on a single weapon.

In front of the right-wing cavalry, Ptolemy placed a specially trained force of light infantry whose task was to prepare the ground to stop the enemy elephants. They came equipped with spiked chains which they spread in front of their own cavalry. The soft feet of the elephants could not cope with either the sharp spikes or with the unyielding iron chains. The light infantry in this area were also the missile men, archers and javelineers, swift moving and operating individually, whose mobility allowed them to approach and harry the elephants and their mahouts.

Diodoros claims that Ptolemy's army 'advanced on the enemy with a great shout', but this is exactly what they did not do, for Ptolemy stood entirely on the defensive. It was necessary that the great mass of elephants and cavalry on Demetrios' left be compelled to attack first. Fortunately for Ptolemy this was exactly the intention. Diodoros also claims that the two opposed cavalry forces fought first before the elephants advanced, but it was surely a more or less simultaneous clash.

The elephant charge failed amid the chains and spikes, and the animals were further harassed by the archers and javelineers, who also deliberately targeted the mahouts. The killing or disabling of these men left the elephants to run amok, and when this was seen, the rest of the Antgonid army fell into confusion. Demetrios' cavalry, already under attack by superior numbers, turned and fled, followed reluctantly by Demetrios and his guard; the infantry was prevented from leaving by Ptolemy's attacking infantry and harassing cavalry, and the great majority of the men were made prisoners. Ptolemy's cavalry followed up the flight of Demetrios' horse sufficiently closely that they got into Gaza before the gates were closed, captured the city, and made more prisoners. Probably two-thirds of Demetrios' army was captured or fell on the field. All the surviving elephants were captured as well.[33]

With his army destroyed Demetrios had no choice but to make a rapid and long retreat. He admitted defeat by asking for a truce to bury the dead, which Ptolemy agreed to; Ptolemy also released some high-ranking prisoners without ransom and returned to Demetrios his captured baggage; these released men would no doubt sow dissension in Demetrios' counsels, while the baggage would slow him down. The other prisoners were sent into Egypt and settled on the land as cleruchs, holding their lands on condition of military service, in effect recruited into Ptolemy's army.[34] Of the four generals whose advice had led to the defeat, three of them escaped: Nearchos, who apparently retired to write his memoirs, Philip, who continued in Antigonos' service for at least another ten years, and Andronikos. Peithon son of Agenor was killed; there is no evidence of how and when this happened but it is surely significant that the one man, apart from Antigonos and Demetrios, who most stood in Seleukos' way in his return to Babylon, was killed.[35] It would not be surprising if Seleukos had deliberately targeted him.

Demetrios did not stop in his flight until he reached Tripolis in northern Phoenicia. By then he knew he could collect a reasonable army from those men who were still in North Syria and Kilikia. Ptolemy advanced northwards with his usual deliberate caution, taking over the towns and cities which Antigonos had captured in the last two or three years. Only Tyre resisted, under the command of Andronikos, who had been at the Gaza battle, and who must have been detailed to hold Tyre by Demetrios during the retreat. When Ptolemy summoned him he was both rude and defiant, but the city cannot have been properly provisioned for this unexpected siege. Fairly soon the garrison, who will have known that Ptolemy had sent their fellows into Egypt to be given land as settlers, mutinied, expelled Andronikos, and surrendered. Andronikos was captured by Ptolemy and, to his surprise and gratification, treated well, presumably after delivering a defiant apology. Nevertheless the resistance of Tyre bought Demetrios time to recover and collect his wits and his forces.[36]

At some point on Ptolemy's march from Gaza to Tyre, Seleukos put his own plan into action. It cannot have been a sudden decision, as it is presented in the sources; it must have been part of the original aims of both Ptolemy and himself in seeking the battle, and in fact it did not depend on the battle being a victory; the only requirement was secrecy and the attention of Demetrios and his generals being directed elsewhere. Ptolemy was mainly interested in driving Antigonos' forces away from Egypt and in regaining control of Palestine and Phoenicia (and possibly of North Syria); but Seleukos was mainly concerned to recover Babylonia.[37] The death of Peithon son of Agenor, and the obvious disarray of the Antigonid forces in Syria gave him his chance, but this will have been his aim from the start. (Even if the Antigonid army was victorious, the aftermath of victory would have compelled Demetrios and his commanders to concentrate their attention and their forces on invading Egypt; this concentration away from his own actions was all that Seleukos required; in addition, the Antigonid forces in Syria, and perhaps in Babylonia, had been thinned out to form the defeated army.) With a force of 800 or 1,000 infantry and 200 or 300 cavalry – surely the infantry were mounted – Seleukos parted from Ptolemy's army and rode hard through Syria into Mesopotamia.[38]

Ptolemy in Syria was soon faced by an army greater than that he had defeated. He sent a detachment under a general called Killes northwards, but it was ambushed by Demetrios, who had recovered his balance and gathered a sizable force. He captured 7,000 men, thereby largely recovering his losses. He also summoned his father, who arrived soon after with more troops. Ptolemy, having discussed the situation with his friends in council, prudently withdrew once again, destroying any fortified place in Palestine as he did so. Antigonos had no intention of invading Egypt, so the two ended up as they had started, facing each other across the Sinai Desert from bases at Gaza and Pelusion.

Chapter Three

Seleukos and Babylon

When Seleukos returned to Babylon in 312 (the journey and its military results will be considered in the next chapter), he was, according to one source, welcomed effusively.[1] He had ruled the region as satrap for perhaps five years (320–315), and from 312 he ruled it again, as satrap and then as king. The people appear to have been notably loyal to him in both offices, and in many respects the region continued to be loyal to his descendants for the next two centuries, which was primarily due to the administration and attitude organized by Seleukos. This is in contrast to the attitude of the Babylonians towards the Akhaimenids, against whom they had rebelled several times, to the extent that, like the Egyptians, they had welcomed the arrival of Alexander in his campaign of conquest in 331. It was also, as will be seen, very much in contrast to their attitude to Antigonos.

Babylon city was in slow decline, having suffered severely under Akhaimenid rule. This was a process which was to be encouraged by one aspect of Seleukos' work, if masked by the general prosperity of the region as a whole. But it was not the only urban centre in the region. It lay on the Euphrates River; a little to the north was the city of Sippar and to the south was Borsippa; on the Tigris somewhat to the northeast was Opis, where the Macedonian army had agitated in an assembly for Philip III to become king; further south, also on the Euphrates, were Uruk and Larsa; to the south and southeast were Nippur, Kish, and Cutha; Ur was in steep decline since a shift in the course of the Euphrates left it in the desert.[2] Many of these cities were even older than Babylon, those in the south in particular having existed from the beginning of city life in Sumer. These seem to have been the major cities in Seleukos' time, but there were plenty of others, smaller, which may be called towns, but still urban on their organization.

In addition, the land was densely populated by an industrious peasantry who lived in nucleated villages. It was seamed by rivers and canals, an organized system of transport and irrigation millennia old. It was agriculturally rich and productive, not only of food, but of taxes. It was also a commercially busy region. The long peace of Akhaimenid rule, once the revolts had been put down, had seen a distinct recovery in the size of the population and the number of villages, a process visible both in the central area around Babylon and in the south about Uruk.[3] This expansion continued through the period of Seleukid rule. As a region and a resource it was almost as important to the Seleukid kings as the Nile valley was to the Ptolemies, but the Seleukids never had the problems of control and resentment, rebellions and strikes, which repeatedly afflicted the Ptolemaic kings. This was clearly due in part to the good relations between the general population and the dynasty.

The prominent men of Babylonian society whom Seleukos had to deal with were sophisticated, numerous, literate, and rich. The merchants had developed a working system of contracts, credit, methods of payment, and markets, and Seleukos and his successors, so far as can be seen, made no attempt to change any of this. There are records of all this activity from the very latest years of Seleukid rule (the 140s), which are very similar to examples from the earliest years, and from the earlier Akhaimenid and later Arsakid periods as well for that matter.[4] Families of merchants carefully maintained archives of records of transactions, written in the cuneiform script on clay tablets just as their ancestors and predecessors had done since the time of Sargon of Akkad.[5]

The heart of every city was the great temple of the city's god; at Babylon it was Marduk (also Bel-Marduk); at Borsippa Nabu, who was the messenger of the gods, a most suitable deity for a commercial city, at Uruk it was Ishtar. However, these were only the most important gods, the patrons of the individual cities, and they all had temples in the other cities, along with lots of other gods – it is claimed that Babylon had fifty-three 'important' temples.[6] However it was the city's patron god which was the most important, both for the citizens and for their rulers. The major city-temples had their own names. At Uruk there were in fact two, Bit Res and Esghal, at Borsippa it was Ezida, at Cutha it was Emeslan, and at both Sippar and Larsa it was called Ebabbar; at Babylon it was Esagila, the greatest of them all. Because for a millennium and a half, since Hammurabi had hoisted it to political grandeur, the city of Babylon had been the political centre of Babylonia, this meant that Marduk was the premier god, and Esagila was the premier temple. This was a fairly normal polytheistic system which the Macedonians could understand and live with without difficulty; the difference lay in the priesthood, which was a rich and important caste and corporation, whereas in Greece and Macedon priests were amateurs and civic officials. The priests who served Marduk in Esagila were the most important group of men in

Babylon. Any king had to deal carefully with these priests, who could be exceptionally awkward and greedy.

Alexander had tangled with Esagila's priests, to his cost and humiliation. They had warned him on his return from India as he approached the city not to enter it at the western gate since it would bring evil on him; before that they had also warned him not to enter the city at all, though if he paid for the restoration of Esagila's ziggurat (destroyed by the Persians a century and a half earlier), he would be fairly safe. Alexander took this seriously for a time, camping outside the city while the army went in, even though to the rest of the Macedonians it was obviously superstitious blackmail. The fact that he eventually disregarded the warnings about entering the city, but then died there, could be pointed to as an instance of the power of the priests and their astrologers.[7]

It behoved Seleukos therefore to have a care to ensure that he kept the Esagila priests on his side. It seems he did so, probably by exercising his power to distribute favours and gifts, such as grants of land, offices, and tax exemptions. The temples were large communities of priests, servants, and hangers-on, and did require a substantial income, which was distributed not only to the priests and used to support the temple establishment, but went out very widely through their associates.[8] What they had wanted from Alexander were funds to pay for the rebuilding, when he gave them permission to do so (which the Akhaimenids had repeatedly refused), whereas Alexander assumed they would find it from their regular income; but they had become so used to spending it on their own comforts that they could not see how to afford the cost of the rebuilding. Seleukos must have sorted the problem out, probably by assigning income from the royal lands for the purpose. He could, of course, also use this method to bring in support from non-priests as well, but the priests' influence was wide and overlapped other social groups, in and out of the city, so they were obviously the primary group to target.

At the same time, Seleukos made sure, as Alexander had before him, that the city held a substantial garrison, and that the garrison had a commander loyal to him personally. That all these measures constituted a generally successful policy is asserted by Diodoros in his description of Seleukos' return in 312. He remarks that the Babylonians had goodwill towards Seleukos because of his earlier generosity, and claims that this applied to both the common people and the priests and the wealthy.[9]

This also supposes that the Babylonians regarded his expulsion by Antigonos in 315 as wrong, perhaps illegal, but also it assumes that it was expected that he would return. Seleukos had been busy as Ptolemy's commander between 315 and 312, but it would seem he had kept contact with the leading men in Babylonia. There is no doubt he wanted to return; his anger at his expulsion was clearly what drove him to spread the news of Antigonos' ambitions to his friends, and his return had been one of the demands of his allies at the start of their war against Antigonos. It seems clear enough that Seleukos therefore worked towards this, partly by his diplomatic campaign around the eastern Mediterranean, but also by encouraging his Babylonian supporters from a distance, though no direct evidence for this survives. Quite likely Antigonos – or perhaps his satrap Peithon – had been less than accommodating towards the priests. He had certainly imprisoned a number of Seleukos' 'friends and slaves', who were clearly still loyal to him. By the time he returned they had been imprisoned for three years, no doubt serving as hostages to keep their associates quiet.[10]

The priests were crucial to the king's control of the region only in part because they were religious officials, landowners, and the administrators of the great temples. This was, of course, the basis of their importance, but it also enabled them to stretch their influence throughout the city and into the lands around. This influence is similar to that attributed to the priests of the giant Egyptian temples, who were capable of organizing strikes among the peasantry, and who could, in times of rebellion, successfully extract concessions from the Ptolemaic kings. In Babylon, however, Seleukos set a more helpful precedent (at least for his successors if not quite so much for the priests). He was generous from the first, but he was not, as Alexander had been, so superstitious that he took their threats seriously.

The priests were important for other reasons. They in effect controlled the schools in which the difficult art of writing in cuneiform script was taught. They were thus largely the creators and preservers of Babylonian literature, much of which centred on religion, by recording rituals, pious tales, and so on. It is not clear how much of the old tales were still read, for it seems that the spoken language in the country was now Aramaic, with Akkadian (not wholly dissimilar from Aramaic) largely relegated to the prestige of a classical language which few could understand – though it remained in use for contracts and chronicles. (Aramaic, using a cursive script, was written on parchment or papyrus, like Greek, and so did not use the more difficult cuneiform developed for use on clay tablets.) As a result the currently produced writings reflected priestly concerns above all. There is, for example, a long series of tablets recording astronomical observations, a series whose surviving examples cover at least five centuries' records, but which started perhaps in the eighth century BC; the earliest example dates from 652 BC. These are mainly a tedious record of sightings of stars and planets, made for astrological reasons, but the priests who wrote them up – every month, it seems – were alert to political, economic and meteorological events. Appended at the end of the monthly stargazing record and after notes of prices of currently needed products, such as barley and dates and wool, there are also, more relevant here, frequently records of particular political events.

These tablets, of course, record events which particularly affected Babylon, but are all the more valuable for that. The entries are in the diary form in which the observations were recorded, unusually precisely dated, so that, for example, we can accurately date the deaths of kings, often to the day. These *Astronomical Diaries*, as they have been entitled, constitute a major advance in Hellenistic history comparable with the revelation of Egyptian affairs obtained from Egyptian papyri.[11]

It was in the same spirit that the priests recorded political events more directly in the form of chronicles.[12] This was an old local custom, and once again, since they are in cuneiform, they particularly reflect priestly concerns – we know a considerable amount about repairs to Esagila, for example. It has taken a long time for these sources to become properly translated and published, and no doubt there are more tablets lying in the ground, or in museums, awaiting discovery and translation.

These Babylonian records were of immediate interest to some of the Greeks and Macedonians. When Alexander first reached the city the travelling historian of the expedition, Kallisthenes of Olynthos, Aristotle's nephew, set about transcribing at least some of the astronomical records, which the Babylonians claimed went back 31,000 years; they were clearly as prone to patriotic chronological exaggeration as any Egyptian.[13] How far Kallisthenes got with the transcriptions is not known, and he did not survive the expedition, but the very fact that he at least began the process suggests that the records were both available and transcribable into Greek on the spot. Seleukos, perhaps not in his first satrapy, but certainly soon after recovering the rule after 312, commissioned the Babylonian priest Berossos to produce a local history of Babylon. This seems to have been produced by about 300, though only some fragments quoted by later Greek historians survive. Its quality is unknown, but the surviving sections do not correlate well with other sources until the last four or five centuries. No doubt he emphasized the antiquity of the local civilization and its major achievements.[14]

The imperial administration which Seleukos set up, however, was Greek in language and practice. It used parchment or papyrus rather than clay tablets, as is evidenced by the survival, not unfortunately of the documents themselves, but of the clay seals (*bullae*) which marked their official nature and authenticity.[15] On the other hand, and even if the language of speech and writing was Greek, the actual administrative practice seems to have been largely that inherited from the Akhaimenid empire.

This is not really surprising. The city had surrendered to Alexander, and its Akhaimenid governor, Mazaios, had led the surrender; it was never damaged (until Antigonos' wars). During Alexander's absence in conquering the east there could be no reason to do more than install some Greek-speakers in the existing system, and get the Babylonian clerks to learn Greek. (They may have been using Aramaic, which could have continued in use.) On his return Alexander showed no interest in changing things, nor did any of the satraps who governed Babylon after his death, including Seleukos. By the time he resumed the government in 312, the Greeks in charge were running things well enough. They had the co-operation of the Babylonian bureaucrats, some of whom added Greek names to their own Babylonian birth names, and who, like bureaucrats everywhere, were more concerned that the correct procedures were followed than who was in charge in the head office. If the system worked, there was no need to change it.[16]

It is the generally accepted conclusion that the direct influence of the new rulers did not penetrate very deeply into Babylonian society. As an example there is Uruk, which grew and flourished greatly in the Hellenistic period, but which retained its full Babylonian identity. The absence of anything Greek or Macedonian – names, inscriptions, even pottery – is remarkable; the only items which had any Greekness to them were Rhodian *amphorae*. In every other respect, however, in mercantile practices, record-keeping, the names of the people, Babylonian practices continued all through the Seleukid period, a mark of the confidence of the Babylonians in their culture.[17]

Babylon itself was different, of course. Being the capital it was subjected to much greater Greek and Macedonian influence. For anyone of any importance or standing it would be necessary to learn Greek. The soldiers in the citadel were, or at least spoke, Greek; the government was conducted in Greek, the kings and the governors were Greek-speakers, and so far as we know, none of them ever learned any Babylonian language. The main priests must have learnt Greek even as they learned to speak (and write) Aramaic and Akkadian, and cuneiform. But the evidence of the written remains indicates that Akkadian and Aramaic and Greek were all employed in the city. There are Greek inscriptions, and the survival of a few *bullae* show that written materials on parchment (or possibly papyrus), existed, and that was the material used for Greek; there are also many clay tablets written in cuneiform dated throughout the period of Seleukid rule and beyond – including, of course, the *Astronomical Diaries*.[18] The contrast between exclusively Babylonian Uruk and Babylon with its layering of Greek-speakers, dual or triple-language speakers, is the contrast of a provincial city and a government centre. No doubt most of the other Babylonian cities were similar to Uruk rather than Babylon, and in all a caste of wealthy priests and merchants and bureaucrats sat on a Babylonian population of the poor, who were tax-payers and illiterate.

No matter how friendly the Babylonians' feelings were towards Seleukos on his return, or Seleukos' conciliatoriness towards important Babylonian individuals or social groups, the situation in socio-political terms was by no means acceptable to the satrap (who became king in 305, but who was regarded as king by the locals from the start, and who was referred to as such in their cuneiform king-lists). Babylon city was never a comfortable place for a Macedonian ruler to live in. It teemed with a busy population which he could not speak to, or understand; even if he controlled the governing system he could not but be conscious that the place was profoundly foreign for a Macedonian.

One of the activities that Alexander had indulged in and which his contending successors could emulate was the founding of new cities. The number of cities Alexander had actually founded has been vastly exaggerated, but the most recent detailed investigation has identified a much reduced number as certain foundations of his.[19] There were, however, many other places where Alexander's mark had been made, and in the romantic recollections of the populations of the Middle East in later years that number of new cities expanded substantially. Many of these were towns which included a Macedonian population. Some were indeed founded by Macedonians, and some were given, or adopted, the name of Alexandria as a claim to prestige. His successors used the founding of a new city as a sign of their claim to power and authority.

The first of these was probably Kassander, who was the least directly affected by Alexander of all the successors, in which case he was probably founding his city – Kassandreia – partly as a gesture of independence, partly as a vanity, and partly as the refutation of the destructiveness of

Philip II, for he chose the site of the destroyed city of Potidaia for his new foundation. He did this as early as 316, and followed it up with another new city, Thessaloniki, named for his wife, who was the daughter of Philip (the man was complicated).[20] Ptolemy meanwhile was beginning work on Alexandria-by-Egypt, as a pious memorial to the dead king, and, not at all by coincidence, as a great naval base and commercial centre, turning Egypt's face towards the Mediterranean.[21] Antigonos could not be left behind in this, and characteristically went rather better than the rest, with new cities at the Hellespont at Antigoneia, which was later renamed as Alexandria-Troas, Antigoneia-by-Daskylion, and Nikaia. At the same time (309) his rival Lysimachos was building his own name-city on the other side of the Hellespont at the root of the Gallipoli Peninsula. Antigonos then began work on another major city at Antigoneia in northern Syria (later engulfed and eclipsed by Antioch), which he was using as a capital by 306; he probably started it in 308.[22]

Seleukos was not to be left out of this aspect of their competition. Each of these cities had been planted at a site notable for its earlier associations – Lysimacheia was on the site of the Greek city of Kardia, Kassandreia was replacing Potidaia, Antigoneia was close to Troy, and so on. These associations were designed either to enhance the new city's prestige, giving it, as it were, a flying start in the fame stakes, or it was designed to obliterate those old associations by gaining a greater prestige by its very existence; the new names clearly asserted this. The replacement of Antigoneia's name by that of Alexandria was a reverse example, attempting to obliterate the memory of an unpopular ruler by adopting an even more prestigious name.

The greatest of these new cities, however, were all founded without any reference to pre-existing settlements. It was, given the long history of the Middle East, impossible to find a suitable site which was completely uninhabited, but the greater cities obliterated the old towns and villages. And, of course, much greater prestige came from founding a new city which was both built from scratch and was very large. Both Alexandria-by-Egypt and Antigoneia-on-Orontes fell into this category. Seleukos could do no less, but other considerations came into it as well. He might have wished to replace Babylon's fame by making it into a new city, but it was so large and so famous that such an attempt would inevitably fail; any replacement on the site would quickly become 'Babylon' no matter what name he might chose to give it. Lysimachos renamed Ephesos with his wife's name, calling it 'Arsinoe', but so far as we can see it remained 'Ephesos' for everyone else.[23]

So Seleukos chose a new site for his new city, that of the Babylonian town (or city) of Opis. This was sufficiently far from Babylon – 70km – not to be swamped by the older city. Opis was a minor place as Babylonian urban centres went and so he would be able to control the population and stamp his prestige on it, starting by naming it for himself, and would be able to define its shape and size and impose his own ruling system on it; it was on the Tigris, not the Euphrates, and it was at the junction of a major canal, the Royal Canal (Nahr Malcha) which brought Euphrates water into the Tigris, and so was never going to be short of water (though the river has since moved away, and the canals have been neglected). It became Seleukeia-on-the-Tigris once he had really set to work founding and giving other places his name.

In order to garner sufficient prestige and fame to outstrip Babylon, and to compete, at least, with the other cities founded by his contemporaries and rivals, the new city had to be special. Even founding it in Babylonia, of course, made it different from the start. Alexander had established cities in the farthest east and India, most of which had already failed by the time Seleukos recovered Babylonia, so to found a new Macedonian city in the midst of Babylonia was a remarkable deed in itself. His rivals' cities – Lysimacheia, Antigoneia, Kassandreia, Alexandria – were all on or close to the Mediterranean, a sea whose shores the Greeks and Macedonians were fully familiar with; the new city was to be inland, hundreds of miles from any sea, in a country where the staple Greek crops of olives and vines would not grow. And it was to be of a size which only one of its contemporaries could rival: it was to be larger than any contemporary city except Alexandria.

The precise date of the foundation of the city is not known, but it took place at some point between 312 and 307 (when Seleukos set off on his eastern campaign – see next chapter), and in that time he was extremely busy until 307, either campaigning outside Babylonia or fighting to hold on to it, and with enemy armies also campaigning in Babylonia. The story we are told of the action of founding the city requires Seleukos to have been present along with a substantial fraction of his Macedonian/Greek army, all actually on the site, which is no doubt correct, given the importance of the city. The only time when this could be done is in 308 or 307, in the brief time between his final defeat of Antigonos and the start of his eastern campaign. Also, of course, his victory over the invading forces of Antigonos gave him the prestige to carry out such a momentous act as founding a new and very large city.[24]

Founding a new city within two days' walk of Babylon was necessarily seen as a threat by the rulers of the older city. Just as when Alexander was seen as a threat to their income, so now Seleukos was an even bigger threat, this time to their whole community. A new city, a royal city, the new centre of the satrapal and royal administration, inhabited by Greeks and Macedonians, and organized and governed as a Macedonian city, was bound to reduce their income and their influence. Quite probably some of the royal lands which had been assigned to temples in Babylon were transferred to the new city. Undoubtedly Seleukeia would attract people from the old city. Perhaps they were offered concessionary rents to get them started; certainly it would cost the satrap/king a large treasure to get it started, and Babylon would no doubt suffer in its income in consequence.

The priests in Babylonia wheeled out the astrologers. Seleukos consulted them on deciding the most auspicious day and hour for the city to be started. They apparently provided the 'correct' date, but shifted the time. The story, as related by Appian, has it that the army, which had been apparently assigned the task of beginning the work, did not wait for the stated hour, but suddenly began work at the 'correct' time, while Seleukos was in his tent waiting for the right time to arrive (the astrologers had clearly pushed the hour back, so that the start would be missed).[25]

This story calls for explication. Accepting that the astrologers did lie about the hour, their purpose must have been to inflict a reputation for misfortune and ill luck on the new city. Yet this could only be done – assuming the actual influence of the stars is nil – if the alteration of the hour was made public, for keeping it secret would have no effect; only if it was known that the start was at the 'wrong' time could subsequent disasters be blamed on divine enmity. But when the secret came out the priests' and astrologers' plot would inevitably backfire on them when it became known what they had done. The plot is therefore a good indication of their desperation.

Then there is action of the army. It is just not credible that this mass of men, presumably several thousand strong, would spontaneously begin work, which must have included such activities as digging, brick making and suchlike physical, dirty, even unmilitary, tasks. Soldiers do not act in that way, partly because none of them would be in the least enthusiastic about the work, but mainly because their whole work ethos – soldiering – relies on discipline and obedience to orders. So we must conclude that someone gave them the order to begin. It was not Seleukos, who was in his tent, but it must have been done with his knowledge and approval. Spontaneity can be ruled out, just as can divine intervention.

The whole story therefore indicates in fact that the astrologer's plot had been revealed to the king well in advance – hardly a surprise, given the known opposition of the priests to the foundation of the new city – and that the spontaneity of the army's response was in fact organized. Seleukos clearly had time to arrange the demonstration, but he was also clearly able to think through the consequences, for what he did was not directly aimed at discrediting or humiliating the priests. These were too powerful to be alienated, so the foundation of Seleukeia was turned into an action which would both conciliate and defy the priests and the astrologers. It would conciliate them by implying divine approval, for it could be argued, with only a hint of irony, that only divine influence could get the army to begin at the 'correct' day and hour, and to act in such an unmilitary way. It was a defiance of the plotters by indicating, and probably revealing, that their plot was both pointless and a failure. This response has all of hallmarks of Seleukos' mind at work; it will be seen in other instances that he was the most cunning and devious of the successors of Alexander – which was one of the main reasons he was to be the most successful of them.

The city itself took a long time to build and to become properly inhabited. Whatever inducements were offered to the potential inhabitants to take up residence it would clearly take years for the necessary construction work to be accomplished and for people to move in. The royal government provided resources, finance, perhaps food, and its planners and surveyors laid out the extent of the city and its basic plan. The site had the Tigris River on the east, where it flowed from north to south; the northern and southern boundaries were formed by two branches of the Royal Canal, leaving a space of about 2km wide, roughly rectangular, in which the city was placed; the western boundary was not quite so well defined and was probably formed by a wall.[26] However, one interpretation suggests that the canals were actually enclosed within the city's boundaries, and that the land to the north and south was part of the city as well.

A harbour was excavated alongside the Tigris, for such a big city would need to import most of its food. The existing settlement of Opis was incorporated, but it seems to have left no real indication of its original layout, except its ziggurat, which was left standing in a plot of its own – and so its temple probably continued. The street plan called for a wide double boulevard starting at the harbour and stretching along the centre of the site, parallel to the canals, with a grid pattern of streets laid out perpendicularly from that line. (It looks desperately tedious on the plan.) A theatre has been located on the south, and a palace not far from the harbour in the east, again in its own open plot. The street layout seems not to have reached the canals or the river in any direction. No doubt the empty spaces thus intentionally left were occupied by the poor and their slums; if the city really spread beyond the canals, these areas could well have been the wealthier suburbs. Because of the difficulty of determining where the city's western boundary lay it is difficult to state just how large the site was. One measurement puts the street layout (the 'gridded area') at 366 hectares, but for the whole city between the river and the canals that should be at least doubled (though we have no real idea of how much of the interior was actually inhabited), and taking in the areas beyond the canals, the whole site would be approaching 1,000 hectares. These figures – 366 and 1,000 hectares – may be regarded as the extremes; this is an indication of the lack of any proper survey of the site.

It took a long time for the city to be properly inhabited. The opposition of the priests in Babylon presumably continued despite the failure of their campaign to prevent the new foundation even getting started, and this opposition would presumably discourage quite a few people from moving from Babylon – not to mention the sensible preference of the people of Babylon for a functioning city over a building site. There are ambiguous comments about the relationship of the two cities. Pausanias claims that Seleukos moved Babylonians to the city; and the Astronomical Diarist recorded that 'the citizens of Babylon went out to Seleukeia' in 274.[27] These have been interpreted as forcible transfers of people, but that puts too much of a strain on the wording. Seleukos could merely be attracting new inhabitants to his city by concessions and low rents; the later item, dating to the reign of his son Antiochos I, looks much more like a ceremonial visit, and was certainly voluntary. The forcible movement is not credible, and even so such actions did not finish off Babylon, which continued to be an active inhabited city for another three centuries – as the continued compilation of the Astronomical Diaries, for instance, shows.

Seleukos' choice of site for Seleukeia is thus one which could provide access for the necessary supplies for a large population. (Surveys have demonstrated that the land to the north, particularly along the Diyala River, was developed substantially during the next centuries, a change attributed to the market provided by the new city.)[28] It was also surrounded on three of its four sides by waterways, and so was eminently defensible – and one of the suggested western boundaries seems to have been a wall. In a wider sense, it was also placed, unusually, on the Tigris (most Babylonian cities were on the Euphrates or in the land between the rivers), and it was further north than any other major city in the region. It was not far from the defensive 'Median Wall' built in the seventh century by King Nebuchadnezzar at the narrowest place between the two main rivers, and just south of the route to the northeast along the Diyala River valley. It was also on, or perhaps just close to, the Babylonian end of the great Royal Road which, from Babylon, reached out and west as far as the Aegean Sea, and east to Central Asia. The route to the east went through the Zagros Mountains at the Bisitun Pass, the major way into Iran. Whereas its destination had been Babylon, now it was Seleukeia, a change which must have contributed to the older city's decline.

The city may thus have been assumed by the Babylonian priests to be a threat to them (though their assumption was belied by the continued prosperity of their own city, if in a declining way, for the next three centuries or so), but this was merely inadvertent on Seleukos' part. His main purpose in founding the great city at that particular place and at that time was as a defence against attack, actual or potential. By 307 he had fought for several years to defend the country against invasion by Antigonos' forces from the east and the northwest. Babylon had been the major fortress on the Euphrates; it was now being augmented by the fortified Seleukeia on the other river. Between them they would (and did) establish Seleukid power over all Babylonia. It also provided a major military base from which to project this power into Iran and into Mesopotamia to the north. It was from his new city that Seleukos set out on his own *anabasis* as far as India in 307. Therefore Babylon's priests were wrong in assuming Seleukeia was intended to be a threat to Babylon; instead the cities were to be twins, providing a powerful defence against Seleukos' (and Babylon's) great contemporary enemy, Antigonos.

Chapter Four

Seleukos' First Kingdom

When Seleukos broke away from the aftermath of the battle at Gaza to chase his satrapy in Babylonia, it is not clear whether Demetrios understood what was going on. Even if he did it seems he could do nothing about it. The advance of Ptolemy to lay siege to Tyre, and of his general Killes and his army northwards into North Syria provided some cover for Seleukos' adventure. But, even if this was the intention, Ptolemy would not have wished to sacrifice Killes' 7,000 men even to help his friend. After defeating Killes Demetrios camped in an area where he was protected by marshes, perhaps in the Eleutheros Valley or in the Ghab area of the Orontes valley, and was clearly not willing to emerge from that shelter until his father arrived with reinforcements.[1]

Seleukos therefore was in no immediate danger of being pursued. What he faced was another matter. He had to travel through two satrapies, and beyond Babylonia was the great command of Media, where Nikanor was satrap. Help and reinforcements could come to Nikanor from Aspeisas in Susiana and from the satrap of Persis, where Asklepiodoros had evidently been replaced by Euagoras, who had been the satrap of Areia.[2] All these are to be presumed to be loyal to Antigonos, and all, particularly Nikanor, had larger armies than the small force Seleukos had led north from the Gaza battlefield. Seleukos, in other words, was tackling half of the Akhaimenid Empire with only his thousand or so men.

It was not, however, quite as one-sided as a count of mere numbers might suggest. In the first place it is reasonable to assume that he had kept in touch with his former satrapy and knew that he had supporters there. It is unlikely Antigonos or Peithon had replaced the whole administration, though some men, loyal to Seleukos, had been rounded up and were jailed in the citadel in Babylon. But there were also presumably still a fair number of men in the government who had originally been appointed by Seleukos. These men included the governors of the sub-sections of the satrapy, usually called hyparchs (such as the man he had disciplined, only to be contradicted by Antigonos), and those in the central administration offices at Babylon.

The welcome he received when he got to the city rather suggests that his governorship was regarded as less unpleasant than that of Antigonos' men. Such at least it is the testimony of Appian and Diodoros.[3] And, of course, Peithon's absence and then his death at Gaza will have left the administration without direction.

There may well have been other factors in Seleukos' favour. After his escape from Babylon, Antigonos had blamed the satrap of Mesopotamia, Blitor, for allowing Seleukos' escaping force to ride through his satrapy.[4] Blitor was sacked, but no replacement is named, and when Seleukos and his men rode into the region in 311, travelling in the reverse direction, no satrap attempted to stop them. In view of Blitor's fate, it is highly probable that a successor would have been more alert, so it would seem there was no satrap after Blitor. It has been theorized that Peithon had added Mesopotamia to his responsibilities along with Babylonia.[5] It is just as likely that Antigonos saw no reason to appoint a new satrap for Mesopotamia. The land was a long stretch of steppe land and semi-desert with only a few population centres of any size; posting small garrisons in such places may have seemed enough, and it was hyparchs of the 'sections' based in the few cities whom Seleukos met on his journey. And, of course, Demetrios will probably have called in many of the men of such garrisons in order to reinforce the Syrian army after the defeat at Gaza. Antigonos, so far as we can see, did not appoint satraps in Syria either, where similar conditions to those in Mesopotamia prevailed, as will be described later. He himself had been in Syria from 315, and Demetrios was in Syria from 314, so probably they acted as their own satraps; Demetrios' position as the king's eldest son would preclude the need to call him satrap.[6]

Seleukos and his men reached the first town in Mesopotamia at Karrhai, having ridden hard from Gaza. It is assumed he set off 'immediately' after the Gaza fight, though it may be he waited to part from Ptolemy until they had reached some way north.[7] He was not apparently detected on his ride through Syria, for neither Demetrios nor Antigonos realized what he was about until after he reached Babylonia. Where he crossed the Euphrates is not known. Thapsakos was the normal crossing place, but it would be well guarded, so he presumably crossed elsewhere. The crossing would be by boat wherever he went – there was as yet no bridge – so perhaps it did not matter where he crossed. He was, as he showed at Karrhai, concerned to keep his adventure secret from Demetrios and Antigonos for as long as possible, so a minor village which had some boats would be sufficient. Since water was always a problem in the region, even in winter, he may have crossed near the confluence of the Balikh River with the Euphrates; it is at this point that there was later founded the city of Nikephorion ('city victorious'), which may well have been named in that way as a commemoration of Seleukos' crossing.[8] Karrhai is further up that river, where the great road from Syria to the upper Tigris crossed it.

When he reached Karrhai he was clearly strong enough to dominate the garrison, and persuaded some of the soldiers to join him. Those who refused were compelled to go with him eastwards in an attempt to keep the expedition secret.[9] (There will have been plenty of people in Karrhai to carry the news to Syria, but civilians are much less likely to hurry with bad news than soldiers.) No other place in Mesopotamia is said to have interrupted the ride, which may be because Seleukos avoided them, or that there were no forces to do so; possibly Demetrios had called them in, or, just as likely, Diodoros simply does not mention them. One would have expected Nisibis, for example, to have a garrison.

The welcome he received in Babylonia apparently began in the north, since Diodoros remarks on it well before he describes Seleukos reaching Babylon city. Another garrison of a thousand men, commanded by a certain Polyarchos, who was the local hyparch, was persuaded to join.[10] It is Polyarchos' reaction by joining Seleukos which provides the best grounds for assuming that Antigonos had left a number of Seleukos' appointees in office. The word of his arrival (and perhaps of Polyarchos' defection) ran ahead of him, but still caught Antigonos' men napping. Those who decided to remain loyal gathered together and took refuge in the citadel of Babylon, under their commander, Diphilos. It is apparent that they were relatively few in number; Seleukos presumably gained still more defections.[11]

Diodoros is very summary at this point, and his account must be supplemented by Babylonian sources. A 'chronicle' from Babylon dated the eventual capture of the Babylon citadel in August of 311. Seleukos had left Ptolemy's army some time after the battle of Gaza, say in January 311, and probably reached Babylon city in the late spring or early summer, certainly after the beginning of the new Babylonian new year in April (since the year-count of the Seleukid era began with that month in 311). How long after April he arrived at the city is not known, but it appears that the capture of the citadel of Babylon took some time. Diodoros implies that the event was over quickly, but the Babylonian chronicle suggests a siege which took some months.[12] Neither side had many troops – Seleukos had only 3,400 men afterwards, even after he had recruited the men at Karrhai, Polyarchos' men, and then more in Babylonia. Diphilos presumably had even fewer, so the siege cannot have been very active. Eventually the citadel was stormed. If Diphilos had only a small force, no doubt parts of the citadel wall were not well guarded.

These exploits were inventive and well attuned to the situation Seleukos was in. He clearly expected to be welcomed, and was obviously aware that Diphilos had only a small force at his disposal. There must have been other outlying garrisons such as that which was commanded by Polyarchos, but they were not relevant when Seleukos had captured Babylon itself. Some now joined Seleukos; others will have joined Diphilos in the citadel or in withdrawing to Antigonos. Already without a satrap, if he could take control of the governing city and remove the temporary governor either by capture or by locking him up in the besieged citadel, he would have returned to his former position as Babylonian satrap. When he took the citadel of Babylon, by rescuing the captives, he would have a group of men who could at once, like him, take up their former posts in the provincial government. Certainly there seems to have been no further overt opposition to him in Babylonia, though any who remained loyal to Antigonos had no doubt escaped into Iran or west towards Syria.

The need to besiege the Babylonian citadel will have become steadily more awkward as time passed. The exploits of Seleukos were no longer secret, and he could expect to be attacked by an Antigonid army as soon as one could be assembled. Antigonos himself was unable to respond. Ptolemy had retired carefully and steadily into Egypt with his forces intact, and was clearly still dangerous. Then Antigonos and Demetrios became involved in a curious war with the Nabataeans of Petra, which can only be considered a pointless distraction. But from the east Nikanor, the satrap of Media, either on his own initiative or as a result of instructions from Antigonos (or, indeed, both) gathered his forces to invade Babylonia.

This would take some time, but Seleukos will have expected something of the sort, hence the need to finish off the resistance in Babylon. Nikanor brought with him Euagoras, the satrap of Persis, and his forces, and commanded an army of 10,000 infantry and 7,000 horse when he came down from Media, presumably through the main pass through the Zagros Mountains at Bisitun, past the old monuments to Akhaimenid victories carved on the cliffs.[13] It may well have been the news of the approach of this army which compelled Seleukos to the desperate measure of storming the citadel at Babylon. If so he would have to turn at once to face his new enemy. It was by now August of 311.

Patrokles was placed in command in Babylon (and guarding the new prisoners). Seleukos had recruited more troops wherever he could in the past few months, but there were not many available in Babylonia, so he set off to fight Nikanor with only 3,000 infantry and 400 cavalry. He was in time to cross the Tigris before Nikanor reached it, and also to spread the disinformation that he had fled when Nikanor arrived.[14] So he was warned well in advance, presumably by scouts posted along the road or in the pass. He had been driven to such cunning by his great numerical inferiority, and this also drove him to the desperate ploy of a night attack on Nikanor's camp, which was poorly guarded – presumably the result of the news of Seleukos' 'flight' and of Nikanor's overconfidence. Nikanor clearly knew that Seleukos had only a small force just as Seleukos clearly knew exactly where Nikanor was all the time, and of the carelessness of his guard.

The night attack had instant success. The Median army panicked. It also seems that Seleukos had deliberately targeted the commanders. The Persis satrap Euagoras 'with some of the other leaders' was killed early on; Nikanor was separated from the rest of the army with only a few men, perhaps his personal guard, and got away. The ordinary soldiers were apparently scarcely damaged. Deprived of their commanders, and probably not under direct attack, they stopped fighting. Seleukos thereupon recruited as many of them as possible into his own army. No doubt he knew of their attitude towards Antigonos, who, not for the first or last time in his career, was shown to be unpopular with his own troops.[15]

Suddenly Seleukos had control not only of his old satrapy but of a substantial army; adding together his and Nikanor's forces gave him something in the region of 20,000 troops (allowing for some casualties in the fighting, and for some of Nikanor's army remaining loyal to Antigonos). Not only that, but Antigonos, counting the losses he had suffered at Gaza and in Babylonia, had seen his huge army of 315 reduced by about 30,000 men (17,000 at the Tigris, 2000 in Mesopotamia and Babylonia, up to 10,000 at Gaza and Tyre); this was getting on for half of his original military manpower. Even beyond that the potential income of 11,000 talents a year which had been calculated for 315, was now well reduced, for Babylonia had been a major source of much of that income (and he was soon to lose more). Again, he had spent lavishly in the last years, above all in building his navy, and so a great deal of the 35,000 talents he had in late 315 had also vanished. If anyone on his enemies' side was keeping count, he could be quietly satisfied that the war which had begun in 314 had been successful in substantially reducing Antigonos' power both in finance and in manpower.

Antigonos, however, had been making progress in the west. Lysimachos had to battle constantly to maintain himself in Thrace; in Greece Antigonos' commander Polemaios was in control of most of the country as far as the borders of Thessaly, and was allied with the Aitolian League. The pressure on Kassander was strong enough to bring him to discuss peace. So while Seleukos was besieging the citadel in Babylon, and Nikanor was gathering his forces in Media, Antigonos received a visit from his envoy Aristodemos who had been contacted by Prepelaos, Kassander's brother, on behalf of both Kassander and Lysimachos. From Greece the two men travelled to see Antigonos at Kelainai in Phrygia. A treaty was quickly made, no doubt because the details had been largely worked out between Aristodemos and Prepelaos on their journey. Lysimachos was included, and Prepelaos spoke for him as well as for his brother. The terms completely ignored the demands of the allies three years before, and the contenders settled on the basis of holding what each had.[16]

This journeying and negotiations will have taken some time. The negotiations took place, it seems, during the summer of 311, but the various journeys (Prepelaos to Aristodemos, then both together from Greece to Kelainai, then their return) can hardly have taken less than a month, and more likely closer to two, even three. Then, once that peace had been agreed, Ptolemy was informed, probably by Kassander (though one must suppose Ptolemy had been kept informed all along). He replied by sending envoys to Antigonos asking to be included on the same terms as the others. Antigonos agreed, but the process was then that he sent three men (Aristodemos, Aischylos, and Hegesias) to take the peace oath from Ptolemy.[17] Again we must expect this process to have taken weeks rather than days. From Kassander's decision to seek peace to Ptolemy's oath-taking must have taken most of the summer, and perhaps into the autumn. Then, of course, the news had to be spread to all the fighting men and the allies of both sides to tell them to stop fighting.

So it was probably after the peace had been made with Ptolemy that news arrived that Seleukos had won his victories in Babylon and over Nikanor. The fighting in Babylon ended in August, and the battle with Nikanor probably took place in September. Seleukos sent a letter to Ptolemy 'and his other friends' – Kassander and Lysimachos, at least – while Nikanor escaped from his defeat and rode off, sending a dispatch of the news to Antigonos, and then returning to his satrapy.[18] It was therefore soon known that Seleukos was still fighting. He went to Susiana after defeating Nikanor; the satrap Aspeisas is not mentioned, but he was presumably removed by Seleukos. Seleukos must have assumed that the war in the west was still on, and will not have heard that his friends had made peace without him until nearly the end of 311.

The death of Euagoras left Persis without a satrap; Nikanor had been comprehensively defeated and was without an army; Aspeisas of Susiana was presumably also removed. By the winter Seleukos was negotiating with the Kossaei (called by the Babylonian Chronicler by the old name of 'Guti'), for the right to march through their territory from Susiana into Media.[19] (Alexander had fought his way through, at some cost; no one else bothered, it was cheaper to pay their fees.) Seleukos appears to have wintered in Susiana. He appointed a new satrap, a man called Euteles; thereby, of course, he was emulating his enemy.[20]

The news of Seleukos' victories, and, perhaps more important, of his capture of so many of Antigonos' troops, undermined the peace agreement in the west. It also probably came as a surprise, since Ptolemy at least can have had little faith in the possibility of success, and it is unlikely anyone else knew of the adventure. But now Seleukos, at a very small cost to Ptolemy, had emerged as a major irritant to Antigonos. And so in the spring of 310, as Seleukos was preparing to move into Media, first Ptolemy, then Polemaios, and finally Kassander, broke the treaty. Ptolemy seems to have been the first since he would be the first to hear the news from Seleukos. He launched an attack into Kilikia, claiming that Antigonos had infringed the terms of the peace by garrisoning Greek cities – the peace terms had evidently incorporated the declarations Antigonos and Ptolemy had both made to respect the cities' autonomy. Polemaios was apparently jealous of the rising importance of Demetrios in Antigonos' counsels and contacted Kassander with whom he made an alliance, then suborned some of the men he had been instrumental in appointing as Antigonid governors. Antigonos was thus under pressure in Greece, Kilikia, and Babylonia.

In this situation, Ptolemy's attack in Kilikia is militarily and strategically the most interesting. He had raided the area once already, of course, but this new attack seems to have been more than a raid. His general Leonides seized control of a number of cities.[21] These are not specified, but one would assume Tarsos and Adana at least, perhaps Mallos, possibly Issos and Soloi. The strategic point is that by holding this area Ptolemy was effectively cutting Antigonos' realm in two, and inflicting pressure on him in yet another area. The passes through the Taurus and Amanus mountains – the Kilikian and Syrian Gates – were the main connection between Antigonos' lands in Asia Minor and those in Syria, unless one went the long way round by way of the upper Euphrates to intercept the old Persian Royal Road. Even if Leonides could not hold his conquests permanently – and he was driven out fairly soon – he compelled Antigonos to devote time and resources to recovering the region. In fact the task was assigned to Demetrios who had done well against the Nabataeans and who now efficiently removed Leonides.[22] But it all took time, and meanwhile Ptolemy had contacted Kassander and Lysimachos.

By the time of this contact Kassander had already persuaded Polemaios to rebel, and he had in turn brought the governor of Hellespontine Phrygia, Phoinix, into the new alliance. Antigonos reacted by sending his youngest son Philippos to deal with Phoinix. Against Kassander he sent Polyperchon, the former regent, who was given Alexander's bastard son Herakles as a pretender to be used against Kassander, and with him he invaded Macedon. Ptolemy, once his invasion of Kilikia had failed, took to the sea and operated in Pamphylia and Lykia and Karia.[23] All this necessarily preoccupied Antigonos and delayed any action he could take against Seleukos. From his winter quarters in Susiana Seleukos, having obtained a right of way through the Kossaean hills, invaded Media. Nikanor had returned there after his defeat and had gathered a new army, but he will have been much weaker than the year before, in numbers, in authority, and in confidence. If his best army had in effect deserted him in the battle, he cannot have been at all sure that the army he had gathered afterwards was trustworthy. In fact, when the two antagonists met, Seleukos is said to have killed Nikanor personally.[24] It looks as if, once more, as at Gaza and in the Tigris fight, Seleukos was striking directly at the enemy commander in the certain knowledge that this would end the fighting.

This, as ever, took a considerable time. Seleukos cannot have got through the Kossaean Hills before the late spring, and though we do not have any clear sign of how long the campaign against Nikanor took, he did not return to Babylonia at all during 310. The Median campaign was thus probably a lot more complicated than the single fight in which Nikanor was killed. It is not clear that Seleukos went as far as Persis, or if he dealt with the satraps of the Central Asian provinces at this stage, but it is likely that he would need to spend a good deal of time organizing his conquests. We know he appointed a new satrap, Euteles, to take the place of Aspeisas in Susiana; he will also have had to appoint new satraps to Media and Persis, since both of Antigonos' satraps were dead, but it is not known who the new men were.

Seleukos therefore had a full agenda in Iran. In Babylonia his governor Patrokles had to face Antigonos' riposte. This was assigned to Demetrios once he had proved, as he did in Kilikia, he was not quite the reckless boy he had been at Gaza and earlier. But having to reconquer Kilikia first meant it was not until well into the campaigning season of 310 that Demetrios could begin. He had a force of 15,000 infantry and 4,000 cavalry at his disposal. These numbers emphasize the cost to Antigonos of his losses, for such an army was not big enough to do the job.[25] It was a smaller army than that now commanded by Seleukos, even if he had to leave a good part of his force in Iran. (He must have been able to recruit more men from Nikanor's second army.)

Seleukos ignored Demetrios' attack for a time, partly because of its relative weakness, but there were other elements involved as well. Ptolemy had promised to send more help when Seleukos set off, and now, while the fighting was still going on in Kilikia, he did so.[26] It could be that Seleukos did not want to expose too many of his own formerly Antigonid soldiers to Demetrios, whose military charisma was such that he was followed faithfully by many an army in the years to come, unlike his father, from whom many soldiers deserted when they could. On the other hand, Demetrios' campaign into Babylonia was a move into enemy territory, where Seleukos' popular welcome had already made it clear that Antigonos was very much disliked. An Antigonid army of less than 20,000 men would probably be enough to hold down Babylonia, if Demetrios reconquered it, and given this force, it is reasonable to conclude that Demetrios expected to fight a single battle, and that the province would then surrender to him – this, after all, is what Seleukos had done. But Babylonian hostility meant that even if he won such a battle, he would still need to garrison several places, so that the size of his field force would quickly dwindle. Even if Demetrios won, therefore, Babylonia would be a heavy drain on Antigonos' military strength.

Patrokles' strategy was based on that which had been followed, perhaps inadvertently, by Diphilos the year before. He had few troops, since Seleukos had taken most of the army into Media, and so he put those he had into the two citadels in Babylon city, which had no doubt been repaired and strengthened in preparation. As Demetrios approached on his long march from Damascus, Patrokles moved the entire civilian population out of the city, sending some into Susiana (where Seleukos could come down from Media to protect them if Demetrios threatened them there), or into the desert west of the Euphrates (and into the southern part of Babylonia as well, to the neighbourhood of the Persian Gulf, a region which Demetrios did not invade). He had a mobile force which made Demetrios' approach difficult by opening canals, flooding fields, breaking bridges, and fighting his patrols.[27]

It was perhaps at this point that Ptolemy sent some men to Babylon across the Arabian Desert, making the journey on camels and carrying their own water supply, taking eight days on the journey. This is only recorded in Arrian's book on India, in what seems an insertion into the main text (it has little to do with India) and Arrian compares it with an exploit said to have been accomplished by some refugees from Kambyses' invasion of Egypt two centuries before.[28] There is no date assigned to this Ptolemaic expedition but if it really was an armed force it cannot have been very large – Ptolemy was busy himself – so we must imagine it as a small force, which was essentially carrying a message, and which crossed the desert because it was not safe to travel by way of Syria and Mesopotamia; undoubtedly Antigonos' and Demetrios' forces were now fully alert to the possibility of an enemy force repeating Seleukos' exploit.

This event would fit best into the crisis of 310, when Ptolemy will have known that Demetrios was setting out to attack Seleukos' position in Babylon – he started his march in Damascus, a region where Ptolemy will have had agents to warn him of possible attacks. It was thus perhaps as much a warning of what was coming, rather than a reinforcement. Seleukos had a greater army than Demetrios, and any Ptolemaic reinforcement travelling the desert route would be so small as to be irrelevant in force terms, but the message and the arrival of however small a force will have boosted morale amongst Seleukos' force in Babylonia. So, warned by Ptolemy of Demetrios' approach, Patrokles will have been able to pass the message on to Seleukos and they could then co-ordinate their responses. It must have been Seleukos' decision to evacuate Babylon city, and it must have been his authority which dissuaded the citizens from complaining – though no doubt they did. Supplies in Susiana had to be stockpiled, and, if many people were sent out into the desert, other supplies were needed there. And, of course, sending such supplies off with the refugees would mean there was less for Demetrios' army when it arrived.

Demetrios therefore faced a difficult problem, perhaps more awkward than Patrokles'. The Babylonian population was hostile (or absent), there were no reinforcements available from his father, who was fully occupied with fighting in Asia Minor and in Greece, and any hopes he had of linking up with Nikanor were extinguished when the latter was killed. (It seems probable that Nikanor's second army followed the first into Seleukos' employ; even if it did not, it would be very difficult for any of the men to reach Demetrios, after Seleukos' victories in Iran.) Delayed and distracted by Patrokles' obstructions and by the unexpected situation facing him, it was some time before Demetrios managed to reach Babylon, probably not until fairly late in 310. He will have left Damascus in the early summer (after the spring campaign in Kilikia), and will have taken at least a month to march to Mesopotamia, so reaching Babylonia in August was not bad going. But he was then stuck in a siege.[29]

At the city he captured one of the two citadels, but could not take the other despite a siege lasting some months – again, the parallel with Seleukos fighting Diphilos is close. Demetrios spent the winter on this, but by February 309 the situation in the west required his return there. He detached a commander, Archelaos, with 5,000 infantry and 1,000 cavalry, to continue the occupation of Babylon and the siege of the citadel. He took the rest of his army on a savage looting raid as far as Cutha on the Tigris, and then marched off to Syria.[30] He reached the coast of the Aegean by the summer of 309.

Meanwhile Seleukos completed whatever he was doing in Iran – Plutarch implies that he was involved in some way in a campaign as far as 'India and Mount Caucasus', but this may refer to his later campaign.[31] He returned to Babylonia, probably in the spring, but it then took some time to drive out Archelaos' force. Even more devastation was the result.[32] It seems that much of 309 can be accounted for in this way.

The years 310–309 saw the final elimination of the family of Alexander the Great, with just one exception. Olympias had already murdered Philip Arrhidaios and driven his wife and half-sister Eurydike to suicide; Alexander's bastard Herakles was used by Polyperchon, but later murdered by him as part of an agreement with Kassander; Kassander himself had acquired control of Alexander IV and Roxane when he eliminated Olympias and, probably soon after the peace of 311, he had them murdered as well. The last member of the family (but one) was Kleopatra, Alexander's sister, who was kept in confinement by Antigonos at Sardis; when she attempted to escape to join Ptolemy in 309, Antigonos had her killed by some of her women, then killed the women and cynically attended her funeral. There was nothing to choose between any of these ambitious and brutal men.

But this did not clear the air. With only Thessalonike, Alexander's half-sister, of the old Argead royal family still alive, there was nothing now to prevent the murderers proclaiming themselves kings in place of the virtually extinct dynasty. Kassander, being married to Thessalonike, could perhaps claim the Macedonian kingship by right of marriage. What other claimants required to lend legitimacy to their self-proclamation was a resounding victory. In 308 Antigonos turned east in search of such a victory, for it must have seemed that Seleukos was much the weakest of Antigonos' competitors, and his defeat would both remove an irritant and recover a very large empire. Kassander had been very difficult to attack in Macedon, where, as Antipater's son and Thessalonike's husband, he had a good hereditary claim to control; similarly Ptolemy had entrenched himself in Egypt, which was no longer easy to invade, and he had a substantial naval force with which he had repeatedly intervened in the Aegean and Greece. Lysimachos was probably actually the weakest of the four, but he was firmly allied with Kassander, and it was certain that an attack on one would be regarded by the other as an attack on both. Seleukos, on the other hand, had a substantial army but one which was composed of men formerly in Antigonos' employ, whom he must have expected would be easy to persuade to rejoin him. Also Seleukos had apparently taken quite some time to remove Archelaos and his small army from Babylonia, which implied a distinct military weakness. Seleukos clearly appeared to be the most vulnerable.

If these were Antigonos' calculations he was wrong, because he did not take into account Seleukos himself. Seleukos had been compelled, ever since the invasion of his satrapy by Eumenes, and then by Antigonos, in 317, to operate on a shoestring. Only since the second battle with Nikanor had he commanded a force larger than his enemy; to survive he had had to be guileful and tricky, and this was the secret of his defeat of Antigonos in the latter's invasion.

Seleukos held the Iranian Plateau and Babylonia. Antigonos controlled Asia Minor and Syria from Kilikia to Gaza. Thinly inhabited Mesopotamia, between the Euphrates and the Tigris, and south of the Anatolian mountains and north of the Syrian desert, was now a frontier area between the two. To reach Seleukos Antigonos had to march his army through Mesopotamia, a long march of at least a month and a half, which would give Seleukos plenty of warning of his approach. Seleukos could afford to await the attack. It must be admitted that this is largely speculative, since virtually no information about this part of the war has survived. The one secure item is a description of Seleukos' victory, preserved as one of Polyainos' *Stratagems*. The two armies met in battle, with no result; then they separated for the night. Antigonos' men camped, disarmed, ate and slept. Seleukos, just as he had done against Nikanor, kept his men alert and made a surprise attack before dawn.[33]

Antigonos escaped, as Nikanor had. So, probably, did most of his army, though it is possible that Seleukos captured some of the men or recruited more. Again none of this is certain, except the victory, and Antigonos' survival. It seems that peace was then made between the two men, sometime late in 308 or maybe in 307.[34] If this is the correct date, it follows that, as usual, most of the detail of the war has vanished from the record, and this time the Babylonian chronicles are of little help. So Polyainos' battle was only one incident in a war which had lasted for at least three years, even four if it can be reckoned from the battle of Gaza. At the end, also, the details of the peace are not known, though it probably amounted to both men keeping what they had gained – that is, that Antigonos gave up any intention of reconquering Babylonia and Iran, at least for the present. The most convincing argument that a peace treaty was arranged is that both men then ignored each other for the next five years. Antigonos, though based much of the time in northern Syria, never attempted to invade Seleukos' territory, and Seleukos went off into the east for the next four years, apparently quite certain that Antigonos would not attack him. It follows that the peace treaty they had agreed was binding, oath-made, and that both respected it.

Chapter Five

Expedition to the East

There were other factors than Antigonos and Seleukos keeping their words in the maintenance of peace between them after the treaty of 307. Above all, Antigonos' attention switched decisively to the west. He sent Demetrios to capture Athens and campaign in Greece in 307, brought him to Cyprus and a great victory over Ptolemy in 306, which he followed by proclaiming himself and Demetrios kings, and then they failed in a great campaign against Ptolemy in Egypt. Then he became distracted into a rather pointless siege of Rhodes until early in 304. This was quite on the pattern with Antigonos' earlier activities: he was never really concerned about the east, though he was certainly annoyed that Seleukos should rise up again and still more that he had taken control of tax-generating Babylonia, but the loss of Media was of as little concern to him as his failure to gain any real power further east after defeating Eumenes in 316.

It may have given him some satisfaction to note that as a result of the fighting against Seleukos much of Babylonia had been seriously damaged. Canals had been broken and fields flooded, which meant that the canals were drained and the water was wasted for agriculture. Some of the cities – Babylon and Cutha at least, and probably others – had been seriously damaged or sacked, and parts at least of their populations had been removed. The displacement of a substantial part of the population into refugee camps in Susiana and the desert had been more than upsetting. 'He plundered city and countryside', said the Chronicler of Demetrios, 'he set fire to the storehouse of Nergal', and 'there was weeping and mourning in the land'.[1] The disorganization of all economic life, and therefore of the production of tax revenue, had been profound and it would take some time for recovery.

The two antagonists may have effectively ignored each other after 307, but neither was convinced that there would not be more fighting. There were always excuses to be found for a fight if any ruler was so inclined and Antigonos by assuming the royal title was effectively putting into institutional form his constant aim of establishing himself as superior to all the rest, if not as a new Alexander, then as a new Philip, who was his contemporary. To be constantly on their guard was obviously a factor in the lives of all these rulers, especially since they had seen so many of their fellows killed in battle, by murder, by assassination, or by execution.

The peace treaty had left both men in control of the lands they held at the time it was concluded. We do not know what these lands were except in the most general terms – Seleukos held Media and Babylonia, Susiana and Persis, Antigonos Syria and Asia Minor. Mesopotamia was divided between them, but this was a large area and relatively easy to cross. Both men had campaigned through it more than once so they understood that there were no natural obstacles in the way, except perhaps three rivers of no great size, the Euphrates, the Balikh, and the Khabur. They therefore seem to have used these rivers as frontier lines, but reinforced them with artificial obstacles to deter or prevent invasion; this, with other cities, produced a defence in depth on both sides.

Another activity of Antigonos in these years of his concentration on western matters was the foundation of several new cities or the refoundation of others. He busied himself in establishing the three new cities facing the Straits, which were noted in Chapter 2, either by founding new ones or by dragooning the people of several smaller cities into one larger one. Clearly one of the main reasons for this was for defence, since across the Straits Lysimachos was finally establishing his control over Thrace and building up an extremely large army.

In Syria Antigonos set about building an entirely new city, Antigoneia-on-Orontes, where he lived during much of the time that Demetrios was campaigning in the west. It was there that he had organized the 'spontaneous' ceremony of being proclaimed king, which suggests that it was intended to be his royal city, as the Babylonians might have put it.[2] This was also a useful post for keeping an eye on any activities by Ptolemy or by Seleukos, the beginning of the development of Syria as a major strategic centre. Antigonos may have slowed down in his battle capabilities, as his defeat by Seleukos implies, but his strategic sense, always acute, had unerringly located North Syria as the crucial point of power in the eastern Mediterranean. This building activity again was a legacy of Philip, one which, of course, Alexander had taken up as well. The exact date of the founding is not clear, though he is said to have been occupied in the process in 306, so the year before, or 306, looks to be likely for the start of work; Diodoros gives a summary description only.[3]

In addition there was a considerable number of smaller settlements scattered through Syria, most of which were probably not 'official' foundations by any of the kings, but were places where Macedonians or Greeks had settled, probably originally forming garrisons to hold the land, and to guard supplies for larger campaigning armies. These places are distinguished from later foundations and from local towns and cities by their Macedonian names; Europos, Pella, Kyrrhos, Doliche, Beroia, and others – whereas later cities, founded by the kings, were normally given dynastic names (such as Antigoneia), and the local names were, of course, in Aramaic. The more or less regular distribution of these Macedonian names through Syria and Palestine emphasizes their military origins. (See also on this Chapter 7.)

There were two groups of these earlier foundations in Mesopotamia. One group lay along the line of the Balikh River and consisted of at least three towns, Edessa, Karrhai, and Ichnai, on or just west of the river; also at the southern junction of the Balikh and the Euphrates was Nikephorion, which, from its name, is reckoned to be a later Seleukid foundation, but may actually have been a Macedonian garrison town of Antigonos' time renamed by Seleukos later; it may have been where Seleukos' small army crossed the Euphrates, hence the reference to a victory. It is an important position if one was guarding the Balikh valley, which is what was clearly intended by all the others; this line of fortified places may thus be interpreted as Antigonos' forward defence line between 308 and 301.

To the east there were two other places, Doura-Europos on the Euphrates, and Nisibis in the upper valley of the Khabur River, which are placed so as to block advances from the west along the two main routes. The eastern part of Mesopotamia is much drier than the west and traffic concentrated along the valley of the Euphrates or along the foothills of the mountains in the north, so these two places were well situated to interrupt movement. Nisibis in the Tur Abdin hills was an old – immensely old – city, but Europos is a clearly Macedonian name which was added to its original local name of Dura. These two may thus be interpreted as Seleukid foundations facing those of Antigonos.[4]

It seems therefore that Antigonos had carefully established military control over the western part of Mesopotamia with a line of garrisons controlling the Balikh valley in advance of his part of the Euphrates, which, without a bridge yet, was another obstacle. Seleukos in reply, or simultaneously, had also established fortified blocks on the main routes, the foothills and the river, which would be used by any invading army heading for his territories. Neither set of garrisons would be strong enough to prevent a major invasion, but by keeping alert they could certainly provide advance warning of any movement, and possibly slow down an enemy advance. Between them, between the valleys of the Balikh and the Khabur, was a no-man's-land. No doubt both forces organized patrols in this area, and no doubt their local commanders carefully established contact with their opponents in order to avoid any accidental conflicts, but it would clearly be necessary for both forces to be fully aware of what each other was up to. There may be peace, but alertness was still required.

These two opposing lines of fortified towns may be regarded as the forward defences in front of the metropolitan regions of Syria and Babylonia. They were all relatively small places and a major attack would never be more than delayed by any of them; indeed any of them could be mastered, blockaded, and/or by-passed relatively easily. For the metropolitan areas the major defences were the great cities which the rival rulers were founding more or less simultaneously. And both Antigonos and Seleukos began work on their new cities just at the time that they made peace. Seleukos' new city of Seleukeia, as noted in the previous chapter was in fact a twin for Babylon, planted to block access from the north or northeast and along the Tigris, just as Babylon blocked the Euphrates route. These two cities were thus in military terms the great bases from which the defence of Babylonia could be conducted, and Antigoneia performed the same purpose for Syria.

Founding cities was one of the marks of sovereignty in the Hellenistic world system, which was one of the reasons Antigonos did it; it may be that Seleukos did so as an indication of his independence of Antigonos, to deny any claim Antigonos had made since his victory over Eumenes had propelled him into revealing that he intended to be the supreme ruler. This is one motive; the strategic one is another. Yet another, as the priests of Babylon perceived, was to provide a rival to the older city, and one which was not so heavily burdened with memories and starched institutions; it was to be a Greco-Macedonian city, with Macedonian titles for the magistrates (*peliganes*), a place where Macedonian kings and soldiers could be themselves, and not constantly on the alert to avoid trampling on local sensibilities.[5]

The more one considers the site, however, the more it becomes clear that it was above all strategic imperatives which dictated not merely its size, but its geographical position and its site. The size of the place was designed to compete in prestige terms with Antigoneia and with Babylon, and perhaps even with Alexandria. Its site was chosen in part because it was three-quarters surrounded by water – the Tigris and the branches of the Royal

Canal – which would be defensive moats, provide plentiful supplies of water, and allow relatively easy transport for food and other supplies into the place.

But it is the overall strategic position of the city which is the most compelling element in the choice of situation. The backstop role against any invasion from Syria has been mentioned already. Babylon had performed that role twice, in 311 and 310, driving home the obvious lesson that a large fortress on the river was an effective defence. Two fortresses were even better. But Babylon was on only one of the rivers, blocking the Euphrates route. Anyone who had been with Alexander's expedition was also familiar with the Tigris route. Alexander had crossed Mesopotamia close to the Taurus foothills, had fought Dareios III near Arbela, and then moved south close to the Tigris; Eumenes had done the same, followed by Antigonos. This was as likely an invasion route as the Euphrates, and Seleukeia blocked it.

It was also close to the junction of the Diyala River route with the Tigris, which was the way into Iran, either to the northwest of that plateau-country, or towards the old Median capital at Ekbatana (by way of the Bisitun Pass). This had been Nikanor's invasion route, and Seleukeia effectively formed a backstop to it also – or a base from which Iran could be invaded.

Taking all these elements into account it seems clear that Seleukos was aiming at several targets with his new city. Its size was a political statement of aspiration among the world of the Hellenistic potentates. It was larger than the cities of Kassander and Lysimachos, and probably larger than any of those of Antigonos. Of course, Seleukos was building a city in a land which had been urbanized for millennia, but even so he was building a greater city than any which had ever existed even in Babylonia in the past. He was building a city which was to be the companion and eventually the successor to Babylon. He was therefore aiming to recruit local Babylonian sentiment, despite the priests, and perhaps to exploit local Babylonian regard for him, since he was clearly well-liked. After Demetrios' invasion and devastation he could put forward a good case for establishing a well-fortified city, a thought reinforced by the memory of Nikanor's invasion out of Iran. He was aiming to outdo his main rival Antigonos by building a greater city than his, possibly even waiting until he found out what Antigonos' plans were before going ahead and aiming even higher. And by emulating Alexander both in founding a new great city and in making it close to the same size as Alexander's greatest foundation, he was bidding to be recognized as Alexander's true successor.

This, as it happened, was not a difficult aim. Seleukos' allies, Ptolemy, Kassander, and Lysimachos, were the rocks on which Alexander's empire crashed. Antigonos may not have been keen on the eastern regions and India, but until Seleukos' war he had controlled most of the old empire, and had he succeeded in bringing in the satraps of the west it is highly probable that he would have made some attempt to deal with the other dissidents – probably by sending Demetrios to do so. But he had failed in the west, both in Europe and in Egypt, and now he was apparently content to abandon everything east of the Balikh River. So none of Seleukos' colleagues, rivals, or enemies now harboured the aim of being Alexander's successor in the sense of ruling his whole empire. Ptolemy, Kassander, and Lysimachos had organized their satrapies as independent kingdoms, and only awaited the appropriate signal to become kings. Antigonos' aim at first had been to rule the whole empire, but he had repeatedly fallen short, by lack of interest in some areas, and by his unpleasant methods – from the execution of Eumenes to the devastation of Babylonia – and by 310 he was old enough to have had much of his ambition burned out, and Demetrios, charismatic though he was, was also erratic and arrogant. Seleukos, however, had risen from nothing in 312 to be the ruler of half of the empire in 310; he had defeated the premier warriors of the age, Antigonos and Demetrios; it is highly likely that he had by this time developed in him a case of Antigonos' original ambition.

This is therefore the significance of the great city founded by Seleukos. It was bigger than any except Alexandria-by-Egypt, Alexander's great foundation. It was close to several places which were vital parts of Alexander's story – Arbela, Babylon, Opis itself. It was planted in a region of great agricultural and commercial wealth, which made it possible to support the existence of such a large community. The mint in Babylon which had been producing coins in the name of Alexander the Great and his son Alexander IV for over twenty years was transferred to the new city; the coins now substituted 'Seleukos' for Alexander's name.[6] That is, Seleukeia-on-the-Tigris was designed from the start as an imperial capital, and as such it was a statement by Seleukos of his own ambition, of his claim, which his competitors had renounced or had never had, to be the only real heir of Alexander; the new city is a statement that his aim was to reconstitute Alexander's broken empire.

This was hardly new. It seems likely that he had formed his ambition by the time he set off from Palestine to recover Babylonia. He is recorded as being the one man on that expedition who was quite confident of success from the start and told a mythical story of his earlier experiences to explain it.[7] This may, of course, be merely a literary trope, but he did set out with only a thousand or so men to face the ruler of most of Alexander's empire, a gesture of self-confidence if ever there was one. And in Babylonia there were stories about him, probably circulating during his war with Demetrios, which imply that his ambition and confidence were recognized locally, stories which may or may not be true, though they are probably based on actual events. This strongly supports the view that he was both lucky and perceived as being favoured by the gods.

One story claimed that on a river cruise with Alexander, perhaps in 330 or 324, the king's diadem blew off and Seleukos dived in to rescue it; the only way to bring it back dry – it had landed in some reeds – was to put it on his own head – and behold! This was a prefiguration of his later kingship. (Another version attributes the action to an unknown sailor, which is perhaps more likely.) Then there were the awkward priests of Esagila, who had worked well on Alexander's superstition but had failed with Seleukos. He did provide subsidies, and he was called 'the custodian of Emeslam', and there are references connecting him with Borsippa as well as Esagila.[8] And he did defend Babylon, while his enemies had ravaged it.

A response by the oracle of Apollo at Didyma was circulated, which Seleukos had visited during Alexander's campaign in Ionia. He had been told that he should ignore Europe, Asia would be enough for him.[9] In this case there may be some basis in fact for the story. Seleukos was later devoted to the shrine at Didyma and presented it with rich gifts, as did his wife; he had passed by the place with Alexander (it had prophesied for him as well), and it would be characteristic of many Macedonians to visit and consult the oracle at the start of what was by then turning out to be a huge adventure.[10] And, of course, the oracle's response is quite unspecific, assuming it was not manufactured later. It is certain that Seleukos was devoted to Apollo all along.

All these stories, whether true or not, circulated sufficiently widely to have been recorded by later historians. The purpose of broadcasting them was, of course, as persuaders. Various groups were the target – Apollo for the Greeks and Macedonians in his army, the local superstitions for the Babylonians, priests and laymen, and all of them for his competitors (who had myth-stories of their own). It did no harm for a man like Seleukos to be thought lucky and divinely favoured. The groundwork for his actions following the treaty with Antigonos may also be seen to be laid; he turned east, as the Didyma oracle had suggested.

   The dating of Seleukos' activities after the defeat of Antigonos is not easy to sort out. The war with Demetrios in Babylonia lasted into 309. Demetrios withdrew during that year. Archelaos kept up the fight for another year or so. Then Antigonos attacked in 308. We know of only one battle – Seleukos' night attack on the unwary Antigonid army – but the distances and enmities involved require several months to have elapsed before Antigonos could admit defeat and the two men could negotiate a treaty, probably still in 308.

   Then Seleukos had to supervise the fortification and garrisoning of Europos and Nisibis, though he would not need to be present for this, but he was certainly in attendance when the layout of the new city of Seleukeia and the ceremony of starting work took place; he also had to attend to the recovery of Babylonia. It is unlikely he could have set off on his next campaign before the late summer of 307 (which is the best date for the founding of Seleukeia), and it might not have been until early 306. As a political control for this estimate, Demetrios' occupation of Athens took place in the early summer of 307, which implies that his father was already at Antigoneia in Syria from where he could supervise the western campaigns. Seleukos could not really feel safe from an attack until he and Antigonos had both agreed a peace treaty and taken the oaths required, but when Antigonos' military ambition and attention were so decisively directed westwards, Seleukos could feel relatively safe.

   So it was either late in 307 or more probably in the spring of 306 that Seleukos took his army through the Zagros Mountains (or perhaps by way of Susiana and through the Kossaean Hills), into Media. He stayed in the east until 302, when he returned for the final campaign to destroy Antigonos' kingdom, but he already knew he had to do so the year before, i.e. 303. The war began when Kassander and Lysimachos sent their joint forces across the Hellespont in early 302, but they only began the war once it was clear that both Ptolemy and Seleukos would join them. Since travel was very difficult in winter, they must have contacted Seleukos and received his agreement during 303. Seleukos therefore knew from perhaps the middle of that year that he had to march west as soon as the passes were open in 302.

   It follows that Seleukos' eastern campaign was very limited in time, from early 306 to late 303, a maximum of four campaigning seasons. Other accounts suggest such dates as 308 to 302 (the maximum) but this would mean ignoring travel time and ignoring also the other work he had to do in the west during 308 and 307. The war with Antigonos may well have ended in 308, but it was scarcely possible to set off to the east immediately;

some time for organizing and preparing must be allowed. Since he had only four campaigning seasons during which he had to attend to any problem in the lands he already ruled – Susiana, Persis, Media – then investigate and impose his authority on the turbulent Baktrian-Sogdian region, and to conduct a military campaign into India, it follows that much of his work was necessarily superficial, though we can in fact reduce the load somewhat.

The measures he would need to take in the Iranian regions were probably not so difficult or time-consuming. He had already spent some time there in 311–310, and we know he had appointed at least one satrap, Euteles in Susiana; no doubt other men had been appointed to Persis and in Media, but we do not know their names. Beyond the eastern boundaries of Persis and Media no western army had penetrated since the year following Alexander's death. Satraps of the Central Asian provinces, in eastern Iran and in India, had been largely ignored in all the manoeuvring since then. Only Eumenes had contacted them, and only Antigonos had replaced any expired satraps. Since 316 they had been ignored by the western contenders.

At least such is the conclusion we must reach on the basis of the written sources available to us – but that was not the reality of the time. Seleukos and his contemporaries will have known a good deal about conditions in the east, from travellers, from letters, from messages, from spies, and the east had only been left to itself because it did not pose any threat to the western rulers. When Seleukos marched east in 306 to plant his authority over the eastern parts of the defunct empires of Alexander, the Akhaimenids, and Antigonos, it is beyond belief that he did so in complete ignorance of what awaited him, and in fact we can make some more or less valid assumptions about what he faced.

First, the Macedonian position in India, with satraps and subordinate local kings, is mentioned until at least 316 when the satrap Eudamos, who had assassinated King Poros the year before, came west with 120 war elephants to join Eumenes when he was summoned along with the other eastern governors.[11] Some time after 316 the Indian adventurer Chandragupta Maurya gained control of the Indus Valley – 'liberated' it – and drove out the Macedonian governors.[12] By the time Seleukos approached, therefore, ten years later, the Indian political situation had been thoroughly transformed. Chandragupta had expanded his kingdom into the Ganges Valley where he had overthrown the old and corrupt Nanda dynasty which had ruled the dominant Magadhan kingdom for the previous half-century. He thus ruled a united North India, from Bengal to the Khyber Pass.[13] His liberation of the

Punjab region may have involved expelling Greeks, and if so, this probably refers only to Greek and Macedonian rulers, of whom, once Eudamos had left, there cannot have been many.

The second major region Seleukos had to deal with, Baktria-Sogdiana, the region north of the Hindu Kush, was formed of the valleys of the Oxus (Amu-darya), the Polymelitos (Zarafshan) and the Jaxartes (Syr-darya). Here Alexander had had very great difficulty in enforcing his rule, and resorted to the savagery which he also displayed in India. In particular the northern regions, the Polymelitos Valley and the lands towards the Jaxartes, had been ravaged, fields destroyed, populations massacred, villages burned. His aim was to dominate the region which until recently had been only lightly governed, if at all, by the Akhaimenids, though it seems that a renewed attempt at control had been made by his immediate predecessors. His demonstrations provoked the nomads of the northern region, from both sides of the Jaxartes, and it was their alliance with the sedentary population which had made Alexander's war so difficult.

Alexander had left a large number of Greek mercenaries in garrisons, in new city foundations, and as settlers in the huge region, but when he died many of these men made a determined attempt to go 'home'. They were stopped by Peithon, sent to do so by Perdikkas, and it seems that most of the rebels were compelled, or more likely persuaded, to return to Baktria. Perdikkas is said to have ordered Peithon to kill all the rebels, but, quite apart from the impossibility of doing so, and pointlessness of it, Peithon did not even attempt it. He did massacre one group, but of the 23,000 Greeks in the rebel army, at least 20,000 survived and returned to Baktria.[14]

This was in 323. In 311, when Seleukos campaigned in Media and eliminated Nikanor, he had probably contacted whoever was in office in Baktria, but he could do no more than that, given the pressures on his position in Babylonia. Maybe he secured a form of submission, but it cannot have been more than a formal gesture, for he had at the time no higher post than that of a usurping satrap of Babylonia. He could not send help, nor could he expect to get any reinforcements from the east. Even Eumenes, who had an official position from the regent, and had acquired armed help from most of the eastern satraps in 316, was sent nothing by the Baktrian satrap of the day, Stasanor. It was evidently thought too dangerous to weaken his position by sending troops away – though he did send some men who were his local opponents, presumably hoping they would never return. (His own aim is not known, but it is likely he was another of those seeking effective independence.) By 306, if Stasanor still lived and ruled, the Macedonian position in Baktria had probably deteriorated further. None of the satraps who were appointed or confirmed by Antigonos in 316 can be traced beyond that year, though given the absence of sources we cannot assume they had disappeared any more than that they had survived.

Central Asia in this period was formed of a series of large provinces which were still those which had been organized by the Akhaimenid empire two centuries earlier. Moving east from Media, there was Parthia, southeast of the Caspian Sea, which was mainly an extension of the high Median plateau; its northern edge was along the Kopek Dagh escarpment, where the land fell away to the Kara Kum desert to the north. The eastern boundary of this satrapy was probably at the Arios River, beyond which was Margiana, centred on the inland delta of the river and modern Merv. Then Baktria, with Sogdiana to its north. It is sometimes claimed that the Oxus River was the boundary between these two regions, but it makes more sense to see the Oxus valley as a unit and the border in the mountain range to the north. (This is where in fact it was placed at some periods later.) This would make Sogdiana the area centred on the Polymelitos River valley (the modern Zerafshan), with the land as far as the Jaxartes added to it; much of this land was inhabited by nomads, and the Polymelitos Valley had been atrociously ravaged by Alexander. It had probably fallen out of the rule of any Macedonian satrap since Alexander. Seleukos' wife, Apama, came from this region, but, given its devastation, it is difficult to see how influential such a connection was. It does not seem likely that she herself had any influence, though the fact that their son, Antiochus, was half-Sogdian, may have had some importance later.

South of Baktria, and separated from it by the giant Hindu Kush mountain range, was the Paropamisadai, the region about modern Kabul; to the east, in the valley of the Kabul River, was Gandara, containing the city of Taxila and opening into the Indus Valley and the Punjab. South of the Paropamisadai was the large province of Arachosia, centred on Kandahar. To the west of Arachosia and between it and southern Parthia were two minor provinces, Drangiana around the basin of the Helmand Lake, and Areia, bordering on Margiana to the north. Along the coast of the Arabian Sea were two desert provinces, Gedrosia and Karmania, the former close to India, the latter bordering on Persis.

Of these the most important from Seleukos' point of view was Baktria, since that had the greatest concentration of Greek and Macedonian colonists.

It has been theorized that the confusion in the region had probably brought about this concentration, partly because it was a wealthy agricultural area with a considerable urban element in the population, and partly because it was well defended by its mountains. If this is so, and it seems reasonable, it follows that some regions had been effectively abandoned.[15]

The most dangerous area, and the most easily let go, was Sogdiana, much of which had been destroyed by Alexander during his campaigns. It can be assumed that any Greeks and Macedonians in that region had retired to Baktria, if they had survived. Others had come in from India, possibly evacuated by Eudamos or driven out by Chandragupta, though it is probable that still others had remained there; Chandragupta was principally concerned to remove the administration, not necessarily the men. It seems likely that there were still Greek-speakers in the Paropamisadai and Arachosia – Kandahar had a sufficiently numerous Greek population fifty years later for Chandragupta's grandson Asoka to publish one of his edicts there in Greek; Kandahar, also, was an Alexandria, one of the king's cities.[16] It seems unlikely that there were many Greeks or Macedonians in the desert regions of Karmania and Gedrosia, though there had been satraps in office in both areas until at least 316. So by the time Seleukos began his march from the west in 306 it was clear that he would need to concentrate on establishing his authority in Baktria first, and in Paropamisadai and Arachosia, if he was interested in recovering control of the Indian regions. In an attempt to revive Alexander's empire, an Indian expedition was absolutely necessary.

It will now be clear that the information we have about the situation in Central Asia is largely conjectural; it has to be said also that the information about Seleukos' accomplishments in Central Asia is almost non-existent. Justin states that he had to fight to secure control of Baktria.[17] This would imply the local desire to be independent, that there was a satrap (possibly still Stasanor, maybe an otherwise unknown Sophytes, who minted coins), and that interference from the west was resented. The only other item known about this expedition is that Seleukos clashed with Chandragupta Maurya. This war is noted only briefly, by Appian, but he is specific that Seleukos reached and crossed the Indus River, which must mean he had marched down the valley of the Kabul, and had therefore secured control of the Paropamisadai, and so probably of Arachosia as well.[18] Whether the 'war' involved much fighting is not known – indeed it has been suggested that the armies never even met – but a 'war' surely involves conflict of some sort. Justin merely says he crossed into India.[19] Diodoros says nothing of it.

Whatever happened, it soon ended. Seleukos will have known of the size of Chandragupta's empire and of his army before he reached India – there will have been plenty of men in Baktria and the Paropamisadai to inform him – and negotiations soon began. This would imply that whatever fighting took place was inconclusive. The talks resulted in a peace treaty in which both men made concessions. Seleukos surrendered several provinces, which he had scarcely controlled in any case – Baktria, which he had conquered, was not one of them. Strabo is the only source to give any details, stating that Seleukos handed over Paropamisadai, Arachosia, and Gedrosia. (Strabo adds Areia to the list, though this has been generally disbelieved.)[20] Certainly the first two of these show later evidence of being ruled by Chandragupta's grandson Asoka; Gedrosia, bordering on India in the lower Indus Valley, might well have gone along with Arachosia. It has been suggested also that Drangiana and Areia were included, though geographically this seems most unlikely. (It may be noted that Paropamisadai and Arachosia are now part of modern Afghanistan, which has often been included in an Indian-based empire; Areia and Drangiana never have – unless Chandragupta is the exception, of course.)

The treaty also included a clause governing intermarriage, presumably between the subjects of the two rulers. There is no evidence, as has been proposed, that one of the two men handed over a daughter as a wife for the other, but some sort of agreement as to the caste-status of Greeks and Macedonians might be involved.[21] Any clause concerning such social relations was probably a dead letter so far as Greeks were concerned, for they were unlikely to pay much attention to Indian social conditions, especially if they were in political control – which, during the Mauryan empire, they were not. Later on is a different matter.

So the treaty included one clause concerning the provinces, and a second concerning intermarriage, a third involved Chandragupta's delivery of 500 war elephants to Seleukos, complete no doubt with mahouts, attendants, equipment, and supplies of food. (Given that it seems that there were only 400 in use at the later battle of Ipsos, it seems likely that Seleukos received a large proportion of the older animals in his batch, or he left some with the Baktrian satrap.) There were surely other clauses in the treaty apart from these three, but the essential background element is never mentioned. This was that the two men had established a degree of trust in each other, and that the arrangements they had made were mutually beneficial. It was easier for Chandragupta to control Arachosia and Paropamisadai from the Indus Valley than for Seleukos to do so from Babylonia. The presence of Indian power in the Kabul Valley would both protect Baktria from attack and was a standing threat to its inhabitants. Seleukos was using Chandragupta and his huge empire to help him keep control over the Greeks in Baktria; Chandragupta knew that no attack from that direction would come while Seleukos ruled there. As one historian has put it, each guarded the other's back. And the elephants represented a decisive increase in Seleukos' military power.[22]

Seleukos' eastern campaign was thus very largely a matter of negotiation and administration, with some fighting in Baktria and some in India. Satraps were presumably appointed to Parthia, Margiana and Baktria, and the provincial administration will have been organized or reorganized. Perhaps some obstreperous locals were disciplined. It would not be surprising if contact was made with whoever had authority in Sogdiana with a view to establishing peace. No doubt fortifications were authorized and begun. And, of course, Seleukos went on to India, fought a brief war, and concluded a peace treaty. There is enough work in all this for a new ruler in a turbulent region for the three or four years which can be allotted to the expedition. Then in 303 the message came from the west, that it was time to settle at last with Antigonos. Seleukos began his march back westwards, with a substantial army reinforced by local recruits, by cavalry collected in Media, and by 500 war elephants.

By the time he began his return from the east, Seleukos was a king. Antigonos had waited for a major victory to claim the title, in 306, and his rivals had then followed suit one by one.[23] Kassander had had Alexander IV and his mother killed at some point after 311, and presumably the others knew this. Certainly Antigonos must have known when he took the royal title.[24] It was implicitly a claim to be the heir of Alexander the Great and Alexander IV to the Macedonian kingship, and to rule in Macedon and all the empire which Alexander the Great had conquered. Antigonos personally made no further attempt to secure a wider rule, leaving actual campaigning to Demetrios, whom he appointed joint-king. The shine of his self-proclamation came off four months later when the two kings were defeated in their autumn attack on Egypt.[25]

Seleukos was therefore in the east when he received the news of Antigonos' self-promotion. Ptolemy, having defeated the new kings' attack on Egypt in 306, was the first of the rivals to take the title; during the following year the others followed.[26] In actual fact Kassander may well have been regarded as king in Macedon since he married Thessalonike, or since he killed Alexander IV, or at least when the news came out that the boy was dead;

he had certainly been acting as king since he took power there. Similarly Ptolemy's position in Egypt, while formally a satrap, was in effect royal, and his activities allowed the Egyptians, and if not the Greeks in Egypt, to refer to him as pharaoh. The same has been detected in Babylonian references to both Antigonos and Seleukos.[27] But for the Greeks and Macedonians, a victory seems to have been necessary, a necessity established by Antigonos when he associated his proclamation with Demetrios' victory at Salamis; hence Ptolemy's claim after defeating both Antigonos and Demetrios. For Seleukos, campaigning in the east, there were victories enough, but it may well have been the Indian campaign which he used as the foundation for his own self-proclamation. The fighting was perhaps not wholly victorious, but it was sufficiently notable to bring respect, it was exotic, it brought Alexandrian memories and comparisons, and he had collected a large force of elephants as a result. He could portray his eastern expedition, including the recovery of rule over Baktria, as a victory without any real difficulty.

For Antigonos the reaction of the others was no doubt a bitter blow. His self-proclamation was a claim to imperial authority, and the others by their own self-proclamations were denying that claim and setting themselves up in direct defiance of him. Only Kassander claimed a specific territorial authority as 'king of the Macedonians'; the others were just 'king'. Therefore all might equally claim to be aiming at the empire, though it was already clear that most were content with their fractions. Seleukos was not. As a sign of his ambition, he began dating his rule by his own period in power in Babylonia, starting at 312 BC, when he set off on his grand adventure. Thus his claim to royal authority did not begin with the death of Alexander IV, or even his imprisonment, but from his own assumption of power, which took place well before Antigonos' claim to royalty. It was another and even more direct denial of Antigonos' claim. As a reinforcement to his claim he included in his job-description the title 'Macedonian'; this was a reminiscence of the title of 'Akhaimenid' used by his Persian predecessors, but it also implied a claim to be Alexander's true successor.

The failure of Antigonos' *coup* is reflected in a famous toast made at a party in Athens in 302, as Demetrios was about to begin his campaign north against Kassander. Demetrios was toasted as king, but the others only as his subordinates or officials – Seleukos as *elephantarchos*, Ptolemy as admiral, Lysimachos as treasurer.[28] It was, of course, an implicit acknowledgment that they were actually independent, but also a claim that Antigonos and Demetrios were the only true kings. Antigonos' *coup* had failed in the most drastic way.

Chapter Six

The Grand Alliance

The origin of the new war into which Seleukos had been recruited lay, as ever, in Antigonos' ambition. Since Seleukos and he made peace in 308 or 307 Antigonos had sent Demetrios on a series of campaigns which were designed to break the ring around him by attacking his competitors one after another. In 307 Demetrios captured Athens, to much pleasure from the citizens, whose tyrant, Demetrios of Phaleron, was expelled. (He took refuge with Ptolemy, though he had been installed originally by Kassander.) From Athens Demetrios collected his fleet and sailed to Cyprus, where he defeated Ptolemy's fleet and captured most of his army and the island. This is the point at which Antigonos proclaimed himself king, and he appointed Demetrios king also. Together the two new kings launched a great attack against Egypt, though Ptolemy succeeded in defending the Pelusion mouth of the Nile against the land and sea invasions.

The apparent defiance of Rhodes now distracted Antigonos into a long siege of that city, which was conducted by Demetrios. This also failed, though the end-result was to bring the city under a modified form of control by Antigonos. By this time Kassander had recovered much of his lost position in Greece, and agonized cries for help were coming to Demetrios from Athens. In a masterly campaign he took his fleet to Greece, landing at Aulis in Boiotia. At once Kassander's whole position in Greece collapsed: his army besieging Athens was isolated, Euboia, Boiotia and Aitolia instantly became Demetrios' allies, then Athens was relieved and soon Sikyon and Corinth were captured in tactically ingenious attacks, and finally much of the Peloponnese fell easily into Demetrios' control. In a few months he had established control over much of Greece south of Thessaly. He then organized his conquests into a new League of Corinth in imitation of that of Philip II and Alexander thirty years before. A new marriage to Daidameia, sister of Pyrrhos of Epeiros, brought the latter's alliance in addition.[1]

As a result of Demetrios' success the position of Kassander became critical. He was all but surrounded; Antigonos ruled Asia Minor, Demetrios controlled almost all Greece, Pyrrhos in Epeiros was his enemy, and

Demetrios' fleet dominated the Aegean. It was obvious that he would be Demetrios' next victim. Kassander tried to evade the issue by negotiating with Antigonos, but the king, confident in his power, would only accept surrender, and then began cementing his control of Greece by his new league. Kassander, therefore, might as well fight.[2] It seems clear, since Kassander had been the one to ask for talks, that Antigonos could have got peace had he been less demanding, but, as so often, he would only make a peace treaty when he was defeated, or on the basis of his enemy's complete surrender. And, of course, everyone involved had been here before. If Antigonos imagined he would only have Kassander to fight in the next phase of his great war, he was mistaken.

Kassander consulted Lysimachos and then resolved on a new strategy. The first element was to inform Ptolemy and Seleukos and recruit them into their alliance.[3] The former was probably still at war with Antigonos anyway after the fighting in Cyprus and at the Nile in 306. Antigonos' attack then had come much too close to success for Ptolemy's comfort, and he now undoubtedly harboured a new resolve to recover control yet again of Palestine and Phoenicia whenever he could. Seleukos, on the other hand, was a long way off, certainly in Media and quite possibly even further east in Baktria. He would take a long time to reach the area of conflict. Not only that, but he was still bound by his treaty with Antigonos; he could not simply invade Antigonos' lands without some excuse; however, excuses for war were never difficult to find, and of the four men in the alliance it was Seleukos who was the most ingenious.

The man with the biggest battalions, as usual, was Antigonos, but he would need some time to gather his forces. He was in Syria when the crisis broke into war, and half of his army was in Greece under Demetrios. To tackle Antigonos alone it would be necessary to gather together the armies of Lysimachos, Kassander, and Seleukos, but it would be best to keep Demetrios' forces from joining his father's. This indicated a campaign in Asia Minor. Since Demetrios controlled the sea this would clearly be difficult. Ptolemy from Egypt would certainly move into Syria, but it was unlikely that he would be able to intervene in the fighting in the north, though it was presumably hoped that he might distract Antigonos sufficiently for the latter to have to divide his forces. Seleukos, providing he could be persuaded to break his treaty, would need at some point to join one or other of the allies' armies. Coming from Iran, and having to defend Babylonia, he would probably prefer to join Ptolemy, as he had in the past. Conventional thinking would therefore assume that Seleukos would march from Iran into Babylonia and west through Mesopotamia to join up with Ptolemy in northern Syria. Their joint armies would then be strong enough to march through the Taurus passes into Asia Minor, to catch Antigonos' army between his forces and those of Kassander and Lysimachos.

The basic strategy of the alliance therefore was for Kassander and Lysimachos to pin down Demetrios and Antigonos respectively until Seleukos and Ptolemy could arrive. It was important to try to keep Demetrios from joining Antigonos, but it must have been understood that this was not likely to be successful. The essence of the plan was obviously communicated to both Ptolemy and Seleukos, but it would be left up to them to organize their marches into the west. Meanwhile Kassander and Lysimachos each took a separate task; Kassander to block Demetrios, Lysimachos to preoccupy Antigonos.

In the late spring, therefore, no doubt when they knew that Ptolemy at least would actively support them, Lysimachos and Kassander set about their work. Lysimachos was reinforced by part of Kassander's forces commanded by his brother Prepelaos, and from Lysimachos' city of Lysimacheia at the root of the Gallipoli Peninsula they crossed into Asia, landing at Lampsakos and Parion. This had to be done quickly and unexpectedly, since the crossing could have been prevented or interrupted by Demetrios' ships. Demetrios therefore became occupied by his attack on Kassander, finding that Kassander's men had occupied and fortified the routes from central Greece into Thessaly through the Orthys range, so he shipped his army from Chalkis in Euboia into the Gulf of Pagasai and so was able to land his forces at Larisa Kremaste, north of the Orthys Mountains. He captured some towns in southern Thessaly, but Kassander had organized a defence in depth and was now on the defensive in the fortified cities of Pherai and Phthiotic Thebes – and north of them were other cities, then the mountains dividing Thessaly from Macedon. The detachment under Prepelaos had therefore reached Asia Minor safely.[4]

Demetrios had already delayed his move north to get himself inducted into the Eleusinian Mysteries in Attika (insisting on a special ceremony on the wrong date, which ruffled Athenian feathers). Now he sat down in front of Kassander's forces to threaten them. Both armies were repeatedly drawn up in battle array, but neither made any real move to attack, and the whole campaign became stationary.[5] It seems that both Demetrios and Kassander were awaiting news from Asia Minor – Demetrios copied Kassander in sending reinforcements to Asia Minor, to his father – but this delay was also much to Kassander's advantage in Europe, and Demetrios should have realized that. The best explanation is that he did not know that Ptolemy and Seleukos had been brought into the alliance, and so he was waiting to hear that his father had arrived and was ready to tackle Lysimachos with overwhelming forces.

Lysimachos in fact advanced without much difficulty into Ionia as far as Ephesos, and then turned inland as far as Synnada, which was in a strategic location just north of the hills and lakes of Pisidia. By occupying Synnada together with Dokimeion to the north, Lysimachos had thereby cut the land connection between the well populated and urbanized west, and the east from which Antigonos must approach out of Syria; he threatened Kelainai, which Antigonos had used as his administrative centre during his time as satrap in Phrygia and on later occasions. At Synnada Lysimachos also captured part of Antigonos' accumulated treasure.[6]

In other words Lysimachos had headed directly for the area from which Antigonos governed Asia Minor. It was also a busy area of Macedonian settlement, or rather of the establishment of several Macedonian lords. Dokimeion was founded by Dokimos, who still held that place as a subordinate of Antigonos; it was he who surrendered Synnada; having done so he was unable to rejoin Antigonos, who viewed such desertions with ferocity.[7] One of the reasons for Lysimachos to reach directly to Synnada was to cut the links of Antigonos' government; another would be to persuade local Macedonian lords to join him, as Dokimos did; he might expect reinforcements as well from Macedonians settled in the area.[8]

Meanwhile Prepelaos with part of Kassander's army was campaigning along the Aegean coast of Asia Minor. He had stayed with Lysimachos while developing a base in the Troad, where they captured Lampsakos, Parion, and Sigeon. They failed at Abydos, where the siege laid by Lysimachos was relieved by a seaborne force sent by Demetrios. Prepelaos then marched south along the coast, taking Adramyttion and Ephesos and several other places. Again, however, Demetrios intervened from the sea, securing Klazomenai and Erythrai. Prepelaos ignored this, for whatever forces Demetrios had installed can only have been small. The places he captured had fallen very easily, suggesting a general unwillingness of the citizens to exert themselves on Antigonos' behalf. Prepelaos marched inland to capture Sardis city, though he could not take the acropolis. In the process another of Antigonos' commanders, Phoinix, deserted, handing over Sardis city. Again this was a major administrative centre.[9] Between them Lysimachos and Prepelaos had effectively destroyed, or taken over, Antigonos' government of western Asia Minor.

This success only lasted until Antigonos arrived. He had set out from North Syria, but it will have taken him some time to gather his forces, and to make the march. Both Antigonos and Demetrios were interrupted in ceremonies by the news of Lysimachos' invasion of Asia Minor. Demetrios was having himself inducted (illegally) into the Eleusinian Mysteries; Antigonos was presiding over a great festival at his new city of Antigoneia in Syria. This was evidently intended to be a great affair, and probably he was aiming for it to become one of the great four-yearly festivals of the Greek world.[10] That both men were so taken by surprise in this way is evidence of their unpreparedness, probably of their over-confidence, and of the success of the allies in keeping their plotting and diplomacy secret.

Antigonos left a considerable force to garrison Syria, clearly expecting an attack by Ptolemy and possibly Seleukos. Even so the army he had with him, together with those men he collected on his march, made him distinctly stronger than Lysimachos and Prepelaos combined. As this became clear, and as Antigonos recovered control of the area around Synnada, Lysimachos discussed the position with his council, then withdrew from the Synnada area northwards to a position which he could fortify and hold.[11] Antigonos could not persuade him to fight and so set about laying siege to the camp. When this became uncomfortable, Lysimachos broke out by night and retired further north to Dorylaion, where he again fortified his camp and defied Antigonos, this time successfully since Dorylaion contained plentiful supplies, presumably collected with this move in view. By this time it must have been clear to Antigonos that Lysimachos and Kassander were deliberately delaying matters, and awaiting reinforcements from Seleukos, or even from Ptolemy. Strategically both Demetrios and Antigonos were doing what their enemies intended.

At some point before Lysimachos retired to Dorylaion, Antigonos had had to do something to prevent these reinforcements arriving. Kassander was well blocked by Demetrios, or so it seemed, but, like Antigonos, Demetrios could not attack since only victory and the total destruction of Kassander's army would serve, and to achieve that would be very costly. If Kassander, like Lysimachos, merely retreated and kept his army intact, Demetrios would have suffered casualties to no purpose. Antigonos, however, thought he could deal with Seleukos and Ptolemy, and once they had been prevented from approaching he could deal with Lysimachos.

Ptolemy turned out to be easy to deal with. He had moved into Palestine with a major army, and then spent his time systematically taking and fortifying the places in the region. He had reached as far north as Sidon, to which he laid siege. Then, it is said, a rumour reached him that Antigonos had defeated Lysimachos and Seleukos and was even then marching south to tackle Ptolemy's army. The rumour had sufficient detail to be credible, including that Lysimachos had retreated to Herakleia Pontike, which was in fact close to the winter quarters he occupied later in the year. But Seleukos was nowhere near either Lysimachos or Antigonos (and probably Ptolemy knew that).

Ptolemy supposedly accepted the truth of the rumour and retreated. But he did not abandon his conquests, nor was his retreat in any way precipitate or necessarily the result of the rumour. If Antigonos really was approaching he would have to move through Syria and Phoenicia into a Palestine which was now thickly sown with Ptolemy's garrisons. This was exactly why Ptolemy wanted to control Palestine; Antigonos was proving once more that to defend Egypt it was necessary to control Palestine. Waiting till the invader reached the Nile – as Perdikkas and Demetrios and Antigonos had done in earlier campaigns – was leaving it too late. In fact Ptolemy retired from Sidon in a leisurely way. He lifted the siege of Sidon only after the commander of the garrison agreed to a truce for four months. This would cover the winter season, when Macedonian armies did not usually fight. That is, Ptolemy's retreat may have happened at the same time as the rumour, but was not necessarily the result of his believing it.[12]

The rumour is presumed to have been planted by Antigonos. It has been supposed that he also sent a force to distract Seleukos and make him turn aside to defend his lands. But neither the date nor the evidence for such an expedition is at all clear or convincing. It would obviously fit best in the late summer of 302, when Seleukos was still in Media, and while Antigonos was trying to force Lysimachos out of his entrenched camp at Dorylaion – or even before, when he was in the entrenched camp just north of Synnada. The problem is that it looks very much like the raid of Demetrios in 310, and there is no evidence for it in 302 or 301. It may have been suggested, but it seems unlikely that Antigonos would have expended a serious force on such a raid. The troops were much more use in Asia Minor or in facing Ptolemy. Only if they could actually pin down Seleukos would an expedition into Babylonia be worthwhile, and Seleukos was in Media at the time. Antigonos was not prepared to leave a really large force in Syria – he made no attempt to do any more than delay Ptolemy's campaign – so sending a force into Babylonia would be a waste of troops.[13]

There is no indication that Seleukos visited Babylonia on his way west (though this is, of course, not definitive). There is a strong sign that he travelled by a northerly route, for he first appeared in Asia Minor in Kappadokia in time to go into winter quarters, so late in 302.[14] If he began the march in Media, he could advance to the west by the difficult route (or routes) through the Armenian Mountains. The possibility of being trapped in North Syria by an Antigonid force stationed in the Taurus passes while Lysimachos and Kassander were being defeated and finished off in Asia Minor must have been his main reason. We do not know which route he took through the mountains, though there are two or three possibilities. There are several river valleys which an army could use – the two branches of the upper Euphrates are the obvious ones. What is known is that he made the march before these valleys were blocked by snow, and that he arrived in eastern Kappadokia in late 302 to go into winter quarters about the same time as every other army in the region. (He had, therefore, resolved any doubts about the propriety of fighting Antigonos; perhaps, if he was formally allied to Kassander, Demetrios' attack provided the excuse; and Demetrios' attack on various Greek cities was clearly against the spirit of Antigonos' 'freedom of the Greek cities' declaration, which had been incorporated in various of the peace treaties.)

Lysimachos had held on in the camp near Dorylaion until Antigonos' army had almost finished enclosing it by a line of circumvallation. This was a minor but strenuous campaign in itself, involving repeated minor fights to prevent or delay Antigonos' lines being completed. In the end, when it was clear that the enclosure would soon be concluded, Lysimachos organized another night-time evacuation. (Antigonos was thus fooled twice by the same method – there was clearly something wrong with his guard system.) Lysimachos' army marched out along a ridge of high land, and Antigonos followed along lower land in parallel. Probably Antigonos would have caught up, having easier ground to march over, but it rained heavily, and the lowland quickly collapsed into mud and overflowing rivers. (The season was clearly late; any rains fall in Asia Minor from October onwards.) Having been so decisively slowed down, and losing men and animals in the conditions, Antigonos gave up the pursuit, and turned aside to go into winter quarters somewhere in the Dorylaion area, quite possibly using Lysimachos' old camp. Lysimachos marched off north-easterly and made his own camp in the plain of Salonia near Herakleia Pontike.[15] This place was carefully chosen, for it was within reach of the sea, and within communicating distance of Seleukos' winter quarters, so that the two men could therefore co-ordinate their moves next spring.

Once Lysimachos had got away Antigonos knew that he and Seleukos would be able to unite their forces next year. Possibly Ptolemy would arrive as well, but Antigonos could assume that the men he had left at the Taurus passes would make that route impassable; and anyway Ptolemy had to capture the Phoenician cities first. But the balance of numbers had now swung away from Antigonos, so he required reinforcements. He summoned Demetrios, who was still camped in southern Thessaly facing Kassander's army. Demetrios and Kassander agreed a truce, which both men so crafted as to be invalid from the start, since to both it was merely a device to disengage their forces and shift the campaign into Asia Minor. Demetrios loaded his army on board his ships and sailed to Asia. Kassander, without a fleet, divided his army. Part of the force, under his own command, he used to recover southern Thessaly – presumably Demetrios had left some garrisons in the towns – and the other part he sent under his brother Pleistarchos to march to the Hellespont and from there to join Lysimachos.

Demetrios took his fleet and army to Ephesos, which his forces had preserved from Prepelaos' attack earlier, and then he reversed Prepelaos' conquests by marching and sailing north along the Aegean coast. He retook the conquests of Lysimachos and Prepelaos in the Troad, so that when Pleistarchos arrived on the European shore he found no way of crossing in the face of Demetrios' fleet, nor anywhere to land, and had to turn aside to try elsewhere. Demetrios placed his army in the lands of Chalkedon, on the east side of the Bosporos, where he was in touch with his father's army at Dorylaion and could also guard the sea approaches. Pleistarchos had to go as far north as Odessos on the Thracian Black Sea coast to find enough ships to take his troops to Asia, and even then he could only find enough to move a third of his force at any one time. He got the first third across to Herakleia Pontike. The tyrant of that city, Amestris, a Persian lady who was the widow of the previous tyrant, Dionysios, had by now married Lysimachos, and so the city was under his control. The second part of Pleistarchos' army was intercepted and largely destroyed by Demetrios' ships, and the third was caught by a storm and largely sunk. Less than half of the men Kassander sent to join Lysimachos actually reached him.[16]

In the winter of 302/301 the five armies were well spread out from Egypt to Greece, though only one was out of touch with the others. Antigonos and Demetrios were at Dorylaion and near Chalkedon respectively, something over 100km apart – a distance which is little more than three or four days' march (or only two if they moved towards each other). Demetrios left garrisons in the cities he had retaken. Lysimachos and Seleukos were probably farther apart, but again if they marched towards each other they would be able to link up within a few days. Ptolemy's army was in Egypt, but he had control of much of Palestine, and so had an easy entry into Syria. Had he wished he could probably march as far as Kilikia, but he must have known there would be no point in such an extension of his forces, for he was too far away to be able to intervene in Asia Minor. Seleukos was in Kappadokia; in Greece, Kassander commanded the larger part of the army with which he had faced Demetrios; like Ptolemy he had no intention of relinquishing his own base in favour of a campaign in Asia Minor. If Antigonos won there, Kassander and Ptolemy had every intention of surviving. It can be assumed that Seleukos had the same idea, though he would have a much longer retreat in the event of his defeat.

In the spring of 301, therefore, Lysimachos marched south-east and met Seleukos marching west, perhaps in the vicinity of Ankyra, on the Royal Road from Iran which Seleukos had been using. At the same time Demetrios marched south from the Bosporos to join his father, and their joint forces moved back to the Synnada area. This remained the strategic key, with Kelainai nearby and Sardis further west. Antigonos held his forces at the village or town of Ipsos, a little east of Synnada, having chosen a battleground which would favour his forces. He had 70,000 hoplite infantry to form his phalanx, and 10,000 cavalry under Demetrios' command, with 75 elephants posted as usual in front of the phalanx. The intention was, as at Gaza, to use the elephants to disrupt any enemy infantry advance.[17]

Lysimachos and Seleukos had a fairly lengthy march to reach the enemy's chosen field, perhaps 200km. No doubt they moved carefully, and fairly slowly, to avoid tiring the men. They had between them 64,000 infantry, mostly men contributed by Lysimachos and Kassander, and probably 15,000 cavalry, mostly brought by Seleukos. Many of these horsemen were light cavalry, archers and javelineers, who could not stand against the heavy cavalry of Demetrios. But Seleukos had also brought with him his huge elephant force, probably by now 400 in number.

Both sides carefully drew up their forces on the battlefield with their own plans in mind. Antigonos mustered most of the cavalry on one wing, with a smaller guard on the other; it was obvious that the intention was to drive the enemy cavalry off and then turn on his infantry, which was to be pinned down by the threatening elephants and the larger Antigonid phalanx. Seleukos put his son Antiochos in command of his cavalry, mostly drawn up to face the main enemy mass, but not all. Of his elephants 100 were placed before the phalanx, facing Antigonos' 75; the rest he placed in reserve.

The problem with Antigonos' plan was that it was all too obvious. It was the normal battle plan of the time and type which Antigonos had used before, like that Seleukos and Ptolemy had faced at Gaza (and perhaps in the battle Seleukos had won in 308). This made it possible for Lysimachos and Seleukos to devise a counter which would be a surprise – for all that was required was to disrupt the even development of Antigonos' intentions, when his army would be rendered confused. Antigonos was over 80 years old by now, and though Demetrios (as he had recently shown in Greece), was alert and imaginative, he was also under his father's control.[18] They were faced by two commanders, equally contrasting in their approaches, but also equal in authority. Lysimachos was an Antigonos-type, stolid, a good tough commander, but without the imagination Seleukos demonstrates over and over again. Seleukos' experience in command had generally been in fights against superior numbers, and this had forced his imagination to devise unconventional means to victory. One can, for example, probably assign the victorious plan of Gaza to him, and certainly he had organized his own victories against Nikanor and Antigonos in 311 and 308. The recruitment of Antigonos' forces on his return to Babylonia in 311 is another example. It would not be a surprise to learn that he was responsible for the mattress of chains and spikes which neutralized the Antigonid elephant force at Gaza. And here at Ipsos he was able to display his imagination again. It concerned the missing 300 elephants. One wonders if Antigonos and Demetrios noticed that they were not present in the battle array. They may not have known how many he had, or they could have assumed that the missing elephants had simply not arrived. Certainly the 'missing' beasts were not taken into account in Antigonos' plans.

The battle began, as intended, with Demetrios launching a charge with his cavalry mass and driving Antiochos and his lighter cavalry force away. Antiochos and Seleukos and Lysimachos must certainly have expected this, so the retreat was partly designed, and did not involve all the Seleukid horsemen – it was perhaps not really a feigned retreat, though it was not far from it. Meanwhile the two elephant forces between the phalanxes joined battle on more or less even terms, a clear recipe for a stalemate. Demetrios pursued Antiochos' force of cavalry off the field, but Antiochos was able to keep him in play for some time – he had fewer heavy cavalry, but more 'lights', so he would be more nimble. No doubt Demetrios' cavalry, cheered by their victory, exultantly charged the enemy and then scattered. In the end, however, Demetrios collected his men, reformed them and turned back to complete his task. He found the way barred by the 'missing' 300 elephants, with the usual light infantry attached to them. He was probably also followed by, and harassed by, Antiochos' 'defeated' cavalry. In the shorthand of the historians, the elephant line stopped the cavalry, though there must be more to it than that. The cavalry Demetrios commanded was by now well used to fighting alongside and against elephants, and the old idea that horses would not face elephants is clearly out of date. Nevertheless it is certain that Demetrios' cavalry was unable to complete their task, which was to rejoin the main battle.

Seleukos' first ploy was therefore successful. The second was to have reserved his force of archers and javelineers, who had evidently not been decisively driven off by Demetrios' charge; perhaps they had quietly withdrawn to one side to let the enemy cavalry through; certainly they were back in action long before Demetrios had rallied his men. These forces now attacked the flank and rear of Antigonos' phalanx (as Demetrios' cavalry had been intended to do on the other side). Meanwhile it seems probable that the elephant battle between the phalanxes had ended, probably in a pyrrhic victory for the allies (who had the greater numbers), and Antigonos' phalanx found itself faced by the surviving elephants, by Lysimachos' undamaged phalanx, and by the bombardment of the archers and javelineers. Maybe some of the elephants broke in on the formation, maybe panic set in when it became clear that Demetrios had failed to return, but Antigonos' phalanx certainly collapsed. Some of the men fled, most of them quickly surrendered, as was usual in such circumstances. Antigonos, always expecting Demetrios to arrive to rescue him, fought on with his guard until he fell beneath a hail of javelins. He had, it seems, been determined never to be captured. Demetrios escaped from the field.

The battle was decisive in bringing the destruction of Antigonos' brief kingdom, but, as such events always do, the other result was to produce a whole series of new problems. Demetrios survived and escaped, collecting a small army on his way; he also maintained control over his fleet and held a number of places scattered about the eastern Mediterranean from Corinth to Sidon. It remained to see what he would do with this curious kingdom. Seleukos and Lysimachos ended the battle by commanding an enormous army; it consisted of Lysimachos' own army, those of Kassander's troops who had been sent to help him and had survived the sea crossing and the battle, and Seleukos' army from the east, plus the soldiers of Antigonos who had surrendered to end the battle. Exactly how many there were is not at all clear, since the casualties in the fighting are not known, but the combined total at the start of the fighting was over 150,000 soldiers (plus the elephants). Those men sent by Kassander were obviously returned to him, and no doubt Lysimachos and Seleukos divided Antigonos' former troops between them. Some will have been discharged, others will have slipped away to rejoin Demetrios, whose force when he reached Ephesos was about 10,000 strong (5,000 infantry, 4,000 cavalry, plus those in garrison who had joined him); others will have simply gone home. The great concentration at the battlefield was therefore probably quickly dispersed, as much for logistic reasons as to divide them into their separate armies, but the two kings remained with very large forces, and there were certainly many soldiers who survived but were unemployed.

We do not know exactly how this matter was resolved, nor do we know how the two kings sorted out the territorial distribution of Antigonos' lands, but it is likely that the two issues were linked. Lysimachos had brought the largest part of the allied force to the battle. He had done, he could claim, most of the fighting, even if it was Seleukos' ingenuity which was as important. Of the 64,000 infantry in the battle on the allied side at Ipsos, Lysimachos had supplied perhaps 40,000 men, more than half; Seleukos, on the other hand, had provided the major part of the cavalry and all the elephants. In terms of military power, however, it was the hoplites of the phalanx who really counted, and in such troops Seleukos, by comparison with Lysimachos and Kassander, was clearly deficient. (Kassander's army had in the region of 30,000 such men.) No doubt Seleukos was interested in recruiting as many of Antigonos' old troops as he could, but he was not in a very strong position for bargaining.

It appears that Kassander had no wish to acquire territories outside the Macedonian area and Greece, where he was no doubt aiming to control Greece as well as Macedon – and this despite his long ago demand for Kappadokia. So the division of Antigonos' territories, which stretched from the Hellespont and the Black Sea to Gaza, was left to Lysimachos and Seleukos to arrange, though Kassander's brother Pleistarchos also had an interest. They decided that those who had fought at Ipsos were entitled to divide what they had gained, but it is clear that the division depended also on the quantity of military power each man commanded. Therefore Lysimachos gained most, because he had the most troops present; Seleukos took most of what was left, and the boundary between them was to be in the tangle of mountains between Asia Minor and Media. Pleistarchos was allocated a kingdom spread in sections along the southern coast of Asia Minor, which included Karia and Lykia but also Kilikia. This last territory was perhaps given him to keep the lands of Lysimachos and Seleukos separated, which may in turn reflect something of the tone of the discussions (if that is the right term), in which the division was conducted.

Lysimachos therefore gained all Asia Minor from the Hellespont to the Taurus Mountains; Seleukos was allocated the lands south of the mountains, but also an area later referred to as 'Seleukid Kappadokia'. This appears to have been the southern part of Kappadokia, perhaps the land between the Taurus Mountains and the upper waters of the Halys River. It is a curious allocation, but may be explained by the fact that it was somewhere in this area that Seleukos' army had wintered in 302–301. Maybe he could claim to have conquered it before the battle.

There can be no doubt, given the history of Ptolemy's policy in Syria, that both Lysimachos and Seleukos knew full well that Seleukos would be faced with a Ptolemaic occupation of Palestine and Phoenicia when he went to Syria to secure control of his part of the spoils. No doubt also Lysimachos was not at all sorry to contemplate the fact that Seleukos and Ptolemy would quarrel. The existence of Pleistarchos' kingdom in Kilikia may have been expected to ensure that any conflict would be confined to Syria and not involve Asia Minor. But, as usual, whatever plans anyone had made were doomed to disappointment. Things did not work out as anyone expected. And that included the immediate collapse of the alliance which had been assembled to deal with Antigonos.

Chapter Seven

New Enmities, New Cities

T he division of Antigonos' kingdom turned out to be quite unequal, bearing no real relation to the contributions the several leaders had made to the campaign and victory. On an objective view Seleukos, Lysimachos, and Kassander had contributed equally, since the war could not have been won if any of them had withheld their participation. Ptolemy had certainly helped, and it was scarcely his fault that the decisive fighting took place where he could not take part, and he could point to a long history of opposing Antigonos, in particular to the crucial victories at Gaza in 312 and the Nile in 306. None of this affected the division of the lands, of course, which was based not on past services, but on present powers.

So Lysimachos took most, having most troops. Kassander held Macedon and dominated Greece, in many ways the decisive geographical area because of its potential for recruiting soldiers. Ptolemy held Egypt and had taken over southern Syria, but he found it impossible to gain control of all Phoenicia, where Tyre and Sidon were held by Demetrios' soldiers and fleet. That left Seleukos, who found he had gained only western Mesopotamia, from the Khabur River to the Euphrates, that part of Syria which Ptolemy had not seized, and perhaps the questionable area called Seleukid Kappadokia. He was not at all pleased, and, since Kassander that was out of reach, and Lysimachos was too strong, he vented his annoyance first of all on Ptolemy, who he claimed had stolen his share of the spoils.

Ptolemy's position was by no means strong. He held Palestine, where the towns were controlled by his garrisons, and probably Damascus. He had taken over some of the smaller Phoenician cities, such as Byblos and Tripolis and Sarepta, but could not take Tyre and Sidon. His northern limit, judging by his later boundary, was the Eleutheros River, which flows westwards to reach the sea just north of Tripolis. Geographically therefore he held the hills and plains of Palestine, the Jordan Valley and the Transjordan plateaux. Damascus could be reached from Palestine relatively easily, and it was a rich and productive oasis. But the Lebanese mountain area was a different matter. If his power reached as far as the valley of the Eleutheros and Tripolis,

Ptolemy had control of the Bekaa Valley, the hollow between the parallel mountain ranges of Lebanon and Anti-Lebanon. Access to this area from the south was not easy. There was a coast road, but with Tyre and Sidon out of his control that route was too dangerous. The route over the flanks of Mount Hermon was far too awkward to be used except by small groups in an emergency. So the route north was by way of Damascus and the gorge of the Barada River, which led into the southern Bekaa. From there the valley gave access to the Eleutheros River valley and so to the coast at Tripolis. Given such a tortuous and difficult route it is not surprising that Ptolemy made no real attempt to reach much beyond the Bekaa, nor is it surprising that he was at once uneasy when confronted by an angry Seleukos and his victorious army, claiming to have been defrauded of his rightful gains.

The country the two kings were about to quarrel over stretched from the Taurus Mountains to the Sinai Desert. It was, as the last paragraph has pointed out, a region of mountains and plains, hollow lands and curious rivers. It had the typical Mediterranean climate of wet winters and dry hot summers. It had been cultivated for 10,000 years; indeed it was the place where agriculture was invented. It was sandwiched between hostile regions; the Mediterranean Sea on the west, the Arabian/Syrian Desert on the east. In effect it was an oblong, 800km from north to south, a maximum of 200 from east to west.

This land was not a unity, however, and, unless conquered by a foreign power, it never has been. Its geography tended to encourage division into relatively small but often vigorous states. It was surrounded by other lands where more powerful states developed – Egypt, Assyria and Babylonia, Anatolia – and these all too often used their power to invade what seemed to be a comparable but much divided land and therefore an apparently easy prey. But the Syrian kingdoms always resisted such conquests fiercely. In the eighth century BC the Assyrians dealt with such resistance by destruction, massacre, and deportation. What they left, the Babylonians in the seventh century destroyed. When the Persians took over the whole Middle East after 550 BC, they allowed some of the deportees' descendants to return, notably some groups of Jews, but did nothing to help the land recover from its devastation. During the Akhaimenid period most of Syria remained a relatively poor land of peasant agriculture with some enterprising port-cities along the Mediterranean coast.

This condition only emphasized the original internal divisions of Syria. A few of the urban centres survived, notably the string of Phoenician cities between the Lebanon Mountains and the sea. Damascus in its huge oasis is a natural city. Gaza was a major fortress guarding the route to Egypt – or blocking the way out of Egypt, depending on one's point of view. But most of the land was de-urbanized. When the rebel army of Cyrus the Younger, in which the historian Xenophon was a soldier, passed through North Syria in 404 BC, only one of these places which the army encountered could be called a town.[1] It had scarcely yet begun to recover from these centuries of mal-treatment. When Ptolemy found he could not march his army along the Lebanese coastal road and so took to the Bekaa Valley, he was passing through a region which archaeologists have found was only thinly populated in the southern half, and not at all in the northern.[2] Ptolemy had in fact seized that part which was, shall we say, least undeveloped, though it had suffered badly from the campaigns of the previous thirty years, in which his army had been one of the worst destroyers.

The coast was the only part of the country with any recognizably urban communities. From Arados to Gaza there were a string of towns or cities, Phoenician and Palestinian, two of which, Tyre and Gaza, had put up a ferocious resistance to Alexander's conquest, while Sidon had just as fiercely resisted an Akhaimenid attack – all within the half century or so before the quarrel of Ptolemy and Seleukos. The Phoenician cities were fortified and very independently minded; it was not at all surprising that, from 301, they were divided between three of Alexander's successors, and none of them was at all pleased at the deprivation of independence this entailed. Demetrios' men had held on to Tyre and Sidon; with Cyprus, this gave him effective naval control of the Syrian seas. Ptolemy had control of the Palestinian coast up to the southern boundary of Phoenicia at the Ladder of Tyre, and had gained control of the northern Phoenician coast from Berytos to the Eleutheros estuary, including Byblos and Berytos and Tripolis. Seleukos, when he arrived, found that the only part of Phoenicia he could hold was Arados, but this was on a fortified island and had its own king, and it controlled the adjacent coastal region, its *peraia*, for seventy or so kilometres north of the mouth of the Eleutheros.

The southern part of Syria, Palestine, contained a number of the urban or near-urban communities, such as Gaza and Ake on the coast and Jerusalem inland; the rest was exclusively rural, but seems to have been more prosperous than northern Syria, if only marginally so.[3] So Ptolemy had gained the marginally richer portion.

Scattered through the whole country there were places where religious shrines were attended by the local people and this had stimulated a certain near-urban development. In the Bekaa the local Baal had his centre at Baalbek; in Judaea Jerusalem was the temple town of the Jews; Samaria to the north was the Samaritans' centre; in northern Syria a temple to Atargatis survived at Bambyke (the only town Xenophon noted). There were others, but they were mainly little more than rural shrines. All the cities had their tutelary gods and temples, of course.

This social and economic detour is important because of the political quarrel which erupted when Seleukos came down with his army from Asia Minor to view his new territories. With Ptolemy occupying the land as far as the Eleutheros River valley, Seleukos had been left with the poorest region. Apart from Bambyke, there were only two urban centres in his section. One was the partly-built Antigoneia-on-Orontes, left unfinished by Antigonos.[4] The other was Arados, on its island 1km offshore; its *peraia* also contained a number of small towns. No wonder Seleukos was annoyed. Not only had he received the smallest share of the spoils in the arrangement with Lysimachos and Kassander, but he now found that half of his share had been taken by a man who had taken little or no part in the war, and what was left to him was the poorest section. He complained, but Ptolemy was unyielding.

There was also another aspect to the whole Syrian region. Antigonos' time had seen the establishment of a series of garrisons scattered throughout the whole of Syria. Some of these would be fairly substantial – Gaza, for instance, was a vital place to hold for anyone who wished to control Palestine – but most were probably fairly small. They can be recognized by their names, usually taken from Macedonian or Greek locations which reminded the soldiers of their original homes, or perhaps they were the names of the units planted there. Indeed some of these places predated even Antigonos' time, going back to the years just after Alexander's death. Gerasa, for example, claimed to have been founded by Perdikkas during his brief period as regent in 323–321; this is surprising but probably convincing, since it is highly unlikely that anyone after Perdikkas' death would have picked him as a founder.[5] Even if the city was not founded by him, however, this does indicate the early origin of its Macedonian occupation.

Several of these places have been noted already, in the Khabur Valley, Nisibis and Europos, and in the Balikh Valley, Karrhai, Ichnai, and Edessa. Of these places, two had local Syrian names (Nisibis, Karrhai); the others were named for Macedonian places. In other parts of Syria there was a

Doliche, which, like its Macedonian counterpart, was a religious centre;
Pella, another Europos (the old Karkemish), Kyrrhos, Beroia (on the site of
the old Halab, now Aleppo), a second Pella, Dion, Larisa (inhabited by an
unit of Thessalian cavalry), Arethousa.[6]

When the kings got busy founding their own cities these kinds of names
were never used; instead, taking up the practice of Alexander (and Philip)
they generously and no doubt pridefully gave their foundations their own
names. There were already several Antigoneias, Lysimacheias, a Kassandreia,
and a Seleukeia-on-the-Tigris to add to the numerous Alexandrias, and
later the names of family members were also used. It follows that we have a
triple layer of new foundations – first the Alexandrias, none of which were
founded after 323 (though some places annexed the king's name later), then
the towns with Macedonian names, which were founded during and after
Alexander's time and in all probability given names by the Macedonian
soldiers who were stationed in them; then the cities with dynastic names,
of which Kassadreia and Thessalonike were probably the earliest, quickly
followed by the Antigoneias facing the Hellespont, Lysimacheia, founded
in 309, on the other shore, and Antigoneia-on-Orontes and Seleukeia-on-
Tigris in 307.

When Antigonos gathered his forces to face what proved to be his final
challenge he needed all the troops he could assemble; it follows that he
will have drastically thinned out the garrisons. He did not totally abandon
them – Ptolemy had to fight his way north through Palestine – and part of
his army was placed to defend North Syria if Seleukos came west by way
of Babylonia. So when Seleukos arrived in Syria he found that there were
several places which reminded him of Macedon, populated in part by small
numbers of Macedonian soldiers who had been in his enemy's service, and
by their families, men who had not been called up to fight; it is reasonable to
assume that any men who had survived the Ipsos battle and who had settled
in Syria came back with Seleukos. His major problem in these years was
always manpower, which is at the root of much of his subsequent policy, so
he will have allowed as many of Antigonos' men as chose to return with him.

Some of these 'Macedonian' places had, after all, been in existence for
two or three decades by the time of Seleukos' arrival. Many of the men
had been soldiers not just of Antigonos, but also earlier of Alexander; in
their garrison towns they had begun to settle down. Perhaps those who had
remained behind in 302 were simply too old to march anymore and so had
been left to compose the garrisons. Those who did march away at Antigonos'

command probably fought at Ipsos, and those who survived would be those who were discharged by the victors, and then returned to their homes. If they left families in Syria this is where they would go. So, as Seleukos and Ptolemy confronted each other, there was also around them and between them a constant flow of returning discharged Antigonid soldiers bent on reoccupying their old homes, some going into Ptolemy's area, some remaining in Seleukos'. They were another factor to be taken into account.

In the face of Ptolemy's occupation of parts of Phoenicia and all Palestine, Seleukos had to decide whether or not to attack him. It is probable that he held superior force, but Ptolemy's troops were well dug in, and a war between the two men would be difficult. The public argument centred on Ptolemy's absence from the great battle, and, when he decided not to start a fight, Seleukos loudly announced that Ptolemy was his friend, so he would not fight him.[7]

This announcement was clever propaganda, putting Ptolemy subtly in the wrong, but – apart from being the truth – it was also in effect an agreement between the two kings to accept the division of Syria, with the boundary along the line of the Eleutheros. By announcing a refusal to fight, Seleukos accepted Ptolemy's occupation of southern Syria, though at the same time he did not renounce his own claim to that territory. This must have been the result of negotiations, and it was in effect the announcement of the conclusion of a peace treaty. As in all such negotiations, however, there had been anger – actual or feigned – on both sides before the agreement was reached.

Ptolemy had been sufficiently alarmed by the threatening and posturing that he had contacted Lysimachos and arranged the marriage of his daughter Arsinoe to him, and thus for the time being to count him as his ally.[8] (This was Lysimachos' fourth marriage, that with Amestris having lasted only so long as it took him to secure her city of Herakleia Pontike; in this he was not unusual for the time, but Arsinoe turned out to be his last wife.) So Seleukos was threatened by enmity from Asia Minor if he continued to quarrel with Ptolemy over Syria, and since Lysimachos and Kassander had been allies for years, he was heavily out-gunned.

But what one king can do, his enemy can do also, and Seleukos was nothing if not politically adroit. Demetrios had regained his fleet after the battle, and had a reasonable force of soldiers with him as well. He had at least 9,000 men when he reached Ephesos, and the fleet will have been manned by more, as were his other bases. He was blocked from returning to Athens, where his arrogant conduct and his extravagance had finally made even the Athenians tired of him, but he had recovered a squadron of his ships from the Peiraios, and he had kept hold of Corinth. Before Pleistarchos or anyone else occupied Kilikia he rescued his mother Stratonike from that area, together with his father's treasure, and had put her safely into Cyprus.[9] It may be that while he was in the area he had made sure that Tyre and Sidon were properly manned and supplied. His sea-kingdom was thus fragmented, but its parts were connected by his ships and his command of the sea. And here was Seleukos' opportunity.

Demetrios had already made it clear that for him the war against the allies continued. He focussed his hostility on Lysimachos, conducted raids against him in the Straits area, the strategic heart of Lysimachos' newly expanded kingdom, where he had built his name city.[10] Once Lysimachos, already allied with Kassander, was also publicly allied with Ptolemy, an alliance of Seleukos with Demetrios was the obvious diplomatic counter-move. Since the symbol of most alliances was a marriage, this would be the symbol of this alliance also. Demetrios sailed to Syria, raiding Kilikia on the way, at which Pleistarchos complained. But he complained to Seleukos, as Demetrios' ally. This shows that Pleistarchos had taken possession, but not only was he unable to protect the land he had been awarded – this was the second time Demetrios had raided it – he was seen as an enemy by Demetrios. Demetrios took the opportunity of Pleistarchos' going to complain to Seleukos, landed yet again and collected the remains of Antigonos' treasure which had been stored at Kyinda.[11]

Pleistarchos clearly understood that Demetrios and Seleukos were already allied before they actually met. The alliance agreement had apparently been made before Demetrios left Greece, no doubt by envoys sent to him by Seleukos – though who they were is unknown. Demetrios' visit to the east was therefore to ratify the alliance, which was done when he delivered his daughter to Seleukos as his new wife. (The raids into Kilikia were thus little extras, which must have annoyed Pleistarchos even more.) The meeting between the kings took place at Rhosos, which is on the border of Kilikia and Syria, but actually still in Kilikia, at the foot of the Amanus Mountains (another insult to Pleistarchos, and through him to Kassander and Lysimachos). The occasion was quite deliberately splendid, with speeches and banquets, ostentatious meetings of the principals without their guards, some on board Demetrios' flagship, and some on shore in Seleukos' tent. This was all designed, of course, to bring the alliance to the notice of the other Macedonian potentates.

This extravagant display has also successfully hidden the content of the talks, but it is likely that we can discern some elements of the agreement by what happened later. The meeting ended with the marriage of Seleukos with Stratonike, the daughter of Demetrios and Phila (daughter of Antipater). Phila was also present at the meeting, and she was also the sister of both Pleistarchos and Kassander. The significant events which followed were that Phila then went off by herself to see Kassander, no doubt to smooth things over with regard to Pleistarchos, while her husband took full control of Kilikia.[12]

At the same time, Seleukos arranged a reconciliation between Demetrios and Ptolemy, thereby severing, or at least undermining, the alliance of Ptolemy and Lysimachos, and making it clear that his own quarrel with Ptolemy was finished, even if his claim to southern Syria had not been abandoned.[13] As a result Lysimachos was partly isolated, though his alliance with Kassander continued. Seleukos and Ptolemy were perhaps concerned that Lysimachos might use that alliance to intervene in Kilikia on Pleistarchos' behalf; both would no doubt prefer it to be in Demetrios' much weaker hands.

None of these alliances lasted much beyond the moment of their making. Ptolemy and Demetrios as friends was a most unlikely partnership, and it soon ended. But it is very obvious that all of these men were feeling their ways to a new pattern of political and diplomatic relationships. Even the antipathies between Seleukos and Ptolemy and between Ptolemy and Demetrios were not yet set in stone. The royal marriages which had taken place were no more than momentary symbols. It was not long before enmity between the three men revived, first between Demetrios and Ptolemy, then between Seleukos and Ptolemy, if it had ever really gone away; no doubt the alliance of Ptolemy and Lysimachos continued, as did the marriage of the latter with Arsinoe. As Ptolemy's brief friendships elsewhere faded away so would their alliance revive. At some point, perhaps now, Lysimachos' son Agathokles married another of Ptolemy's daughters. (So father and son were married to sisters.)

After a year or so the alliance of Seleukos and Demetrios became badly frayed, and the reconciliation of Demetrios and Ptolemy lasted no longer. The issue was Tyre and Sidon. Seleukos asked that Demetrios hand over to him either Kilikia or Tyre and Sidon. He offered to pay for Kilikia, but Tyre and Sidon he claimed as his by right of the victory at Ipsos and the partition treaty later. He must have known Demetrios would refuse; he affected to be insulted at the offer of money. Plutarch claims he said he would not pay to be Seleukos' son-in-law, so perhaps Seleukos was asking for these places as a dowry payment.[14]

So Demetrios point-blank refused, and sent reinforcements to his eastern lands, including the two cities, from one of which a raid went out into Palestine as far as Samaria.[15] Demetrios appreciated full well that Ptolemy was as eager as Seleukos to acquire these two cities. Tyre had been comprehensively destroyed by the sieges of Alexander and Antigonos, and by its repeated captures by Ptolemy, but Sidon had survived by judicious surrenders, and was still under the rule of its own king. It was about this time that Abdanolymos of Sidon commissioned a sarcophagus decorated with scenes of battle, which has become called the 'Alexander Sarcophagus'; he seems to have been succeeded as king not much later by Philokles. Arados, in Seleukos' sphere, was also ruled by its own king at this time.

Demetrios campaigned insistently, restlessly, much annoying the others, particularly as it was quite likely he would succeed in building up his power once more. A coalition of Lysimachos, Ptolemy, and Seleukos was formed in about 296 – Kassander had died by this time – which was aimed specifically at restricting Demetrios' ability to cause them mischief. More or less in concert the three kings moved against different parts of Demetrios' isolated dominions. Lysimachos seized control of the cities along the Ionian coast, including Ephesos, which Demetrios still held; Seleukos took Kilikia; Ptolemy seized Cyprus. Ptolemy was the only one of the three who had to do some serious fighting, since Demetrios' forces on the island stood siege at Salamis. When he took the city, Ptolemy sent Demetrios' mother and his children back to him unharmed and honoured.[16]

It is noticeable that Tyre and Sidon were missing from this concerted campaign, no doubt because Ptolemy and Seleukos could not agree on who should take them. Without any other bases in the east, however, Demetrios was now severely handicapped in maintaining them. That was so until 294, but then by a careful mixture of diplomacy, aggression, and murder he eliminated the last of Kassander's sons and took over Macedon for himself as king. The kings will have congratulated themselves on having moved against his other possessions when they did, for he set about vigorously developing his military and naval strength with the aim of recovering his father's kingdom.[17]

Seleukos probably had other motives, besides momentary protection, for his early alliance with Demetrios. Virtually all the men in his army had originally served with Antigonos. They had joined him at various times –

in Babylonia, in Iran, and after Ipsos – and Antigonos was now dead. But Demetrios was alive, very active, and a much better liked commander than his father ever was. There can be no doubt that, given the numbers of men involved, some of Seleukos' soldiers had guilty consciences over deserting Antigonos and might salve their guilt by joining Demetrios, but if Seleukos and Demetrios were allies those men had much less inducement to go over, and with Seleukos married to Demetrios' daughter the conflict of conscience some might feel was surely much less.

Seleukos had also another aspect of his policy in Syria which could reconcile any Antigonid loyalists who still felt badly about the outcome of the war. He made great efforts to settle Syria with his soldiers and with other immigrants. The places with Macedonian names were inhabited by the old Antigonid soldiers, but the arrival of immigrants – almost entirely, so far as can be seen, from Greece – diluted the Macedonian element in the population, by adding people who owed allegiance directly to Seleukos himself. As time went on, of course, the old soldiers died off, and the problem of their allegiance faded. This was, however, not the only reason for Seleukos' intensive development of North Syria. To explain it the international situation needs to be considered again.

For Lysimachos, Seleukos, and Ptolemy, the old nightmare revived when Demetrios seized Macedon, but this time it was much more serious. Antigonos had been bad enough, but Demetrios with the resources of Macedon and Greece and in command of his huge fleet, was an even greater threat. Sheltered by his fleet he could recruit and organize in Macedon at leisure. Then he would be able to attack at any of a number of places. And as a commander he was much more to be feared than 80-year-old Antigonos; he was swift, ingenious, and commanded the loyalty of his men much more securely than Antigonos ever had.

The coalition of the three Antigonid enemies gradually reformed yet again. Demetrios was kept busy in Greece for several years, where the Greek cities and leagues were as averse to Macedonian control as ever. He developed a flamboyance and arrogance towards his Macedonian subjects which left them annoyed and alienated. But the threat he posed continued. Of the three coalition partners Lysimachos was still the most powerful in military terms, and he was proving surprisingly adept at diplomatic intrigue as well. Ptolemy had a substantial fleet, and was the most distant from Demetrios' base, and was therefore the least likely to be immediately attacked. Seleukos had no fleet, and was clearly extremely vulnerable to any attack by Demetrios. The landing of a large force from Demetrios' fleet at Tyre or Sidon might well see Seleukos' control of North Syria collapse at once.

Seleukos' vulnerability lay in several areas. He was probably militarily still the weakest of the kings, a condition aggravated by his lack of warships. His contribution to the Ipsos campaign had been mainly in cavalry, much of it light cavalry and horse archers, and elephants. Of the cavalry much of it had been recruited in Media and the east, and had no doubt rapidly returned there after the campaign. Of the elephants, he had begun with 500 in India, but had only 400 in action at Ipsos, an attrition rate (assuming the reduction was due to death and disability), which would eliminate the whole elephant corps within ten years.

Seleukos had always been short of hoplites for the phalanx, which was the essential basis of military power. Such soldiers were recruited in Greece and Macedon and in parts of Asia Minor, to none of which Seleukos had easy access, unlike his rivals. These men were the real strength of any army, hence Seleukos' vulnerability. If Demetrios arrived in his fleet of 300 ships, carrying perhaps 20,000 soldiers, Seleukos could well be overwhelmed. But he had always known that this was his weakness – that was one of the reasons Lysimachos had been able to secure the lion's share of the spoils after Ipsos – and it was one of the strengths of Ptolemy's position, for he had diligently recruited soldiers to settle on Egyptian land as cleruchs (military colonists), which gave him the ability to call up a major force in emergencies to reinforce his regular army of young conscripts and mercenaries.[18]

Seleukos had therefore begun in Syria with a blank sheet. He had fewer troops of the necessary type than he felt he needed, he had acquired a land which was no more than a thinly populated peasant region with few towns, and those had few Greeks and Macedonians amongst their inhabitants. The only military resources in this land were the old Macedonians settled in the scattered Antigonid garrisons; as Antigonid soldiers for up to twenty years, they were not likely to have any real loyalty to Seleukos, and they might well revert to their old allegiance if Demetrios arrived.

On his mettle, Seleukos showed once again that he was the most inventive of Alexander's successors. Maybe it was the sight of the partly-built Antigoneia, possibly the arrival of the Antigonid survivors of Ipsos, perhaps the memory of Alexander's work in founding cities, which propelled him to a radical solution. Most likely, however, it was the pressing need for military manpower and to provide for the defence of these new territories in the face of Demetrios' and Ptolemy's and Lysimachos' hostility. His answer was to set about building cities in his new lands almost as soon as he acquired them. He had, of course, done this in Babylonia, at Seleukeia-on-the-Tigris. That was a single huge city, established partly as a political statement but also as a fortified defence for Babylonia.

Seleukos' plan for Syria was altogether grander and more practical.[19] He established four great cities, spread out in a quadrilateral, so that they established fortified control over the territory directly north of Ptolemy's chosen boundary along the Eleutheros Valley. The region consisted of a narrow plain along the coast, much of which was part of the Aradian *peraia*; this was backed by the Bargylos Mountains (now the Jebel Alawiyeh); east of the mountains was the valley of the Orontes River, which here flows from south to north, and which was in a trench, the northward extension of the Great Rift Valley, which was mainly occupied by marshland (the Ghab); east again of the river was a scarp slope and then a plateau which sloped fairly gently and more or less evenly away to the distant Euphrates, becoming desert only a relatively short distance from the Orontes. Two of Seleukos' four cities were placed so as to form a block on the coastal route (Laodikeia) and the inland route, between the river and the desert (Apameia); the other two were, in a sense, the citadels of the region, Seleukeia-in-Pieria on the coast just beside the mouth of the Orontes, where it blocked a way into the interior, and Antioch on the river inland; the river broke through the mountains at this point, and the valley formed a route connecting these two cities.[20]

The two northern cities were each about 600 hectares in area within the walls, with an acropolis on some high land overlooking and dominating the site. The walls enclosed not just the site of the inhabited city on the lower land but the slopes leading up to the acropolis as well, so that the settled parts were perhaps two-thirds, or even less, of the total area of the two cities. The two southern cities, Apameia and Laodikeia, did not have mountainous sites, and so all the area within the walls was available for settlement; they were thus about the same size in their inhabited areas as the two northern cities. Each of these had its acropolis, Apameia on an old tell beside the new city, a tell which is still inhabited today (as the town of Qalat el-Madiq); Laodikeia had a purpose-built acropolis at the northern end of the site. Between them the four cities enclosed the Bargylos highland, controlled both the coastal road and a route along the escarpment overlooking the river. And to make it absolutely clear that this was his work, his territory, and his kingdom,

Seleukos gave them all dynastic names, even Apameia, which had been called Pella earlier (and had the Syrian name of Niya before Alexander's passage).

The four cities were obviously planned as a single system. Seleukeia, being a port and one of the largest cities, seems to be the main city of the region, like Seleukeia-on-the-Tigris in Babylonia. It was founded in 300 BC, which means the other cities were also founded then. Seleukos decommissioned Antigoneia almost as soon as he arrived, and used the building materials already assembled to begin the construction of Seleukeia. The site of the city of Antigoneia was then enclosed within the bounds of Antioch, and reduced to a suburb of the main city, a satisfying revenge, no doubt.

It is worth emphasizing the priority of Seleukeia, since this did not last, and Antioch eventually overtook it. But it was to be the burial place of the kings, it had the founder's own name, it was unpolluted by being the site of a former enemy's city, and it was the first to be begun. It was, like its fellow in Babylonia, to be the 'royal city'.

The first priority would necessarily be given to Seleukeia's construction because it commanded the entry point of Syria at the mouth of the Orontes. It seems probable that the materials from Antigoneia were used not just as a means of destroying Antigonos' city, but because they were available to build the initial fortifications. A defended port with a harbour basin connected to the sea by an artificial channel was also excavated. Seleukos clearly intended to defend his new land, and, as Seleukeia's harbour suggested, to build himself a navy.

These four cities divided between them all the territory in their vicinity, plains, hills, marshes, and desert. From evidence dating to the Roman period it has been possible to plot the approximate boundary between the territories of Apameia and Antioch, and it is clear that there was no intervening political community between them; it is therefore reasonable to assume that the four cities took up all the territory from the Eleutheros Valley to the Amanus Mountains, and inland as far as the desert.[21] But there was also a series of other cities founded in Syria outside this quadrilateral; they were clearly separate from the big four, independent of them, and in control of their own lands.

These places have generally Macedonian-derived names, in contrast to the royal names of the big four, which means that they had originated before Seleukos' arrival as garrisons or at least armed posts occupied by the Macedonian soldiers who gave them these names. They lay east of Antioch, between that city's territory and the Euphrates. Seven cities occupied this land, five of them with Macedonian or Greek names. In the north was Doliche, the site of a local shrine which became important in the Roman period, and presumably acquired its Macedonian name because Doliche in Macedon was also a local shrine. On the Quweiq River Beroia had been the Iron Age (and earlier) city of Halab; both the Syrian and the Macedonian cities of that name were on rivers. There were also Kyrrhos, in the hills, and Chalkis near the intermittent Jabboul Lake – Chalkis was a Greek rather than Macedonian name, a reminder perhaps that many of the soldiers in these Hellenistic armies were Greek mercenaries – but there was also a Chalkidike in Macedon. On the Euphrates was Europos, the defunct Karkemish; Thapsakos, the Euphrates crossing, had acquired the name Amphipolis.[22]

These places were more or less evenly distributed across the land between Antioch and the Euphrates and it seems probable that their promotion to city status was by deliberate selection; they would be prime settlements for Seleukos' Greek settlers, and he could organize a new local government by which he could establish control over them. There may well have been other small Macedonian posts which did not earn such favour, and which no doubt would be enclosed within the territory of the other cities, as Antigoneia was within Antioch, or Pella within Apameia. But there were also two other cities which he founded but which were not of Macedonian origin. One was Bambyke, a major local shrine of the goddess Atargatis and her less important husband Hadad. This was an important enough place even in Alexander's time for the local chief priest to mint his own coins.[23] The town was renamed Hierapolis – 'holy city', a recognition of its local importance – and probably given a Macedonian-type civic constitution, which gave the royal government some control, but it always remained essentially a temple-city; Queen Stratonike is credited with patronizing the temple.[24]

The other city was another Seleukeia, and therefore a royal foundation, on the Euphrates. It was built around a bridge across the river, probably at the old crossing point of Thapsakos (which name disappears, as does its Macedonian name of Amphipolis). It was distinguished from other cities of the same name by being known as Seleukeia-Zeugma, Seleukeia-'the-Bridge'.[25] This appears to be the first time the Euphrates had been bridged (Thapsakos had been a ferry point, as had Karkemish-Europos). Apart from being an example of the superiority of Greco-Macedonian engineering, the bridge was a vital strategic link between the old dominions of Seleukos in the east, and his new Syrian territories; the eastern suburb was Apameia, the bridge symbolizing the royal marriage joining the two.

Two more of these pre-Seleukid towns are known, this time situated on the Orontes south of Apameia. Their names, Larisa and Arethousa, were Greek rather than Macedonian, and it is known that a regiment of Thessalian cavalry had settled at Larisa.[26] The sites of these places were primarily strategic. Both are on the Orontes, and Arethousa in particular was a highly defensible site occupying a peninsula encircled on three sides by the deeply entrenched meander of the river.[27] Pella (which became Apameia), Larisa, and Arethousa established control along the route of the river, first for Antigonos, and now for Seleukos; they began to outflank Ptolemy's boundary at the Eleutheros Valley, and kept open the most obvious invasion route to the south into the Bekaa Valley.

These pre-Seleukos places, even though erected into *poleis*, were all considerably smaller than the four greater cities. Those to the east, between the Orontes and the Euphrates, were all about 100 hectares in size, but the two along the Orontes were smaller – Arethousa was about 70 hectares. The four in the quadrilateral were considerably larger, about 300 hectares (Apameia and Laodikeia) or 600 (Antioch and Seleukeia) – though these last two included large areas of steep hillside which were (and are) uninhabitable.

The sheer work involved in organizing, building, but above all populating these cities is astonishing, but it is the populating of these cities which raises the most difficult problem; in a nutshell, where did all the new inhabitants come from? There were, of course, as the pre-existing towns of Antigonos' time indicate, already a fair number of Greeks and Macedonians living in Syria when Seleukos arrived, but there cannot have been nearly enough to populate a dozen cities.

The size of the populations of these places is unknown, and thus controversial. Only one population figure has reached us from the ancient world, for Apameia, which is said to have had a population of 117,000 in the early Roman period.[28] This is taken to be a total for the whole city area, city and *chora*, and probably represents adult males only (though even that is not clear). The urban portion of this number is also not known. Further, this figure comes from a time of great prosperity in Syria, when the population was probably at a very high level; its population at the start of the city's history would be much smaller.

Two other figures are available. Antioch is said to have begun with 5,300 citizens;[29] Seleukeia-in-Pieria is said to have had a population of 6,000 citizens after its recapture by Antiochos III in 219.[30] Neither of these can be taken in any way as indicating the normal population size. First, they referred only to adult males, and to reach a number for the population of that social standing they must be multiplied by four or five (to include wives and children). Slaves, of course, are also omitted, but the number of slaves in Syria was probably not a large proportion of the overall population. The real omission is of the native Syrian population, the people who were living in these places when the cities were founded and those who moved into the new cities from the surrounding regions.

It has been argued earlier that North Syria was fairly thinly populated before Seleukos took possession, and it is true that then there were few places which could be reckoned to be urban. But the land is fertile, reasonably well watered by regular winter rains and by rivers, and the peasant population was probably omnipresent. In just about every case where evidence exists, these new cities included within their walls a pre-existing village. Notably, the street plan of Beroia still shows the contrast between the irregular layout of the old village with the regular grid of the new Seleukid city.[31] That is, the cities from the start had a Syrian population upon whom the Greeks and Macedonians were imposed, and which increased by the process of the natural attraction of an urban centre. The cities acquired a constitution delivered by the king, probably on a standard pattern, which placed power firmly in the hands of the Greek and Macedonian immigrants. They were the citizens, the voters, they controlled the city government, and they were awarded lands for their support. But they did not form the whole population and indeed were probably not at any time the majority part of it.

The absence of surviving ancient calculations for city populations forces us to use the actual sites as a basis, their areas and situations. Naturally there are problems – how much of a city was actually built over, were the houses of one or two storeys or more, what of the extra-mural suburbs? Uncertainties abound. But, bearing these in mind, a start can be made with the area of the cities inside their walls. Yet here again there is an instant problem – what density of population should be assumed? Colin McEvedy measured many ancient sites, and for many of them suggested possible population numbers. But his assumed densities of population vary from 370 per hectare (Alexandria) to 100 (for most places) or even less.[32] A more interesting calculation has been made by G. G. Aperghis, based on the density of population in villages, where it was seen that the larger the village the lower the density. He ended with the assumption that about 200 people per hectare would be a reasonable figure for ancient cities.[33]

Taking these three figures – 370, 200, 100 – as the possible range, some possibilities for total populations can therefore be suggested. The highest figure, for Alexandria, may be taken as the likely population-size for a major government centre. This would put Rome's population at 130,000 (rising to double that in the time of Augustus), Seleukeia-on-the-Tigris at double that, and Antioch (assuming 400 hectares' occupation out of 600 within the walls), at about 150,000. The lower density figure would apply to the secondary cities – so Seleukeia, Apameia, and Laodikeia had perhaps 50,000 to 80,000 inhabitants, and the smaller cities, Beroia and so on, perhaps 20,000. If the lowest figure of 100 people per hectare is taken these numbers must be halved.

However, these figures, using whatever density one chooses, can only be applied once the cities were built, populated, and operating (not to mention any special features which could operate, such as plagues, famines, and wars). At the start there can only have been a relatively small contingent of Greeks and Macedonians for each city, and a larger number of Syrians. This is where the note that the citizens of Antigoneia numbered 5,300 becomes relevant. This may well be the size of the original Greco-Macedonian settler group when the city was constituted, and possibly that of succeeding Antioch. And that regiment of Thessalian cavalry at Larissa cannot have been very large; it had previously been one of Alexander's regiments which had then fought for Antigonos, so that by the time the survivors settled down their numbers were much reduced, quite likely to be a good deal less than a thousand. These then may well be the sorts of numbers which Seleukos had available as founders for his cities. And that would mean he had to attract many more immigrants if the cities were to be adequately populated. This would be a process that could last for many years, and meanwhile he had to deflect threats and challenges which might have interrupted or prevented the work.

The marriage of Seleukos and Stratonike came in the early stages of the city-founding process in Syria and, as noted earlier, it was probably part of the same policy, which was aimed at planting Seleukos' power and authority in North Syria. Since one of the new cities was named for his first wife, it seems probable the city was founded before the new marriage took place (no cities were named after Stratonike until much later). It is not known if Apama died before the new marriage, though it is quite possible that Seleukos had two wives.

Stratonike's presence in the royal family produced a crisis which had a major effect on the family itself, and more broadly on the government of the kingdom. Apama, the daughter of the Sogdian enemy of Alexander,

Spitamenes, is rarely heard of at any time. We know she and Seleukos had at least two children, perhaps three, Antiochos, who had commanded the cavalry at Ipsos, a daughter whom Seleukos is said to have offered to Chandragupta, and perhaps another son, Akhaios. The marriage customs of Seleukos' generation of Macedonian kings took after that pursued by Philip II, who had multiple wives simultaneously. Some of the kings married serially rather that simultaneously, discarding one wife as they took the next. This seems to have been Lysimachos' practice (four wives), for he sent Amestris back to Herakleia when he married Arsinoe. Demetrios, however, was married to Phila while a series of extra and younger wives came and went, not to mention numerous affairs with courtesans. Ptolemy was of Lysimachos' persuasion in this, marrying serially, though each discarded wife retained access to him, a practice which eventually caused him trouble. Kassander, on the other hand, seems to have been content with one wife, Thessalonike, a daughter of Philip II.

Seleukos' marriage to Stratonike took place in 300 or 299; his first wife, Apama, was honoured in 299/298 at Miletos. That is, Seleukos seems to have joined the royal group of kings with simultaneous wives. The relationships thus set up in the royal family were apparently tense. Apama was honoured along with her eldest son Antiochos by her gifts to the temple of Apollo at Didyma, close to Miletos.[34] Apollo was Seleukos' chosen divine sponsor, and there was of course a story that the Didyma oracle had encouraged Seleukos' ambitions. (The temple had been in ruins since the Persian conquest in 494; the oracle had revived as Alexander approached – no doubt the encouraging oracle was the sensible enterprise of an ambitious priest of the temple). Seleukos was paying for its restoration. The family was thus united in this enterprise, which just coincidentally lay on the edge of Lysimachos' territory, and close to the Aegean, which was dominated by the sea power of Demetrios. In religion, we are also in politics and foreign affairs.

The position of Stratonike in the family is unclear but was probably difficult. She became notorious for extra-marital dalliances, and the subject of later stories. Lucian of Samosata has a story of a friend of Seleukos mutilating himself to avoid (or perhaps confirm) his feelings for her.[35] She was, of course, much younger than her husband, indeed younger than his son Antiochos, and as the daughter of the formidably intelligent and independent Phila and the flamboyant Demetrios it is unlikely she was reticent in venting her opinions. She and Seleukos had a daughter, another Phila, but no other children.

Stratonike was, of course, very largely a symbol of the brief alliance of Seleukos and Demetrios, but such diplomatic marriages were not intended to be more than a mark of the conclusion of the treaty, not a binding tie for the future. No war ever began when one of these wives was discarded. On the other hand, as the daughter of Demetrios and the granddaughter of Antigonos she had another symbolic value to Seleukos in reconciling the former subjects of those two kings to his own rule. The presence of Stratonike at his court was helpful in directing her father's former subjects' loyalty towards her husband.

That consideration can only have assisted Stratonike in her independence, and her continuing status as royal wife, and it made it difficult to discard her when the alliance faded away. By 294, when Demetrios became king in Macedon, and when Seleukos had seized Kilikia from him, the tension in the royal family had apparently become dangerous. Stratonike might well become a focus of loyalty in herself, and so a source of disloyalty towards Seleukos, particularly if Demetrios' power approached Syria. To Antiochos the possibility of her producing a son would be a clear threat.[36] If Stratonike was isolated in the court, and the subject of malicious rumours and gossip, she may well have felt she had nothing to lose by breaking up Seleukos' kingdom.

Much of this is perhaps over-interpretation of source-material which is thin, late, and oblique. But it is a fact that in about 294–292, Seleukos removed her from his court by handing her on to Antiochos as his wife and making Antiochos joint-king and governor of the eastern provinces, the 'Upper Satrapies'. This is wrapped up in the sources by having it explained as a romantic passion of Antiochos for his stepmother, a story which is partly ludicrous, partly hilarious, possibly true, but more importantly, wholly political. The unwanted wife was therefore discarded in the contemporary royal fashion, but kept within the family by a peculiarly Seleukid twist – so her father Demetrios, who was now, just at this time, king in Macedonia, could hardly object. A major government problem was solved by sending a capable and loyal man to rule the turbulent east, a family crisis was defused, a possible disruptive influence eliminated. It was a typical Seleukos-type solution to a variety of problems, all at once.

Chapter Eight

Antiochos in the East

The elaborated explanation of the marriage of Antiochos to Stratonike as a love story has some success in concealing the basic political content of the event, but the politics was the essential heart of what had happened. The possible disruption of the royal family was involved, but the politics is clear, whereas we can only guess at the family issues. The growth of the power of Demetrios, Stratonike's father, during 294 or 293, was a clear threat which concerned all the kings. Seleukos, the king with the highest proportion of Demetrios' old soldiers in his kingdom, was the most vulnerable. Demetrios still controlled Kilikia to his west, and Tyre and Sidon, only a little to the south of Seleukos' border in Syria. Unless he could gain control of these cities and regions they would be a standing threat to his position in Syria, and even if he did seize the cities he would find himself embroiled with Ptolemy. So, from the point of view of the international politics of the kings, it was necessary to move Stratonike away, but not to inflict insult on her or her father. Delivering her to Antiochos, covered by a romantic story, was a cleverly devious move, very much what one might expect from Seleukos. The seizure of Kilikia took place at about the same time as the new marriage, the coincidence of the two events no doubt also contributing to confusing the issue.

Seleukos went further, not only separating himself from Stratonike in this clever way, but also separating Stratonike from any surviving Antigonids in his kingdom by sending Antiochos and his new wife to govern in the east, a region where there were few old Antigonid soldiers. The east was always in need of attention, but with the threats of his western neighbours ever present, it had not been possible for the king himself to attend to eastern matters personally for the past ten years. Sending Antiochos, Apama's half-Sogdian son, to take over, neatly solved that problem, and also equally neatly inverted the threat Statonike posed in Syria to an advantage in the east. Antiochos was a capable commander even at the age of twenty or so, as was shown in the battle of Ipsos; he had already attended to the royal responsibilities in Babylonia, and he took with him to the east – or they were already there – some of his father's senior commanders; he had seen his father operating in Syria and with regard to the other kings, which was an invaluable political education. By 292, aged about 30, he probably also had ideas of his own. So a further advantage in this appointment would be the separation by some distance of two highly capable men whose political ideas and aims may not have been fully compatible. Antiochos, for example, seems to have been much more willing to resort to war than Seleukos, who in turn seems to have been more intent on using intrigues and diplomacy to gain his ends, though the contrast may be as much the result of the circumstances they faced as of their characters.

Even before the marriage to Stratonike, Antiochos had evidently been active on his own in Babylonia. A part of a chronicle in cuneiform recorded his activities. He is referred to as 'crown prince' in modern terminology (*mar sarri* in Babylonian). He was, from at the latest 292, linked with his father as joint-king, so the chronicle appears to apply to his actions before 292, or at least before his appointment as king.[1] The text is broken and has serious gaps, but the prince is referred to in connection with at least three temples in Babylon, giving offerings, with a canal, with the city of Seleukeia, and with the army. This is a set of activities normally associated with, or carried out by, any Babylonian king, so it shows that he was operating with full royal authority and standing in for Seleukos even before being made king.

The story in Plutarch of the transfer of Stratonike from Seleukos to Antiochos appears to link the marriage directly with Antiochos' appointment as joint-king, but this link may not be quite as direct as is implied.[2] The first problem is the date of the marriage. I have assumed until now it was in 294 or 293, for there is a link with Seleukos' seizure of Kilikia, which took place in 294. So we have four successive events – Seleukos' takeover of Kilikia from Demetrios' rule, the marriage of Stratonike with Antiochos, the appointment of Antiochos as joint-king, and this was followed by his posting to the eastern provinces. This seems to be the order of the events but exactly how they were connected is less clear. Since the marriage might have been construed by Demetrios as an insult and a usurpation of his rights as a father, it seems probable that it was not directly and temporally connected with Seleukos' seizure of Kilikia, for had the two happened at the same time, it might have been too much for Demetrios to bear. The connection between the marriage and Antiochos' appointment as joint-king is certainly possible, for Stratonike would thereby continue to be the wife of a king, and so any insult to Demetrios would be mitigated. Also, since the marriage must have been in part aimed at mollifying any pro-Antigonid feelings amongst Demetrios' old soldiers in Syria, it must have taken place only when it became clear that Demetrios' power had seriously increased, which was not the case until after 294. It may well be worth pointing out also that the appointment of an adult son as joint-king was in fact copying what Antigonos Monophthalamos had done for Demetrios back in 306; if imitation is the sincerest form of flattery, then Seleukos was laying it on fairly thick; Demetrios, of course, was susceptible.

The Babylonian evidence on these issues is not clear-cut. There is one dated clay tablet which names both men as kings in 292, but an Astronomical Diary names only Seleukos in 291.[3] A list of kings who ruled Babylonia which was compiled much later separates the two, and makes Antiochos' reign begin in 281 and last twenty years (281–261), rather than the thirty-one he should be credited with (292–261).[4] So there was some doubt in Babylonian minds as to who was the reigning king between 292 and 281. On the other hand, they must have been used to Antiochos' authority even before he became king, and the contemporary documents refer to the two men and joint-kings.

It therefore seems most acceptable to see these three changes in the Seleukid royal government as successive and linked. The sequence would thus put Kilikia first, concerted by agreement between Seleukos, Lysimachos, and Ptolemy. The achievement of the Macedonian kingship by Demetrios may have been the trigger for this, or it may have been plotted independently. The divorce and remarriage of Stratonike could seem to be the result of Demetrios' increase in power as king in Macedon, and so it happened sometime after his seizure of power in Macedon. If the acquisition of Kilikia happened in 294, it might be best to put the transfer of Stratonike later, in 293 or even 292. Antiochos was certainly joint-king by the end of 292, according to one Babylonian document, but the Babylonians did not know before September of that year, when Seleukos was still named alone. The appointment as joint-king led to his eastern command.

The internal court intrigues and discussions involved in all this are wholly invisible to us. Little credence can be put on the love story, if only because the doctor said to have been the catalyst, Erasistratos, has been identified as being alive much later, and was therefore too young to be really involved.[5] (Though this does not, of course, invalidate the story, only Erasistratos' involvement; the doctor is unnamed in other versions.) A second marriage by a king was, of course, a threat to the king's earlier children – the problems of Philip and Alexander at the end of the former's reign, when his final wife produced a son, were surely in everyone's minds. The only child of Seleukos and Stratonike was, as it happened, a daughter, named Phila after her grandmother. They were married for seven or eight years, long enough to have produced more children, and the absence of these children is very suggestive. Passing Stratonike on to his son – they were much closer in age, of course – therefore also solved the tension within the royal family. Not only that, but Antiochos, at last married at nearly thirty years of age, could set about establishing the dynasty more firmly. The number of potential problems – internal relations with former Antigonid soldiers, the dynasty, government to the east, recognition of Antiochos as heir, snubbing the troublesome Demetrios – which were dealt with by this marriage and the allocation of the east to Antiochos are remarkable.

Antiochos' area of responsibility as king was the 'Upper Satrapies', which by its very name probably excluded the low-lying Babylonia, which was closer to Syria than to Baktria, which had to be Antiochos' primary area of operations, but precisely what was actually included is less clear, and perhaps no precise division was ever made. He is recorded as acting in the farther east, and in Persis, but not in Media, which was later to be the central part of the viceroyalty of the Upper Satrapies. Common sense and geography would suggest that Media was part of his area, in part because he would need the military and financial resources of that country if he was to impose his rule successfully in the more turbulent Baktrian region. It would therefore probably be wrong to assume that there was a strict geographical division between the responsibilities of the two kings: they were joint-kings of all the kingdom, and both exercised authority throughout it; they are certainly both named as kings in Babylonia ('King Seleukos and his son King Antiochos') and this probably applied in the rest of the kingdom as well. On the other hand, it would be more comfortable for the two men to stay apart, not least if the transfer of Stratonike had involved serious family and dynastic troubles.

Antiochos' work in the east had become necessary because of the instability which neither Alexander nor Seleukos in their brief visits had done much to calm – indeed the instability was largely the result of Alexander's campaigns. Antiochos, however, was on the spot for a full decade, from about 292 until his father's death in 281. For the first time for four decades therefore the east had the benefit of constant royal presence and attention, and it may well be the first time since the Akhaimenid conquest by Cyrus I in about 530 BC that a royal ruler had made a sustained effort and paid detailed attention over a fairly extended period to the needs of the region.

Antiochos was accompanied to the east by two of his father's prominent supporters. Demodamas of Miletos had sponsored the connection of Seleukos and Apama with his home city in 299, and had been involved also with the rebuilding work at the Temple of Apollo at Didyma.[6] Patrokles had been with Seleukos as far back as 311, when he was left in command in Babylon while Seleukos went off into Iran, and was probably one of those who were with him in Egypt, and perhaps earlier.[7] Both of these were military men, who could be trusted to command without royal supervision, which is possibly why they were sent, quite apart from their loyalty to Seleukos – for they no doubt also functioned as supervisors of Antiochos on behalf of his father. The geographical range of the necessary activity of Antiochos in the east was huge, from the Zagros Mountains and the Caspian Sea to the Indian border, and from the Iaxartes River to the Arabian Sea, whereas in the west Seleukos could stay in Syria and deflect the major threats to the kingdom which were all within 100km of Seleukeia-in-Pieria.

It may also be during Antiochos' time in the east that Megasthenes went as an envoy to India on more the one occasion. His first visit to India was after the peace made between Seleukos and Chandragupta in about 305/303. He is described as an envoy of Seleukos, but that does not exclude him from working also with Antiochos.[8] More certainly Daimachos of Plataia, another envoy to India who visited Chandragupta's successor Bindusara (Mauryan emperor from 297), may have been part of Antiochos' entourage.[9] Even if these two men were originally sent by Seleukos from Syria, they surely reported also to Antiochos as they posted through his area on the way to and from India.

We may therefore see these men as part of the power-group in the east. Megasthenes and Daimachos went to India, and both of them wrote books about that country, and no doubt they advised both Antiochos and Seleukos on policy in that area. The lands taken up by Chandragupta after the peace of 303 made his empire a close and immediate neighbour of Baktria, even if their mutual boundary was the Hindu Kush mountain range. There will always be issues to be addressed between neighbours, and both Megasthenes and Daimachos were no doubt concerned in ensuring that none of the problems which arose developed into something serious.

One of the issues was presumably the status of Greeks and Macedonians who continued to live in the formerly Macedonian territories Chandragupta had taken over. None of these people who were in the Indus Valley are known, but there was a Greek-speaking population in Arachosia, specifically at Alexandria-Kandahar in Asoka's reign (272–c.230), who were presumably survivors and successors of those who settled there in Alexander's and Seleukos' time.[10] They might naturally feel a greater loyalty towards their fellow Greeks and Macedonians in Baktria, and to a nearby Macedonian king, than to an absent and distant Indian emperor. It will have been part of the tasks of the Seleukid envoys to prevent them causing trouble, and at the same time they were also no doubt committed to ensure that these people were treated fairly by the Indians. Then the trading contacts across the borders would need to be regulated. There was a longstanding trading connection between India and Central Asia, which the Indian emperors would wish to continue.

One of the problems the Mauryans had in their western territories was with Taxila, which rebelled against them at least twice, aiming for independence.[11] The city was in a very sensitive strategic position, controlling the entrance to the Khyber Pass, one of the main routes linking the main body of the empire with its Central Asian provinces. It was also, as the excavations there have shown, considerably influenced by Hellenic culture, and this may well have been unsettling, particularly given its close geographical position next to Greek Baktria.[12] Should the Seleukids be interested in attempting to 'recover' their 'lost' lands in India, Taxila's disaffection with Mauryan rule would be a useful point of leverage. As it happens it does not seem that any ruler in Central Asia made any such attempt, at least while the Mauryan Empire existed. Antiochos I certainly had quite enough to do without tangling with the huge Indian armies.

In the work of establishing full royal control in Baktria, there seems to have been a division of labour among Antiochos, Demodamas, and Patrokles, though this may be an accident of the surviving sources. Patrokles is known to have explored the region of the lower Oxus River and the Caspian Sea, which presumably means the region anciently called Chorasmia, south of the Aral Sea.[13] By about 300 B.C., or perhaps before, there was a coin-producing kingdom in this area.[14] Patrokles is credited with an exploration, but his expedition was surely military in nature, unless he had made very careful diplomatic advance preparations. His conclusion was that the Caspian Sea was open to the world-encompassing ocean in the north, so it is evident that he did not really explore much of it, though for the Seleukid state, it was only the southern half which was important.

Patrokles will have worked out the political situation in the area between Baktria and Sogdiana to the east, the Aral Sea to the north and the Caspian Sea to the west. This was partly the valley of the Oxus, and partly the deserts of the Kara Kum and the Kyzyl Kum; in fact it was the region of the Parni, who were to invade Parthia (and take that satrapy's name), a generation later. The people of this area, notably Chorasmia, became, or were already, in contact with the Greeks in Baktria, as artefacts found in excavations of the sites in the area show.[15]

Demodamas, on the other hand, operated in the valley of the Iaxartes, that is, in the north of Baktria, beyond the mountains which separate the Oxus and the Iaxartes Rivers. The Iaxartes formed the northern boundary of Sogdiana, which essentially consisted of the Iaxartes Valley and the valley of the Polymelitos (the modern Zarafshan), a region which had slid out of Macedonian control before Seleukos' expedition. However, only part of the Iaxartes was accessible, for the western part of the river swings north before reaching the Aral Sea, and the eastern part lay among the great mountains of the Pamir Knot. The essential place in the region where Demodamas operated was the city founded by Alexander and since called Alexandria-Eschate – Alexandria-the-Farthest. This was close to an array of triumphal altars which had been set up by Cyrus and Alexander (and, it was claimed, by Semiramis – perhaps really Darius I) to mark their conquests; Demodamas added another, to the Apollo of Didyma.[16]

A campaign so far north from Baktria, plus Patrokles' 'exploration' in the Caspian Sea, Chorasmia and the deserts, means that Antiochos was deliberately expanding his and his father's kingdom to include, at least, Sogdiana. The details of Demodamas' campaign are absent, but it is not without significance that he was associated with Queen Apama, whose father led the great Sogdian insurrection against Alexander, and her son, the half-Sodgian Antiochos. Whether or not Apama was still alive, it must be presumed that Antiochos' ancestry carried some weight in his time in the east.

But Antiochos' essential purpose, through Demodamas and Patrokles and others, was to fasten his family's rule not only on Baktria and Sogdiana but on other regions east of the Zagros Mountains. The most powerful institution which was developed to do this was the fortified city, the Macedonian version of the Greek *polis*, an urban foundation which had some elements of self-government but which was ultimately under royal authority; it had a garrison of royal soldiers in the acropolis, and a royal representative supervising the elected council. Antiochos had seen his father using such cities to secure his grip on Babylonia and then on Syria; in Central Asia and the Upper Satrapies it was Antiochos who was the real founder of these cities.

The cities Alexander had founded in the east had mostly failed, partly because of lack of support from the kings and the satraps, partly no doubt in the more remote frontier regions because of local hostility and desertion by the settlers. There had been plenty of warfare, even as shown in our exiguous sources, in the region to bring out military settlers to fight in armies since Alexander's time. It is clear that Alexandria-Eschate was no longer in existence; when Demodamas reached the country he had to 're-found' it.[17] This would mean importing a substantial Greek-speaking population, supplying them with two or three years' provisions, ensuring that the city had adequate defences, and perhaps campaigning to suppress local hostility, at least for a time. (Founding the city, W. W. Tarn commented, was hard work for a king.)[18] Demodamas is also said to have crossed the Iaxartes, as Alexander had, which implies that he waged a deliberate campaign against the local nomads. Since there was never any attempt from Alexander onwards to rule north of the Iaxartes, such a campaign was presumably designed as a brutal warning to the nomads of the area to stay north of the river.

But Alexandria was very remote – it was not called 'the farthest' for nothing – and it could hardly be left to fend for itself. Other cities were needed within helpful range. We do not know of any. The seven 'cities' Alexander is said to have planted along the river were long gone. Samarkand (Marakanda) was revived (it had been smashed by Alexander), but it is 150 miles (240km) away and across a mountain range.[19] Further, the Polymelitos Valley had been extensively ravaged by Alexander, and while it had probably been resettled by the time Antiochos came to rule, it was not a serious power source. An active satrapal government for the region, with command of a substantial armed force, must be presumed, but it does not look as though there was much in the way of support for the northern outliers from any other source, and the satrap's army was always liable to be elsewhere when needed.

Within Baktria, that is, the valley of the Oxus, rather more urban centres were encouraged. Baktra was an old fortified administrative centre, and so it remained and continued. To the west, a firm grip was established on the valley of the Arios River, where the city of Antioch-in-Margiana was actually the old centre in the delta of the river where it made an oasis before evaporating in the sands; its name indicates that it was 'founded' by Antiochos, which must mean the planting there of Greeks and Macedonians, the presence of a royal garrison, the organization of the city government, a refurbishment of the city's walls and of its civic buildings, but on the basis of an existing population.[20] South along the river's courses there were two other cities, Artakoana (another Alexandria) and Herakleia, both newly named cities, but founded on old settlement sites.

It was probably Antiochos who oversaw the founding of the new city at the site which is now known as Ai Khanum. This has gained fame because it has been extensively excavated, and the continuous wars in Afghanistan since 1979 have then permitted the excavators to concentrate on publishing their findings in detail.[21] Not that this has been by any means definitive. It has taken much more research to produce some clear conclusions as to the purpose, history, and setting of the city.

It is, however, producing a clearer understanding of the history of Greek Baktria. The more it is studied, the more it becomes clear that Ai Khanum – we do not even know its ancient name – is by no means a typical Greek city, even for the eastern territories. This, of course, should have been clear from the start since it had been founded on a more or less virgin site, and has not been re-occupied since its demise. It was therefore a more than usually artificial urban settlement. The area in which the city was placed was a land of villages, whose people farmed the valley by means of irrigated agriculture.[22] So there was a peasant population already in the region and thus a food supply available. In this, of course, it was not unusual, for this was the pattern of Greek colonization both before and after Alexander. What is unusual about Ai Khanum is that it failed. After the Greco-Macedonian population left, or was driven out, the place remained deserted ever after. Further, the city itself is clearly anomalous both in its layout and in its geographical context. Internally, it consists very largely of large public buildings – theatre, temples, palace, a gymnasium, and the acropolis – but there is little evidence of private buildings, shops, houses, and so on. This may be in part the consequence of the archaeologists' preference for excavating such buildings, but in total these large public buildings occupy something getting on for half the area within the walls. This is clearly an unbalanced condition, and the place has therefore all the appearance of an administrative centre with little or no connections with the surrounding territory. There is evidence of a few large private houses outside the city walls, but not many, and a suggestion that private housing occupied the (unexcavated) areas, but this looks too much like a guess to be relied on. The purpose of the city – if it can be called that – was thus evidently to control the nearby area by means of a garrison, bureaucrats, presumably a governor, and tax collectors. Of these last there is clear and abundant evidence.[23] But the geographical location of the city is also significant. It lies at the junction of the Kokcha River with the Oxus, and in fact uses their streams as part of its fortification system. Upstream along the Kokcha were sources of various minerals, including copper and iron and perhaps tin, but most importantly lapis lazuli, of which this was (and still is) the only source in the world. So the city is best seen therefore as a government centre devoted to the supervision and taxing of the mining region upstream.

The date of this foundation is put at about 300 B.C. It was thus not one of the Alexandrias which are frequently sought. It also seems unlikely that anyone in Baktria had the resources before Antiochos' arrival in 292 to develop such a site, so we may assume that Antiochos was the founder, and that the foundation date must be shifted later, to between 290 and 280. It is, of course, possible that the place was begun by Seleukos during his eastern expedition, but only Antiochos was active in the region long enough to see such work through to an approximate conclusion.

The other cities founded during Antiochos' viceroyalty are more difficult to identify with any certainty, but some can be suggested on purely strategic and economic grounds. The main city of Baktria was Baktra, where several attempts have been made to locate the Seleukid levels, with little success, but there is no doubt the city existed and was heavily fortified (it stood a long siege eighty years after Antiochos' time).[24] The site of Termez was the main crossing point over the Oxus, and Hellenistic Greek-type city remains have been located there.[25] Qunduz, located between Baktra and Ai Khanum, was a city before Alexander came and continued to flourish after the Greeks ceased to rule. No doubt Antiochos had something to do with it. Above all Baktra itself was developed still further as the administrative centre of the whole region, as well as for the Baktrian satrapy. There were undoubtedly other such places, though the fabled 'thousand cities of Baktria' was a wild exaggeration. Nevertheless the quality and quantity of archaeological, numismatic, and epigraphic evidence for this period in Baktria has grown enormously in the past half century or so, though it is still largely scattered and difficult to collate, being in several languages, but it seems certain that it will continue to grow.[26]

The rest of Antiochos' responsibilities have produced rather less evidence of his work, but some inferences can be drawn. Baktria was connected with

Babylonia and Syria by the eastern half of the Royal Road, and this route became dotted with cities. Some already existed, of course, as at Ekbatana, the old Median kingdom's capital. It recurs in the sources throughout the Seleukid period, and indeed exists as a city still (Hamadan). Nearby were two other cities, Nihavand, which was given the name Laodikeia, and Kangavar, whose name became Konkobar in Greek. Together these formed a fortified guard some way east of the Bisitun Pass, blocking the route to the farther east.[27]

Only Laodikeia-Nihavand had a dynastic name, but this was a region of castles and fortified towns, many of which were probably garrisoned. It was obviously a vital strategic position. Along the Royal Road, the next such position was at the Caspian Gates, a narrow valley just south of the Elburz Mountains. Just to the west was Rhagai (in the southern suburbs of Teheran), which was given the name Europos. Beyond the gates was an Apameia, whose name suggests an early foundation, probably by Antiochos. The ten-mile channel of the Gates was guarded by a garrison at a place called, suitably enough, Charax (fort).[28]

This system of fortified cities along the road probably did not take all that much effort to organize, for it quite evidently rested on the foundation of pre-existing Akhaimenid and Median towns. Such organization as was required could have been done by Seleukos in his eastern expeditions, or by Antiochos. The intention was evidently to arrange a reasonably comprehensive guard for the vital route. The basic reason was that, to the north, between the Caspian Sea and Armenia, was the independent kingdom of Media Atropatene.[29] The kings there showed no obvious inclination to revive the old Median kingdom, but the possibility would have concerned any Seleukid satrap or king. A pair of caves, Qalah Karafto, 200km or so northeast of Ekbatana, were taken over to house a guard, overlooking one of the routes southward. There was another facing Atropatene at Avroman to the northeast.[30] One must assume there were others of these guard posts in old castles and on ancient tells all over northern Iran.

Apart from founding and refounding the cities, and reinforcing the defences of the region, Antiochos had also to plant the imperial administration on a firm basis. This work would involve careful delineation of satrapies, organizing the collection of taxes and setting tax rates, setting out legal practices and procedures, delimiting the powers of satraps, placing the governors of sections of satrapies (the Baktrian-Sogdian satrapy was enormous; the satrap would certainly need several subordinate officials).

Mints had to be set up, and they appear just at this time.[31] It is almost certain that he will have concentrated much of his energy on Baktria and its immediate surroundings, which was the area where the population was densest, and the Greek settlers had become concentrated, but he is also recorded as operating in Persis, beyond the southern boundary of Media, on the shores of the Persian Gulf, where a settlement became another Antioch.[32] This means he was busy also in Media itself, concerned with all these cities, and probably he ensured that his authority was accepted in the thinly populated satrapy of Karmania along the Indian Ocean coast, and even perhaps in Gedrosia.

Antiochos ruled these eastern territories, the Upper Satrapies, for a decade and more while his father concentrated on the west. It was his work to establish the authority of his family as the accepted rulers there. In this he seems to have been successful to the extent that after he moved back to the west when his father died (he was also in the west in 283) the work he had done in the east lasted for another generation or so. In one sense that was eventually a failure, for the Baktrian area eventually broke away into independence. In a wider sense, however, Antiochos was successful, since the breakaway state was a fragment of his kingdom which continued to be ruled in the same way, as a Seleukid copy. And in the end, when the nomad invasions died down and the Kushan Empire controlled the whole region, it was still very much a Greek-type empire, erected on the foundations laid by Antiochos.

Chapter Nine

Seleukos in the West

From his situation in his new city of Seleukeia-in-Pieria, Seleukos could watch events in all the necessary directions. Eighty kilometres to the south along the coast was the boundary between his autonomous but subordinate city of Arados and then the territories of Ptolemy; to the west he faced the Mediterranean Sea, dominated either by Ptolemy's fleet based at Alexandria and Cyprus or by Demetrios' ships from the Aegean; to the north was the great area of Anatolia, much of it under Lysimachos' control, separated from Seleukos' territories of Kilikia and north Syria by the Taurus Mountains; to the northeast he is said to have ruled in Armenia and Seleukid Kappadokia, bordering on Lysimachos' lands. These boundaries were clear enough – the mountains and the Anatolian desert to the north, and the Eleutheros River in the south – but the size of the lands he had acquired as a result of the victory over Antigonos was still much smaller than those secured by his former colleagues. Above all North Syria was enclosed on three sides by the lands (and seas) of his rivals: he ruled a salient thrust between enemies.

A good deal of his energy and attention in the 290s and 280s was devoted necessarily to his work of fortifying this small region to defend it. This was, after all, what the cities he founded in Syria were mainly for. Each of them was provided with surrounding walls in the latest pattern, enclosing a wide area by placing the walls on the best defensive positions, usually on hilltops and ridges, utilizing rivers as boundaries, and where no natural obstacles existed, building walls with regularly spaced towers of formidable strength. Then the new cities had to be populated. They were all founded on the sites of existing villages or small towns, and the people of these places were incorporated into their populations, but what Seleukos really needed was Greeks and Macedonians, particularly young adult men, preferably men who were already trained to arms. He could offer a life in a new city, citizenship, and an allocation of land in exchange for their agreement to be available for military service in an emergency, and quite possibly a subsidy to get them started. Families would be welcome. His aim was to populate these new cities with people who were loyal to him, and who would support him in any future crises. Thus the cities were both fortified positions planted to defend his lands, and places where the population of the kingdom would be increased.

The cities were equipped not only with defensive walls, but with temples, gridded street plans, and public buildings. But perhaps most significant was the placing of the acropolis. In every single case this was established on the edge of the city site, with one wall separating it from the city itself and the other looking out at the surrounding lands. This was hardly the normal plan for a Greek city. In Athens or in Thebes, for example, the acropolis was in the centre of the city, in fact had clearly been one of the reasons for the city's original development: it was as a final refuge in case of attack, and perhaps the place of the original settlement. Seleukos' acropoleis were designed partly to protect, of course, but primarily they were to dominate the city and its population. They were the visible signs of Seleukos' royal power and his ultimate control over the cities.[1] It will have taken some time to set the cities up, build the defences (probably the acropolis first), bring in the people, and organize the city government, but after some years – say ten or so, by the early 280s – a substantial part of the work will have been accomplished. Much will have remained to do, probably the city walls were unfinished, which in the larger cities will have needed a great deal of stone, but many of the houses within the enceinte were built of wood by the new inhabitants.[2] But in that relatively brief period all north Syria was transformed from a thinly populated, unfortified territory into one studded with a dozen cities, all fortified in some way, all populated and growing. And just by publicizing that the cities existed, even if they were not fully built, Seleukos was proclaiming that the region was much better defended than it had been.

This was a major work of social, political, and military engineering. The sheer size of the work dwarfs anything accomplished by any other ancient state. It took twenty years to build the Great Pyramid of Giza, twenty years to build Hadrian's Wall, and less than twenty years for Seleukos to organize the building of four great cities and half a dozen smaller ones in North Syria. They were then – this is the key difference – populated by living persons, not a sterile defence like the Wall, or a useless tomb for a megalomaniac ruler. Seleukos' work transformed the strategic condition of the Mediterranean and the Middle East, promoting North Syria – now quite rightly referred to as the 'Seleukis' – into the heart of his enormous kingdom and the one region it was absolutely necessary for any power to control; putting it another way, it had now become necessary to control the Seleukis if a power was to be seen to dominate the eastern Mediterranean. There were other areas with a similar charisma – the Aegean, Egypt, Sicily – and now Syria had joined them. For Seleukos it had become the power centre of his kingdom, and it was the region which remained with his family to the very end.

In the immediate term, however, Seleukos was concerned to defend his new territory. The threat from Demetrios was contained by the great cities of Seleukeia and Laodikeia, both fortified ports, that from Ptolemy by Laodikeia on the coast route and by Apameia and its satellites along the Orontes (Larissa and Arethusa), while the danger from Lysimachos was largely countered by the difficulty of the Taurus passes and the old cities in Kilikia, which were also fortified, as well as by his fear of Demetrios, who controlled Macedon and the Aegean to the west.

The acquisition of Kilikia had brought to Seleukos a land which was already a good deal more urbanized than North Syria. There were several cities of modest size already existing in the plain land which was called Flat or Smooth Kilikia, where a whole series of vitalizing rivers flowed from the Taurus to the sea – Tarsos, Adana, Magarsos, Mopsuhestia, and others. Seleukos also founded one new city in the area, Seleukeia-on-the-Kalykadnos. This was formed by a synoecism, bringing together the inhabitants of several smaller places into a new city. Once again this was quite evidently done with a view to defence. The new city was sited at the point where the Kalykadnos River reaches the sea, and so it blocked the mouth of the valley. That valley was a traversable route from Central Asia Minor – it had been used by Alexander – so it defended Kilikia from the direction of Asia Minor; it also sat on the difficult coastal route around Rough Kilikia to the west, a region where Ptolemy had intermittent control of several small towns. So Kilikia was defended from that direction as well. Forming the city might well have been pleasing to the moved inhabitants; it was also a major defence move by Seleukos.[3]

Demetrios was the main threat to the other kings from the time he seized the Macedonian kingship in 294. One reason (added to the several already noted), for Seleukos' divorce of Stratonike was to convince Lysimachos and Ptolemy that he was no longer allied to her father, though they probably took little convincing; he also no doubt pointed out that the divorce not only broke whatever fragments of their alliance still existed, but was an insult which made Demetrios unlikely ever to be willing to revive it. It does not matter that this was not necessarily true, but it might well be accepted by the others as a clear indication that Seleukos was now aligned with them.

Demetrios busied himself with attempts to gain full control of Greece and to build up his military and naval strength. By 288 he is said to have developed a fleet of 500 ships and an army of perhaps 100,000 men.[4] These figures are of the usual vague and suspiciously rounded sort, but there is no doubt that he had developed a formidable armament. This growing menace was quite sufficient to keep the other kings in suspense and fully alert, their attention fixed on Macedon all the time during his reign. The threat was also potent enough to dissuade them from quarrelling with each other. From Seleukos' point of view Demetrios was possibly less of a danger than to the other two, particularly Lysimachos, but even so the need to develop his defences was clear. This meant that from the time of his arrival in north Syria in 301 and his announcement that Ptolemy had defrauded him of his just rewards by occupying Palestine and Phoenicia, Seleukos had a dozen years (301–288) to build his cities, enlarge his army, and perhaps develop a small fleet. When Demetrios' power in Macedon collapsed in 288 when the Macedonians rejected him, Seleukos' position was much stronger than it had been.

Demetrios was felled by a combination of threats from outside and discontent within his kingdom. As his military and naval power reached its peak at the end of 289, the three kings formed another alliance designed to bring him down, in the same way that they had brought down his father.[5] This time it was Seleukos who was in the position of Ptolemy in 302, unable by reason of his distance from Macedon to intervene directly. Ptolemy could reach the Aegean and Greece with his ships, and could help Athens, for instance, in its revolt against Demetrios; Lysimachos had a common boundary with Demetrios between Thrace and Macedon and could effectively threaten an invasion of Macedon from the east. Pyrrhos of Epeiros was brought into the alliance, he was a friend of Ptolemy and had been briefly his son-in-law, and was also admired by the Macedonian fighting men, who had fought him before; he was assigned the really dangerous part, the invasion of Macedonia from the west.

The alliances worked because the Macedonians had wearied of Demetrios' arrogance, carelessness, and overweening ambition – and of his tax extraction. And they found that, in effect, they had friends in Pyrrhos and Lysimachos. The Macedonian army mutinied and refused to fight. Demetrios found that his kingdom, founded as it was solely on the army, melted away beneath him. He retreated to his fleet, but retained control of a good deal of Greece, in particular Corinth, the Peiraios, Chalkis in Euboia, and his own foundation of Demetrias in Thessaly.

Lysimachos took over the eastern half of Macedon, Pyrrhos the west. Athens rebelled against Demetrios, who laid siege to the city. Ptolemy and Pyrrhos intervened, with the result that a peace conference was held at Peiraios, which suggests strongly that the several kings were very wary of each other and were all too well aware of their various strengths, and of the unlikelihood of a clear victory. But they were also less concerned with Athens than themselves and anxious to get on with their own aims. Athens became in effect independent, but Demetrios held on to Peiraios and other forts in Attika.[6]

Pyrrhos was pleased with what he had gained, but was annoyed that Lysimachos had taken over part of Macedon. Demetrios seems to have focussed his anger on Lysimachos, whom he apparently blamed for his downfall. Ptolemy had meanwhile used the crisis to gain control of Tyre and Sidon while everyone was watching what was going on in Greece and Macedon. This seems to have been a well-laid scheme.[7] The Sidonian king, Philokles, was taken into Ptolemaic employ along with a squadron of Demetrios' ships he was commanding, and became almost a viceroy of Ptolemy in the Aegean in the next years. Ptolemy had also no doubt taken note of Demetrios' enmity towards Lysimachos and fully appreciated that only the presence of his own power in the Aegean was likely to prevent Demetrios from attacking Lysimachos. The seizure of Tyre and Sidon was also calculated to annoy Seleukos, who was surely hoping to be able to do so himself.

As a result of Demetrios' fall, Lysimachos had become what Demetrios had threatened to be and what Antigonos had been; the most powerful of the kings, and therefore the most threatening. Had Demetrios waited before seeking greater power and revenge, he could well have engineered a new alliance with Ptolemy or Seleukos or Pyrrhos or any combination of them, in the same way as he had recovered in 300. Instead, after losing control of Athens, he launched himself on Lysimachos' Asian territories and for the next year campaigned across southern Asia Minor. He was as successful as usual when it came to fighting battles, but this time he faced a commander as careful and as strategically sensible as Seleukos in Agathokles, Lysimachos' son.[8]

For a dozen years Demetrios had been betrothed to Ptolemais, one of Ptolemy's daughters. When he had been driven from Macedon his first wife, Phila, had finally despaired and committed suicide. At Ephesos Phila's sister Eurydike brought her and Ptolemy's daughter Ptolemais out of her cold storage and at last he married her.[9] This may well have been a diplomatic gesture, an attempt to appeal to Ptolemy for a revival of the old momentary alliance which the betrothal represented, but Demetrios had the timing all wrong. The gesture would have had some meaning had it taken place at Athens before his campaign began; it would have suggested to Ptolemy a possible alliance after all those years. But by carrying out the marriage at Ephesos after having already attacked Lysimachos, he had spoilt his chance, for it looked too much like either a momentary lust or a despairing appeal for help. Ptolemy was not going to join in an alliance with Demetrios in order to fight Lysimachos. So Demetrios was either too late or too early in using this marriage.

Ptolemy does not seem to have reacted, and once Demetrios was campaigning through Asia Minor it is unlikely he would be able to contact Ptolemy. It was in any case a fairly futile gesture. If the adventures of Stratonike showed anything, it was that marriage alliances were extremely fragile diplomatic instruments. And anyway Lysimachos was already married to Arsinoe, and his son Agathokles to Lysandra, both of these also daughters of Ptolemy. Whatever these kings were doing in negotiating marriages and dispatching daughters to other kings it was not to create anything like permanent political alliances. It is just possible that the marriage stopped Ptolemy from sending help to Lysimachos, but there is no sign that Lysimachos needed any.

So Demetrios had to fight his own campaign. Agathokles carefully avoided any pitched battles and gradually shepherded Demetrios' army eastwards, picking off detachments, encouraging deserters, denying supplies – much the same sort of campaign as that waged by Patrokles against Demetrios in Babylon nearly thirty years before – and Patrokles was present in Syria, as an adviser to Seleukos. His army reducing in numbers all the time, Demetrios eventually crossed the Taurus Mountains into Kilikia.[10] Now at last Seleukos became involved.

Demetrios had no difficulty in gaining control of Kilikia. The cities of the area, even Seleukeia-on-the-Kalykadnos, were apparently not sufficiently well fortified to stand against a modern Hellenistic army – they had changed hands repeatedly in the past fifty years, generally without resistance. And

Demetrios had ruled the area himself for a time until almost ten years before, so possibly he had some local support. On the other hand, Kilikia was not just separated from the rest of Asia Minor by the Taurus Mountains (which Agathokles promptly fortified); it was separated also from Syria by the Amanus range, across which there was only one decent pass, the Syrian Gates. The Amanus was even more heavily wooded than the other ranges of Syria and Lebanon, of which it was a northward continuation. That is to say, by moving into Kilikia Demetrios had put himself into isolation. Agathokles could easily prevent him from breaking back to the north by occupying the main passes, and if he headed east he would face Seleukos.

Demetrios waited for some time in Kilikia, where he could at least replenish his supplies and rest his troops. He opened up negotiations with Seleukos, who supplied some provisions. Demetrios' army was in a bad way by this time and the negotiations were probably intended to gain time for the men's recovery. Seleukos was being advised at the time by Patrokles, of course, and by others, who had presumably returned from the east, perhaps because of the growing threat which Demetrios had posed over the past year. Eventually Seleukos moved into Kilikia and drove Demetrios northwards, first into the Taurus Mountains and then probably beyond the mountains into the region called Kataonia. Here, as Plutarch remarks, he felt he was trapped in a small area, surrounded by enemies.[11]

Kataonia is probably much the same area as the 'Seleukid Kappadokia' which Appian includes as part of Seleukos' spoils from Antigonos' collapsed empire in 300. It was a small region centred on the temple-city of Komana, between the main Taurus range and the Anti-Taurus further north. It does not feature until this point in Seleukos' story, which is mainly concerned with Syria and the eastern territories, but strategically it gave him a vital gateway into Asia Minor. Demetrios was able to get out of Kilikia, probably by way of the valleys of the Saros and Karmalas Rivers, and this means he had entered that land by another route, probably along the Kalykadnos. This was therefore one of the routes which was now blocked by Agathokles' forces – the other being the narrow Kilikian Gates – and now that he had driven Demetrios into Kataonia, Seleukos also blocked the passes he controlled. Demetrios contemplated moving still further east into Armenia and then Media, but his men were against this idea. Hence his feeling of being trapped.

There were the usual skirmishes and minor battles between Demetrios' and Seleukos' forces, in which Demetrios is said to have been generally successful. But every fight reduced his strength, and Seleukos' forces were vastly more numerous to start with. Eventually Demetrios seized control of a pass and broke back into Kilikia, but Seleukos had fortified the passes of the Amanus between Kilikia and Syria, so Demetrios was as trapped as ever. Agathokles offered to help, but Seleukos was too suspicious of Lysimachos to accept the offer. Demetrios fell ill, some of his troops deserted, and others scattered to find food (and presumably loot) on their own account. Their welcome in Kilikia must have been worn out by this time.

When he recovered Demetrios gathered up his forces once more and succeeded in breaking through Seleukos' defences in the Amanus. He was still able to spring a surprise, despite the necessary alertness of the enemy, this time by beginning a march away from his objective, then turning back when it was dark and approaching silently, 'without using his trumpets', as Plutarch says. But once over the mountain pass he was in a country even more difficult for him, narrow valleys and wooded hills, and he faced the prospect of attacking the many cities Seleukos had spent the last fifteen years developing. He may have hoped for support from some of his and his father's old soldiers, but by this time they were fifteen years older, and they were heavily outnumbered by Seleukos' colonists, and anyway they would surely by now not wish their new homes to be a battleground. Demetrios was, specifically, in the territory of the city of Kyrrhos, called the Kyrrhestike, a region of hills and winding valleys. He does not seem to have got anywhere near the city itself, but even if he did, and captured it, he would be faced with having to attack and capture a dozen more cities – and Seleukos' army still outnumbered his.[12]

Seleukos had no wish to fight a long damaging campaign in his own country. The cities he had founded cannot as yet have been very strongly fortified, nor were their populations very large as yet, and Demetrios' men were highly skilled soldiers. It takes more than a decade and a half to build and populate so many places. Some of the people might have responded to the appeal of Demetrios' charisma, but any old soldiers were getting on in years by this time and it seems unlikely they would have been keen to set out on campaign again. For the only thing Demetrios offered was more war. His aim was to recover his Macedonian kingdom and his father's, and to do so he must fight Seleukos, Ptolemy, Lysimachos, Agathokles, and Pyrrhos. He offered, in effect, continued, even everlasting, warfare. The old soldiers of Antigonos cannot have been too pleased at the prospect.

In the end they did not have to make the choice, or perhaps, by not responding to his appeal and his arrival, they implicitly rejected it. Seleukos brought his army close to that of Demetrios, outnumbering it, and when the latter tried another night attack, Seleukos was warned by some deserters. 'He started up in alarm, and ordered the trumpets to be sounded, while at the same time he pulled on his boots and shouted to his companions that a terrible wild beast was about to attack them.'[13] This is Plutarch's description of Seleukos' reaction, and as he also points out, it was highly effective. The noise which was made in Seleukos' camp made it clear to Demetrios that he was approaching an alert enemy – one is reminded that Seleukos had twice won battles in that very same way; it seems likely that he was nowhere near as close to being surprised as Plutarch assumed. All Seleukos had to do apparently was to 'pull on his boots' to be ready.

Seleukos was able also to get his forces moving, even in the dark, so that he was close to Demetrios' camp when dawn came. Given that he outnumbered the enemy it seems that Seleukos was about to surround Demetrios' army, for, according to Plutarch, Demetrios sent one part of his force to drive back one wing of Seleukos' army while he attacked the other. But before the fight became general and deadly, Seleukos pulled off another of his tricks.

He dismounted, and advanced ahead of his own men, alone, carrying only a wicker shield (which is probably what a cavalryman would be carrying), took off his helmet and hailed Demetrios' soldiers. He explained who he was and appealed to them, pointing out that no one would benefit from continued fighting and claimed that he was refraining from attacking them. (This was a further indication that Demetrios' troops were more or less surrounded.) He asked them 'to come over to him' – which means he was offering to recruit them on the same, or better, terms than Demetrios had offered. The point was, of course, that they were mercenaries and the longer they fought, and the more who died, the lower was the bill for their pay that Demetrios would have to face.

The men he was appealing to accepted his terms.[14] Demetrios found that his army, like that of Macedon, melted away. (It must be assumed that Seleukos swiftly sent most of them well away from the battle region, in case they had a change of heart; he will also have split them up into smaller groups and scattered them in different places. Any who wished to go on fighting he would send to Antiochos in Baktria.)

Demetrios, with a small group of followers, turned back towards the west, towards Kilikia, but found that the Amanus was held even more strongly against him therefore. Seleukos had the guards light many watch fires, which made it clear that there was no way through. Demetrios was sufficiently disheartened by this, and by the continuing desertion of his small following, that he was persuaded by those still with him to agree to surrender. He made a suicide attempt, which was easily thwarted – either it was not really serious, or his friends were expecting it.

His surrender was negotiated. Seleukos promised to treat him as a king, sending a friend of both of them to convey reassurances. Even in captivity he retained the fame of his extraordinary career, but he rapidly became too fascinating to a number of Seleukos' courtiers, some of whom were Demetrios' old companions, so Seleukos quickly had him sequestered, probably at Apameia or near Antioch, at a place called the Syrian Chersonese. There were too many former Antigonid and Demetrian subjects in Syria for Demetrios to be allowed any real freedom; he surely understood this. He sent word to his son Antigonos Gonatas, who had been left in control of Corinth and the fleet, and to his old commanders in other places, that no messages from him were to be acted on, since he was in captivity and not a free agent.[15] He does appear, however, to have been visited by his daughter Stratonike and her husband; he probably never saw the son born to Ptolemais, who was named Demetrios in his honour.

Seleukos commemorated his victory in the most suitable way; he founded another city, calling it Nikopolis.[16] It was placed in the valley of the Kara Su below the Amanus where he had persuaded the enemy to surrender. This was especially suitable since it was the other cities which had blocked Demetrios' progress. They had already done their job.

With Demetrios in captivity the other kings could relax somewhat, or rather they could turn to their other projects. Lysimachos turned to deal with Pyrrhos in Macedon. He instituted a campaign by letter to persuade those Macedonians who had supported Pyrrhos that he was a foreigner – Macedonians and Epeirotes were never really friends – and then he invaded Pyrrhos' part of Macedon. He was able to blockade Pyrrhos' army at Edessa until Pyrrhos withdrew back into Epeiros.

So the main result of Demetrios' fall from power was to enhance the power of Lysimachos, and once again the others felt threatened. His last campaign had shown up the strong suspicions that existed between Lysimachos and Seleukos, while Ptolemy had failed to prevent Demetrios from attacking Asia Minor though he probably could have stopped him by intervening with his ships. Lysimachos, when he heard of Demetrios' capture, is said to have offered Seleukos a large fortune if he would have Demetrios killed. Seleukos carefully publicized this offer together with his revulsion at the very idea;

thereby successfully putting Lysimachos in the wrong, just as he had with Ptolemy over the latter's seizure of southern Syria.[17]

With the removal of Demetrios from active power, there were now three of the main kings still alive, together with a slowly increasing number of lesser rulers and relatively powerful cities around them and in the interstices of power. Seleukos, Ptolemy, and Lysimachos were all in their seventies by this time, but all three had capable adult sons. It is to be assumed that all three wished to be founders of dynasties, but they had before them two contemporaries who had aimed to do the same and had failed. Alexander's dynasty had failed in large part because he died while his heirs were either too young or too dim to have any chance of surviving in competition against such power-hungry and unscrupulous men as Kassander and Antigonos. Kassander's dynasty had failed because his eldest son died within months of succeeding him and his younger sons quarrelled, leaving the way open for Demetrios. Antigonos' dynasty was not yet finished, but Antigonos had been killed in battle and his son had failed through arrogance and ambition; the next generation, in the person of Antigonos Gonatas, was reduced to a few fortresses and a fleet; it looked like another failure. That is, not one of the Macedonian kings had yet succeeded in establishing a dynasty of rulers. (One might include the last Akhaimenid dynasty, potentially begun by Dareius III, which fell before Alexander's assault and then at the hands of rebels.)

All three of the surviving kings had organized things so that their eldest sons had been marked out as their heirs, though in different ways. Seleukos had been the earliest and clearest on this, and Antiochos had both the post of joint-king and explicit and heavy responsibilities; Ptolemy's son, also Ptolemy, was publicly given much the same position in 285 or 284, to the anger of another son, Ptolemy Keraunos, who left Egypt and voiced his grievances first to Seleukos, then to Lysimachos.[18] Ptolemy I's delay in naming his heir was due in part to the conflict between these two sons, but also to the possibility that a clear nomination of a successor might well be an invitation to his seizing power. Seleukos had avoided this by sending Antiochos off to the east.

Lysimachos, however, fell into a version of this trap. Agathokles, Lysimachos' eldest son, had been given the command against Demetrios, and this seemed to contemporaries to mark him as the old man's primary heir. But all of these kings had taken full advantage of their position and had fathered other children with women who were either extra wives or mistresses or concubines. Seleukos seems to have been the most restrained, with just two wives, Apama and Stratonike, and only two sons, Antiochos and Akhaios (though it is not actually certain that Akhaios was his son), and perhaps two or three daughters. Ptolemy had several daughters by several wives and concubines but only two sons (or perhaps only two survived). Lysimachos, having had at least three wives, had several sons.

Not surprisingly, given the numbers and the situation, it was Lysimachos who had the main family trouble. Ptolemy Keraunos and his half-sister Arsinoe, Lysimachos' current wife, engineered the old man into a suspicion of Agathokles, procured his execution, and so opened the way for Arsinoe's son to be in a position to succeed. Agathokles' wife was, understandably, furious, and was clearly in danger herself, as were her children. She went off to Seleukos. Lysimachos impatiently turned on those at his court who complained and purged them, some being executed, others leaving rapidly.[19]

Arsinoe was interested primarily in securing the succession for her own children, Keraunos in securing either that or the kingship of Macedon. The whole sordid drama was played out within the court, but on the outside it became clear that this was a development which was one unpleasantness too much for the general population. Lysimachos, as his reaction to criticism had shown, was a hard, even brutal, ruler, and was all too avid for taxation revenues; he was unimpressed by the idea that cities were to be free and ungarrisoned; he was thus unpopular. Agathokles had been the obvious hope for improvement, and his succession was clearly imminent, given Lysimachos' age. But with Agathokles dead and the succession headed for the sons of Arsinoe, as tough and hard as her husband, the dislike of the king spread.[20]

The first of the three to go, however, was Ptolemy, who died late in 283 or early in 282.[21] His successor was the recently promoted Ptolemy II, surnamed Philadelphos. He was adult and capable, but inevitably his first years were uneasy. In particular he was threatened by the ambitions of Keraunos, whose erratic aims could well include attempting to displace his half-brother. So, during the growing instability in Lysimachos' kingdom, the Ptolemaic state was under new control, with an inexperienced king who would not be able to adventure abroad with confidence for some time.

With Lysimachos embroiled in a crippling internal crisis, and Ptolemy II uneasy and preoccupied with establishing his own position in Egypt, this was an opportunity Seleukos seized with both hands. He had made some general preparations for almost any eventuality. His captive Demetrios died in 283, after two years in captivity, which he had spent in hunting, eating and drinking. He was, it seems, visited by his daughter Stratonike when she and Antiochos came to the west, and when he died his remains were ceremonially delivered to his son Antigonos, who took them on a tour to various places in the Aegean before interring them at Demetrias in Thessaly, the dead man's name city.[22] One of the objects of Seleukos' gesture was obviously to establish friendly contact with Antigonos, who had been left in political isolation by his father's campaign and failure, but he had a considerable naval power, and controlled major fortresses in Greece. He was generally ignored by the others, but Seleukos was not so short-sighted; his generosity towards his father-in-law was to bring its reward later. (Incidentally, it was in a ship or ships of Seleukos' fleet that the remains reached the Aegean – so we know that he had a small fleet, though it was hardly used.)

Seleukos also received and listened to the refugees driven from Lysimachos' kingdom by that king's anger. The leader was Agathokles' widow Lysandra with her children, but there were others who came with her or followed her.[23] From them he learned of the unrest in the kingdom and the unpopularity of Lysimachos. The temporary political paralysis of Ptolemaic Egypt meant that no immediate danger threatened from that direction. He was in contact with Ptolemy Keraunos, who eventually returned to Lysimachos. But if Ptolemy II threatened to intervene he could well let loose Keraunos on him. He must have known Keraunos' ambitiousness, by which he wished for a kingdom. It may also be that Ptolemy Philadelphos was in contact with Keraunos; he was certainly in contact with Arsinoe; though how much of what happened later was down to Ptolemaic family intrigue is not known. It was certainly in Philadelphos' interest to direct Keraunos away from Egypt, and this he may well have succeeded in doing.

Probably late in 282 (but before the winter, when the Taurus passes were closed), Seleukos invaded Lysimachos' kingdom. He had already contacted, or been contacted by, some of the more important men in Asia Minor, including the guardian of part of Lysimachos' treasure, Philetairos of Pergamon. So in his military campaign Seleukos was leaning on a house of cards. He was able without difficulty – at least as far as we know – to march all the way to western Asia Minor, as cities and principalities surrendered to him. Lysimachos' son Alexander (by a concubine), who might now claim to be Lysimachos' heir, though there is no sign that Lysimachos had recognized one, went on an independent campaign in which he captured the town of Kotiaion in the northwest; Seleukos himself captured Sardis, the old capital of the region. The decisive encounter, after campaigning into mid-281, of which we know nothing, took place not far from Sardis, deep within Lysimachos' territory, at a place called Koroupedion. Lysimachos gathered his considerable forces, and sought a decisive battle; he was beaten and killed. Lysandra almost succeeded in denying him a funeral, but Alexander insisted on the proper rites – another indication perhaps that he had hopes of the succession.[24]

Arsinoe and her children had been at Ephesos when the battle took place. She escaped with a substantial treasure, and went to Kassandreia, presumably intending to make her son (another Ptolemy), king of Macedon.[25] This cleared the way for Seleukos, setting aside Alexander as an illegitimate son, to claim the kingship. Nor was he going to be denied the ultimate prize. He must have seen himself as the true heir of Alexander the Great, reuniting his broken empire. He had with him Ptolemy Keraunos, who had apparently opportunistically changed sides after the battle, and whose ambition overrode any gratitude he might feel. Seleukos spent several months dealing with the new situation in Asia Minor (see next chapter), then he crossed the Hellespont into the Gallipoli Peninsula, staying at Lysimacheia, the great city which the dead king had founded as his capital, and which, with a fleet, could control the Straits. Keraunos suggested a visit to a local shrine or tomb, and killed Seleukos when they were alone.[26]

Chapter Ten

Antiochos I and the Galatians

One of the main purposes in appointing Antiochos as joint-king was so that he would be in office (and an experienced ruler) when Seleukos died. Ironically the same precaution taken so apparently reluctantly by Ptolemy I had worked well, whereas Seleukos' aim was, in the short term, unsuccessful. Even so, Ptolemy II needed time to establish his own authority after the old man died. Seleukos' careful plan failed because he was assassinated; his unexpected death meant the transition was anything but smooth. It appears that this was a contingency not anticipated, which is surprising given the casualty rate amongst Macedonian rulers from violence of one sort or another. Indeed the whole adventure of Seleukos in his war on Lysimachos was hazardous in the extreme. He was, after all, in his late seventies, at an age at which men died naturally (Antipater, Ptolemy), if not in battle (Antigonos), if they had survived so long, and Alexander and Kassander and Demetrios had died at much younger ages. He could surely be expected to die at any time, though presumably it was assumed that there would be some warning.

So for all his planning, Seleukos' death was sudden and unexpected, it happened far from the centre of his government, and it occurred in the absence of his fellow king. We do not know where Antiochos was at the time of Seleukos' murder except that he was certainly not in Thrace, Asia Minor, or Syria; there were instant disturbances in both these latter regions, which would probably not have happened had he been on the spot. It is possible he was in Babylonia, but more likely he was even further east; Babylonia would be a sensible place for him, given that Seleukos was leaving Syria (for perhaps the first time in years), and going on a new campaign, so Antiochos' relatively nearby presence would have been a good precaution. Unfortunately there are no contemporary Babylonian records except a record of the king's death, recorded in Babylon in August or September 281.[1]

One historian, Memnon, does remark that Seleukos assigned the government of 'Asia' to Antiochos when the old king headed off to Europe.[2] There are problems here; first in divining what he meant by 'Asia', and in determining if Memnon really knew what was going on. He was from Herakleia Pontike, and that city was in contact with the Seleukos in Asia Minor, which might suggest local knowledge. But that still does not solve the problem of where Antiochos was at the time. It could be that Memnon was simply making an assumption from later events, for it was obvious that Antiochos really was in command in 'Asia' when Seleukos was killed. The difficulties of a single item of information are encapsulated in this notice. Another fragment, this time a papyrus which recorded the installation of a king, gives a hint of the ceremonies, though it is not easy to understand.[3]

The troubles which followed the spread of the news of Seleukos' death, stimulated no doubt by the violence and unexpectedness of the event, affected both Asia Minor and Syria. The first is hardly surprising since Seleukos had only recently gained some sort of control and there were plenty of groups and commanders and lords looking to their own fortunes. Indeed Seleukos' work in bringing the region into his control was no more than partly done. He had clearly felt enough had been accomplished so that he could move on to establish control in Thrace and Macedon, a matter of some urgency, but it was by no means finished, and his death effectively cancelled, or at least delayed, the achievement of much that he had done so far. Asia Minor was in a state of some confusion, not really surprising in the circumstances.

The news of his death spread rapidly, for this was the death by violence of the most powerful ruler in the world. This spread was powerfully helped by the murderer. Ptolemy Keraunos sent letters in all directions, presumably justifying his deed. His half-brother Ptolemy was told, the king of Bithynia and the city of Herakleia Pontike were informed, and so was Pyrrhos of Epeiros. He was hailed as king by the army at Lysimacheia, a force which had been Lysimachos' and consisted of Macedonians. This was as legitimate an accession as any. He then headed off into Macedon, where he proposed marriage to his half-sister Arsinoe, who was in Kassandreia, claiming that he would thus be able to defend her and her children by Lysimachos.[4]

The troubles in Syria are not well understood. There is only one, rather vague, even ambiguous, reference to the Syrian difficulties, in an inscription from the city of Ilion recording honours offered to a King Antiochos by the city. It includes an explanation that soon after his accession as sole king he 'sought to bring back to peace and their former prosperity the cities of the Seleukis' – meaning Syria – 'which were suffering from difficult times because of the rebels from his cause'.[5] The rebels are not identified. It is natural to assume that the cities referred to were the rebels, but that is not actually what the passage says. The cities were, in fact, suffering as a result of operations by the rebels, and were not necessarily in rebellion themselves. So, if not the cities, who was in rebellion? Possibly some of the Syrians native to the land. It had been a difficult area for Alexander to conquer half a century earlier, and Antigonos and Ptolemy had both marched through it several times, so it is quite likely that the native Syrians were less than enamoured of Macedonian rule; Seleukos' extensive settlement policy, involving as it did the confiscation of land, the imposition of new landlords, and the importation of large numbers of foreigners, may well have provoked a powerful resentment which boiled over on the news of his death.

The possibility of external interference clearly also exists, with the accusing finger pointed at Ptolemy II Philadelphos. He may well have tried to stir up trouble; after all, it was his half-brother Keraunos who had killed Seleukos, and this possible conjunction might suggest that it was a family plot. It would be very attractive to argue this way, but there is no evidence for Ptolemy's involvement. Certainly Keraunos was the murderer; certainly Philadelphos was likely to be pleased to see his alienated half-brother busy with his own kingdom, and to see the new Seleukid king in trouble. But of any collusion between them, and of any action by Philadelphos in Syria at this time, we have no evidence; the suggestion must be rejected. It follows from this that any 'War of Succession' was an internal Syrian affair, not an international conflict. The problem in Syria was fairly quickly dealt with, which suggests that the cities were not involved, and that the rebels were annoyed native Syrians seems therefore most likely.

The real problem for Antiochos was in gaining control of Asia Minor. There he faced a very different political problem. The combination of the murder of the king, the rebellion in Syria, and the general collapse of royal authority in Asia Minor brings home the general fragility of the kingdom. It was a briefer version of the break-up of Alexander's empire, or of the collapse of Demetrios' authority in Macedon. In each case it was the absence or incompetence of the ruler which was the basic fault. It seems likely that it was the realization of this which was at the root of Ptolemy I's political caution, and of Ptolemy II's initial unadventurousness – an example, perhaps of politicians learning from history. The Seleukid kingdom therefore can be said to have owed its survival to the training Seleukos had given his son in ruling in the east. Antiochos inherited his father's ambition to reunite Alexander's empire, and his ability in military and diplomatic affairs, but his task turned out to be one of recovery rather than conquest and reunification.

Of the three regions he had to deal with, the Syrian revolt was quickly suppressed, Asia Minor was much more difficult; and Macedon was out of reach.

Asia Minor, despite having been subject to two powerful kings, Antigonos and Lysimachos, for over thirty years (315–281), was actually divided among a large number of political authorities. To start with, there were dozens of Greek cities spread all around the coasts, from Trapezos in the east of the Black Sea to the cities of Kilikia; many of these were rich, venerable, busy, independent states, and had to be treated with care.[6] In addition the interior contained a number of autonomous principalities.[7] Seleukos had already encountered some of these 'dynasts' as these rulers are called, during his conquering campaign; indeed at least one had contacted him in advance. Others probably joined him during his campaigns, for they existed both before and after his march to the west. Several of them had defected from Antigonos in 301, and now did so again, from Lysimachos. It is evident they were hardly primarily loyal to any king, but aimed to be as autonomous, or independent, as possible.

Seleukos also installed his own dynasts, who might well be more loyal. The preliminary contact had been from Philetairos of Pergamon, who both offered to support Seleukos before he invaded Lysimachos' kingdom, and collected Seleukos' body after his death (he bought it from Keraunos), and handed it over to Antiochos.[8] In return he kept control of his Pergamon city and continued to guard the treasure Lysimachos had entrusted to him.

The children of Lysimachos were notable absentees from the people who were later revealed as prominent in Asia Minor. Alexander had campaigned on Seleukos' side in the war, and was surely entitled to some reward. He then disappears completely from any record. Similarly Lysandra, the widow of Agathokles, whose importuning had been one of the triggers for Seleukos' invasion, disappears, as do her children. Alexander was the son of an unknown concubine, which might have limited his chances in gaining the inheritance, but Lysandra could have claimed Lysimachos' inheritance for her children, though the survivors were girls. Lysimachos' final wife, Arsinoe (II) had fled to Macedon, where she evidently aimed to have her eldest son installed as king, with herself as regent. But she was persuaded to marry Keraunos, her half-brother, and he forthwith murdered two of her children by Lysimachos.[9] Her eldest son, Ptolemy, was obviously in the contest to be the Macedonian king, and he survived Keraunos' hate. But Keraunos was a more acceptable king for the Macedonians, being adult, vigorous, ruthless, and experienced. Ptolemy and his mother eventually went to Egypt; he was later installed in a small principality in southern Asia Minor by his stepfather.[10]

This seems to have been the fate of Asia Minor, to be used by the greater Hellenistic dynasties as a reservoir of estates and minor principalities which could be awarded to scions of those dynasties. Several such principalities of various origins and sizes already existed. This was not a new phenomenon. There had been a group of Iranian lords established, particularly in northwest Anatolia, under the Akhaimenid regime, and some of these at least still existed.[11] After the campaign of Alexander through the country in 334–333 it was the scene of much fighting until Antigonos established his rule in 315. Cities and garrisons were the tools used to fasten his control, but in the confusion commanders had often planned to carve out a lordship for themselves.

Western Anatolia had already been well urbanized for centuries, and much of the urbanizing work of Antigonos and Lysimachos in this area had been in the form of synoecism, gathering groups of small communities into cities, or refounding and expanding existing cities. So Antigonos had brought several small cities close to the Hellespont into a new Antigoneia, and for several years had used Kelainai in Phrygia as his administrative capital. Lysimachos had expanded Ephesos and renamed it Arsinoe after his third wife.[12] But within the west there was a limit to what these rulers could do in terms of colonization because of the existing dense spread of cities.

In the interior of the peninsula much of the urbanizing work was left to prominent Macedonians, usually men who had survived from the time of Alexander, and these were the dynasts. Some had been eliminated by Antigonos, but by the time of Lysimachos the survivors were quite willing to join any winning side, and they did so when Seleukos came. Philetairos of Pergamon was one of these men, though he was not an Alexander man. He was from Tios on the Black Sea coast, where a relative of his, Eumenes, had been tyrant for a time. Philetairos had joined Lysimachos before the battle of Ipsos, being given charge of the town and castle of Pergamon, which he retained for twenty years. He contacted Seleukos in advance of the latter's invasion of Anatolia, thus for a second time anticipating the arrival of a new lord. He clearly had very sensitive political antennae. As a result of his service to Antiochos in securing Seleukos' body after the murder, he retained Pergamon.[13]

Philetairos is the best known of the Anatolian lords who executed nimble changes of allegiance in these difficult circumstances because his successors developed his city into the centre of a kingdom. In central Anatolia Dokimeion had been founded by a Macedonian commander who, like Philetairos, adapted himself to the new rulers. Dokimos was a former officer of Alexander who had become notorious for his easy switches of allegiance, but he was instrumental in founding a city of modest size in the region partly inhabited by Phrygian-speakers. There are two gravestones from the place, one with a Phrygian inscription but where the names are Greek, one in Greek to a girl with a Phrygian name; evidence of the hellenization, and its limits, which was also going on in Syria.[14]

Dokimeion was founded on the frontier of hellenization, some way north of the old Royal Road which linked the urbanized west with the rest of the Akhaimenid Empire, and facing Kappadokia, which was a frontier region. Dokimos had been in this area since at least 319, when Antigonos I put him in charge of Synnada, one of the important garrisons on that road – Dokimeion is perhaps 50km northeast of Synnada. Further along the road were the cities of Lysias and Philomelion, whose names proclaim that they were founded by members of the family whose menfolk were named Lysias and Philomelion in alternate generations. A Lysias served as a commander under Seleukos I in 286 in his defence of Syria against Demetrios, and the family can be traced for the next century and more into the 160s (if the regent Lysias was one of them).[15] But if he was fighting for Seleukos in the 280s, the earliest Lysias was not yet an estate-holder in Asia Minor, which was Lysimachos' territory, so we must assume he was rewarded by Seleukos or by Antiochos with a wealth-producing estate after the conquest. He, or other members of his family, then developed the two cities. For a man who had served Seleukos while the king was building a dozen cities in Syria, founding two more would be both homage to the king's memory and serving his own interests. These two cities are also situated so as to reinforce control of the Royal Road. They were undoubtedly founded with royal permission, by a family whose loyalty to the dynasty was totally reliable.[16]

Lysias' dynasty took a minor role in events in Asia Minor for the next century. More prominent, though without having founded cities, so far as we can tell, was the family founded by Akhaios, who is claimed as a son of Seleukos I, and the younger brother of Antiochos. The evidence is indirect. Akhaios' children became very prominent in Asian affairs in the next generation; one daughter married Antiochos II, another married the

Pergamene king Eumenes I, a third became governor of Lydia, and the prominence of the family continued into the next generation (see Table B). So for a family totally unknown before Akhaios (I) in 267, their rise was astonishingly rapid. Then there are the names of the children; Laodike, Antiochis, and Alexander, all names also used in the Seleukid royal family. This suggests an even closer connection than mere intermarriage. The strongest drawback – apart, of course, from the lack of any direct evidence – is that the male names, Antiochos and Seleukos, do not appear; these may have been reserved for the direct line.[17]

It is quite certain, however, even if Akhaios was not the second son of Seleukos I, that the family was a major force in Asian political affairs, partly because, as is shown by an inscription, the first of the family, Akhaios himself, was a major landowner, and partly because of marriage into the Seleukid family.[18] No other family of an obscure origin climbed so high; the presumption that Akhaios was the son of Seleukos must be seen as not proved, but to be very likely, and is the easiest explanation for his rise. Like Lysias, he was probably a new arrival in Asia Minor, placed there by Seleukos or Antiochos as a means of developing their own local political support in the newly conquered territory.[19]

There are several other towns of similar foundation in various parts of Asia Minor, but usually smaller and less prominent. The city of Themisonion, for example, was presumably founded by a man called Themison.[20] In Karia a Macedonian called Eupolemos, who had been one of Kassander's commanders, and then with Pleistarchos, set himself up as an independent chieftain after Pleistarchos' death; he vanished in the late 280s, possibly a victim of the war of Seleukos and Lysimachos.[21] Even fainter traces exist of others, presumably Macedonians, but of whom little is known. Karia and Lykia seem to have been fertile of such men all the way until the Roman period. It was, of course, in part a consequence of the geography of the Anatolian peninsula.

These examples are of dynasts and settlers established in the west and centre of Asia Minor, but there were others whose authority rested on their control of areas on the periphery, and who aimed for as much independence as they could secure. These could be either dynasts or cities. Before he moved on to cross into Europe Seleukos had been visited by a delegation from the city of Herakleia on the Pontic coast. The leader of the group, Chamaileon, spoke to him using a Doric dialect, which he could not understand, and he wearily dismissed them. Herakleia was effectively an independent state, but was also at enmity with the Bithynian ruler, Zipoetes. In turn Zipoetes had won a battle against a general of Lysimachos' and had proclaimed himself king.[22]

Further east was Pontos, stretched along the Pontic coast for 500km, ruled by another self-proclaimed king, Mithradates, a descendant of an old Akhaimenid aristocratic family, whose father had quarrelled with, and been executed by, Antigonos, and who had therefore joined Lysimachos.[23] Seleukos had sent one of his friends, Aphrodisios, to persuade Mithradates to submit to him, but, like Herakleia and Zipoetes, Mithradates temporized or refused; Seleukos reacted by sending a force under a commander called Diodoros to enforce Mithradates' subjection; Diodoros was defeated and Mithradates took the royal title; he became referred to as *ktistes*, 'the founder', the man who had formed a new kingdom.[24] In the interior of Anatolia, between Pontos and the Royal Road, was Kappadokia, another region in which an Akhaimenid aristocratic survivor had been gathering authority.[25] Ariarathes was not yet a king, but could well be soon. Further east Armenia had another Iranian aristocratic dynasty, and in Media Atropatene there was an Iranian king; from the Bosporos to the Caspian these states were independent and generally hostile to the Macedonians.

Along the south coast, Seleukos had fastened his authority firmly in Smooth Kilikia, but not in the mountainous area of Rough Kilikia to the west; nor had he attempted to do so in Pamphylia. In these areas Ptolemy had some influence, as he had further west in Lykia, but only in some of the cities, and his authority never spread very far inland.[26] This was often the case also on the west coast, where Ptolemy held some of the cities, though many others were independent. Seleukos had again made little attempt to extend his power into this heavily urbanized region, not presumably because he regarded the wishes of the cities to be free of the kings, but because he did not have much time.

So the authority inherited by Antiochos was concentrated geographically in the interior of Asia Minor. He controlled Smooth Kilikia and the Kilikian Gates, which led into Anatolia. He controlled the Royal Road, even though some of the dynasts had established themselves astride it, and he had gained control of the old Persian administrative centre in the city of Sardis (as well as that favoured by Antigonos at Kelainai). From this elongated geographical base his authority spread as far as his forces could make it reach.

This complicated political and geographical diversity was in marked contrast to the situation in Syria, where, with some exceptions, the native Syrian population was fully under the control of the immigrant Greeks and

Macedonians in the new cities, and especially so after the suppression of the rebellion in 281–280. But Antiochos, after a decade in which he had governed the very diverse Baktria, Media, and Persis, where the local population included nomads and peasants, lords and cities, Baktrians, Greeks and Macedonians, Medes and Persians, and was even more geographically divided by mountain ranges than Asia Minor, as well as even larger, was well-trained for coping with the new conquest. It is therefore significant that, while he was dealing with Syria, he sent on ahead one of his colleagues from Central Asia, Patrokles, with an army.[27]

The conquest of Asia Minor by Seleukos I had thus been no more than an easy preliminary to the really hard work of organizing and administering the region. He had found that it was composed of an awkward set of varied problems once his victory over Lysimachos had been won. But he had also to attempt to establish his authority in Macedon, which Lysimachos had ruled as well, and both tasks were clearly urgent. Macedon was a target for its surrounding enemies, and Seleukos' new conquest in Anatolia might be regarded also as a tempting target for the peripheral states. His suddenly expanded power will no doubt have excited the apprehensions of Ptolemy, hence the suspicion that Ptolemy II had encouraged his half-brother in his murderous attack.

All these problems descended on Antiochos, with the addition of that of the murderer Ptolemy Keraunos ruling in Macedon. Macedon was also the target for Pyrrhos of Epeiros and Antigonos Gonatas, and the future of Italy and Sicily as well as Macedon and Greece soon became one of his concerns as well. All of this was new to Antiochos. We have no idea of how much, or if, his father had kept him informed of western affairs, but he must have come up to date rapidly as he travelled from his eastern realm to take up his western inheritance. Keraunos was proclaimed king in Macedon, but was only one of several claimants.

Macedon's kingship could be claimed by Ptolemy son of Lysimachos, by Antigonos Gonatas, the son of Demetrios, and by Pyrrhos of Epeiros, who had ruled part of the kingdom before Lysimachos took it all, and by Antiochos, as the son of the conqueror of the previous king. In fact Pyrrhos' new adventure was to rescue the Greeks of Italy from the menace of Rome, and he persuaded Antigonos, Keraunos, and Antiochos to provide ships, men and elephants respectively for the cause; no doubt they were pleased to get rid of such a troublesome gadfly.[28] He sailed to Italy early in 280, and was out of Balkan affairs for the next five years.

Keraunos travelled to Kassandreia in ships provided by Herakleia Pontike and those inherited from Lysimachos. When Patrokles reached Sardis he sent a commander, Hermogenes, north, with a modest force to attempt to enforce the suzerainty which Seleukos had claimed over both Herakleia and King Zipoetes of Bithynia. Meanwhile at Kassandreia, after his marriage and murders, and Arsinoe's flight from him to sanctuary in Samothrace, Keraunos faced and defeated an attempt by Antigonos Gonatas to dethrone him, using the ships of Lysimachos, plus those loaned him by Herakleia.[29] In the north Hermogenes succeeded in making terms with Herakleia, but when he turned to tackling Zipoetes he was defeated and killed.[30] Meanwhile Ptolemy II had at last taken a hand. The evidence is thin, but by the next year, 279, he was in control of the city of Miletos, and had reinforced his domination of the southern Anatolian coast.[31]

The situation was clearly very confusing for everyone, but a few gestures soon sorted things out. For one thing Keraunos does seem to have agreed that he would no longer aspire to the Egyptian kingship. Ptolemy II no doubt publicized this, and was also careful to avoid any overt clash with Antiochos, so it will have become clear that Keraunos was on his own. Ptolemy II had certainly taken over at Miletos, where Antiochos had been honorary *stephanephoros* the year before, but the change does not seem to have been violent, and perhaps the change was only a set of gestures to pay honour to the kings. The presence of Ptolemy's fleet in the Aegean, where he took over the Island League and used Philokles of Sidon as his viceroy, did not prevent Antiochos from gathering his own fleet – presumably including some of Lysimachos' old ships – in an attempt to tackle his northern problem.

Herakleia had gathered to itself a group of other northern powers who felt threatened by Seleukos, and now by Antiochos. Patrokles had sent Hermogenes against Bithynia before Antiochos' arrival, but he was defeated and killed. This was one of the reasons for the formation of the 'Northern League'. At first it was an alliance of King Zipoetes with three cities, Byzantion, Kalchedon, and Tios; Mithradates of Pontos later joined after defeating Diodoros' attack, but the essential strength of the group was at sea, and Herakleia had put its fleet at Keraunos' service, since Keraunos was also threatened by Antiochos (though it had to fight for him against Antigonos first, perhaps unexpectedly).[32] Antiochos sent his fleet into the Sea of Marmara, and this could be seen as an immediate threat by at least two of the allies, though it is more likely that Antiochos' purpose was to create a situation in which he could cross from Asia into Thrace on his way to attack Keraunos and make himself Macedonian king. Into this came Antigonos Gonatas, who was interested in blocking any move into Europe by Antiochos. The two kings' fleets did clash, but without result.[33]

Keraunos thus fastened himself successfully on to the Macedonian throne by first being accepted by the Macedonians, and then by removing in various ways three of his competitors; Arsinoe and her surviving son had fled, Antigonos had been defeated; Pyrrhos was intent on his expedition to Italy. He had forsworn any ambition in Egypt, even if Arsinoe should agitate against him, which deflected any hostility from Ptolemy II. Whether he had in some way contrived the confrontation of Antigonos and Antiochos in the Sea of Marmara is unknown, but one would not be surprised if he had. This was a remarkable record and boded well for a successful and vigorous reign. But then he had to go off to the northern frontier to confront a barbarian invasion of Macedon. In this he and his army were overwhelmed. Keraunos died.[34]

The invaders were bands of Keltic warriors, travelling with their families. After their victory at the frontier they poured into Macedon, and then moved on into Greece.[35] This soon overshadowed the non-war between Antiochos and Antigonos, and they soon made peace. Antiochos' fleet was now facing that of the Northern League, but meanwhile a succession dispute had broken out in Bithynia, with Zipoetes' son Nikomedes in rebellion and supported by Herakleia; this crippled the league. Antiochos took the part of the second son, another Zipoetes, and the death of the father (after a reign of forty-eight years), then left Bithynia divided between his warring sons.[36] Mithradates of Pontos had withdrawn from the League, or at least he took no part in the action. Antiochos was therefore now free of pressure from Antigonos, did not need to worry about Keraunos or any other Macedonian, and so he could press on against the northerners and Nikomedes, who were thus likely to lose. But the Galatians were approaching.

One force of the Galatians in Macedon went south, where they were eventually defeated by a coalition led by the Aitolians, but only after looting the sanctuary and temple at Delphi. Other groups turned east, and just as his war with the Northern League approached victory, Antiochos was partly distracted by the pressure of Galatian bands roaming the European shore, one band led by Leonnorios, hovering near Byzantion, and another, captained by Loutorios, in the Gallipoli peninsula. Antiochos used his ships to block their obvious intent to cross the Hellespont, and the Byzantines blocked any crossing of the Bosporos. (So part of the Northern League was co-operating, if distantly, with Antiochos.) But Nikomedes, and perhaps the other cities of the league (though only Nikomedes gets the blame), arranged that the group near Byzantion should be brought across to help to eliminate Zipoetes. The treaty listed a string of Greek cities which were his allies and were therefore protected by the treaty. As they came across Loutorios' band also managed to get across the Hellespont into Asia.[37]

Once their contract with Nikomedes was fulfilled, and the younger Zipoetes was removed, the Galatians set off on a career of raiding throughout western Asia Minor, keeping scrupulously clear of the cities of the Northern Alliance. The Galatians were organized into three major tribes, which had allocated among themselves different sections of western Asia Minor for exploitation, the Trocmi in the north-west, the Tolistobogii against the cities of Aeolis and Ionia, and the Tectosages in the interior, which rather implies a fairly good advance knowledge of the region.[38] Some of their victims defended themselves, some paid blackmail, some were occupied and looted, though there is no instance of a walled city being taken, at least in this early period. It fell to Antiochos, naturally, to lead the resistance. This was particularly difficult, for the raiding bands were liable to split up, and were able to move quickly, sometimes, indeed often, catching their victims unawares. The details of this war are almost entirely lost, and all we have are isolated comments and inscriptions in which single incidents are noted, and a few literary sources which are just as fragmentary, and which betray indications of bias.

Kyzikos suffered first, caught between the two bands who approached from both sides, and had its lands ravaged.[39] Ilion, still unwalled, was occupied briefly, and no doubt looted and damaged; the Trocmi considered the place as a base, but the lack of fortification deterred them.[40] Pergamon survived, and Philetairos used his wealth to help useful friends.[41] Erythrai was one of those who paid the raiders to go away, which would only mean they would return later.[42] Apollo of Didyma was robbed, as was only to be expected; the riches heaped on the shrine by Seleukos I and his wife were thus put back into circulation.[43] It was noted that the raiders desecrated shrines and temples, but since these were places often holding treasure, they were a standing invitation to them. Miletos preserved a story that the women of the city were captured outside the city during the annual festival, and several of them are said to have committed suicide as a result of their treatment.[44] An Ephesian woman did the same.[45] At Priene, the raiders met some serious resistance; when engaged in ravaging the city's lands they were attacked by a sortie of the citizens; Sotas son of Lykos was honoured by his fellow citizens for heading the counter-attack.[46] At Thyateira a father set up an inscription to give thanks for the rescue of his son from the invaders.[47] Other places relied more on divine aid than self-help. Themisonion's citizens hid in a divinely-revealed cave until the danger passed.[48] At Apameia-Kelainai the city was saved when the river rose in a sudden flood, which was ascribed to the intervention of the river god, Marsyas.[49]

A Babylonian source suggests that Antiochos was based at Sardis until 274, when he went south into Syria to attend to an Egyptian invasion.[50] It seems likely that he had been in Anatolia all the time since his arrival in 280, such were the constant crises of the region. The fight against the Galatians was no doubt difficult, particularly given their divisions and liability to unexpected attacks – when they crossed the Straits they were said to have had seventeen individual leaders, and each of these men would no doubt want to scavenge for himself.[51] Once the shock to the local communities was survived, however, resistance had hardened, both at the level of the cities themselves and at the level of the royal government. Philetairos of Pergamon was active in helping cities in his region, notably Kyzikos, where a record of his gifts exists, and probably elsewhere.[52] But the only way to stop the raids was to defeat the Galatians soundly, and then either drive them out or settle the survivors in a place of their own (assuming one would not simply kill them all, which was Antigonos Gonatas' solution; this is what he is reported to have said when he beat a band of them in the Chersonese – the battle of Lysimacheia – in June 277).[53]

At a date which is placed variously between 275 and 268 Antiochos managed to meet a major Galatian army in battle and defeat it. To bring them together for a formal battle Antiochos had presumably defeated a number of their smaller forces and was on the way to defeating larger ones in detail. However, little is known of the armies involved and nothing of the composition of the Galatians' force, though the battle was remembered for Antiochos' use of elephants in the victory.[54] Afterwards, probably by a treaty with him, the Galatians were allocated a region of north-central Anatolia as a new home.[55]

This did not stop all the raiding, and there were other attacks recorded at various times throughout the next five decades, but it did reduce them drastically. One of the results may well have been that people such as Akhaios and Lysias became involved in city founding; the failure of the raiders to capture fortified cities surely encouraged widespread defensive preparations. Akhaios is first recorded in an inscription implying that he was the major landowner in the area of Laodikeia-ad-Lykon; Lysias was active in the deeper interior, where his cities were clearly vulnerable to attack by the Galatians.[56] Antiochos himself was also active in city founding particularly in the area of the Royal Road near the central Anatolian lakes. His work consisted largely of re-forming existing urban settlements into *poleis*, but some others were founded anew. The shortage of new foundations may reflect the damage done by the raids and/or the drying up of the availability of colonists coming from old Greece. New cities included Stratonikeia in Karia, and another Stratonikeia in Mysia, named for his wife, of course; refoundations included Kelainai moved from its hilltop site into the valley and renamed Apameia, after his mother. Several of the Antiochs must have been his work, though it is difficult to date their origins, especially as the dynastic name sometimes faded away later. The results were a combination of places along the Royal Road, again intended to block raiders from penetrating further west, and to maintain control of communications with Syria.[57] In the face of this Galatian crisis Antiochos had abandoned his apparent original intention to move west into Macedon to seize the kingship. It is possible that he made peace with Herakleia and Nikomedes of Bithynia, though given their responsibility for introducing the Galatians into his territories this may well have taken some time to arrange. The victory of Antigonos Gonatas over the Galatian band in the Thracian Chersonese, together with his recruitment of a large force of Galatian mercenaries, with which he drove out their still-marauding fellows, gave him the prestige and strength to move into Macedon, evict the current ruler (a descendant of Antipater – there had been several others since Keraunos), and make himself king.[58] He set about removing, or settling, the Galatians who were still there, and so far succeeded in making his rule accepted that Antiochos formed an alliance with him, sealed by providing him with a wife in the form of the daughter of Seleukos and Stratonike, Phila.[59] (Antigonos and Stratonike were siblings, so he was marrying his niece; Ptolemy II had by then married Arsinoe, his sister; royals made their own rules.)

The date of the elephant victory is a difficult matter. Originally dated to 275, it has more recently been suggested to be in 268 or 267. This latest suggestion is based on the information in the inscription from near Laodikeia-ad-Lykon which names Akhaios. This makes it clear that raiding was still going on until not long before the date of the stone (267).[60] However, the elephant victory is not mentioned, and the raids on the cities of the west and the interior can mainly be dated to between 278 and 275, and seem to have ceased from then on. In 274 Antiochos left Sardis to campaign south of the Taurus against an Egyptian invasion. In combination the raid dates and the willingness of Antiochos to leave Anatolia suggest very strongly that the Galatians were no longer active on a large-scale by 274. If he had deserted the Anatolians while the raids were still on, its seems unlikely that the surname 'Soter' – 'saviour' – would have eventually been given him.[61]

The elephant victory may thus be best placed at the original 'traditional' date of 275, followed by the settlement of the Galatians in the centre of Anatolia, a task which would keep them occupied for some time.[62] A revival of raiding to the south after some years seems to have taken place, as the Akhaios stone suggests, and as might be implied by a raid on Themisonion[63] and by others into Lykia, but these were on a much smaller scale than before.[64]

Therefore it is probable that the major Galatian crisis in Anatolia was over by 275, and that it is in the year following that the long series of cities in central and southern Anatolia began to be founded and organized. Antiochos may well have won the main battle, but he was also seriously weakened by the war. In 280 he had inherited a huge kingdom which extended from the borders of India to the Hellespont, with Thrace and Macedon waiting to be occupied, and but for the Galatian invasion he would surely have attempted to gain control of Macedon. But now, as a result of the fighting in Asia Minor, he had lost any chance of gaining Macedon or taking possession of Thrace, and he had been compelled to abandon his attempt to secure control of the northern coastlands of Anatolia. Furthermore, he had had to settle the invaders in the interior as his neighbours.

In addition, he had been prevented from imposing his authority more directly on those lands he did rule. Philetairos, Akhaios, Lysias, Dokimos, and others were clearly now almost autonomous rulers, and their autonomy had been encouraged by their need to fortify their cities. Philetairos had extended his benevolent influence as far as Kyzikos and down to the Aegean coast and Aeolis; Dokimos and Lysias were lords of cities of their own foundation; Akhaios was locally wealthy enough to ransom Galatian captives and receive the thanks of their relatives, all without any reference to the king. The cities of the west that had fought their own battles against the invaders were also no doubt inclined to emphasize that fact when any of Antiochos' officials turned up, so that any prospect of imposing his authority on them was clearly delayed. All this, of course, was no more than a local version of the independence asserted by Bithynia and Pontos (and the Galatians) in other parts of Asia Minor, but it does show how limited was the king's authority, and how fragmented was Asia Minor.

Chapter Eleven

The New State

When Antiochos I moved from Sardis into Syria in 274 it was to combat an Egyptian invasion of his Syrian territories. At least that is the reason given by the Babylonian chronicler who recorded the move.[1] This was the result of a series of diplomatic actions over the previous decade, and Antiochos cannot have been surprised at the outbreak of war. There is a very good case to be made out for him being the aggressor, though it was Ptolemy II who made the first military move.

Ptolemy II had perhaps been taken by surprise when Seleukos' attack on Lysimachos in 282–281 succeeded so quickly. His father and Lysimachos had been allied against Seleukos, at least in formal terms, though there had been no call for action for years, and that alliance had ended when Ptolemy I died. Ptolemy II, like his father, always acted cautiously, and clearly had not renewed the alliance, or perhaps had not had time, and the internal collapse of Lysimachos' kingdom will have prevented any serious diplomacy. When Seleukos invaded Lysimachos' territories in 282 Ptolemy stayed out of the war. Seleukos' quick success cannot have been expected, even if the steady deterioration of Lysimachos' internal position had been only too obvious. Ptolemy must have hoped the two old men would become locked into a lengthy and mutually destructive conflict.

Seleukos' death at the hands of Ptolemy Keraunos, Ptolemy II's half-brother and rival, does not seem to have involved Ptolemy II, though one has one's suspicions. It was, however, a clear threat to him, since Keraunos had made it clear earlier that he was ambitious for a kingdom, and Egypt would do just fine. When he seized the Macedonian kingship, therefore, Ptolemy II might be pleased that Keraunos had gained his ambition, but concerned that this ambition might not be satisfied with just one kingdom. Hanging over every king in the Hellenistic world was the memory of Alexander and his great empire, and Keraunos was clearly the sort of man who would harbour an Alexander-longing.

Ptolemy II's caution was justified when Antiochos I became involved in the repeated crises in Asia Minor – a version, in fact, of the hoped-for war which

Seleukos I had launched, but with different enemies. Keraunos rid himself of a sequence of rival claimants for the Macedonian kingship, including Arsinoe and her son and her other children, and then made it clear to Ptolemy that he was no longer ambitious for the Egyptian throne.[2] Meanwhile Ptolemy had used his fleet to collect a series of bases along the southern Anatolian coast and in the southern Aegean, but carefully avoided becoming entangled in the fighting in Asia Minor. His caution was clearly justified and as events unfolded his position seemed only to strengthen. However, Keraunos was killed in the Galatian invasion, and his position in Macedon was eventually seized by Antigonos Gonatas, who quickly allied himself with Antiochos, at least by marriage. This then looked like Ptolemaic isolation.

Having successfully used one daughter in his diplomatic game, Antiochos soon deployed another. His daughter by Stratonike, Apama, was of marriageable age by 275, and was offered to, and accepted by, Magas, who was a stepson of Ptolemy I.[3] He was ruling in Cyrenaica as Ptolemy's viceroy, first for the old king then for his successor, and Ptolemy II had left him there. So by marrying the daughter of the Seleukid king, Magas was in effect indicating his independence, and to Antiochos this was clearly a major diplomatic success, a reply perhaps to the veiled hostility he must have felt emanating from Egypt and the Egyptian fleet in Cyprus and the Aegean.

This was perhaps the extent of Antiochos' intentions, to detach Magas and his land from Ptolemy II's rule and influence, and to be content that Magas stood as a threat to Ptolemy, and, by being independent to sensibly reduce Ptolemy's power and resources. It was not, however, the intention of Magas to remain quietly in Cyrene, a mute threat. He had ambitions to displace Ptolemy II as king in Egypt, and had in fact already taken the title of king. Antiochos cannot have been ignorant of this; the marriage to Apama was a green light for Magas' ambition.

So the allies were at cross purposes; Antiochos made the alliance to give him a connection which was a standing threat to Ptolemy; Magas' purpose was to acquire Seleukid strength and support so as to allow him to attack and displace Ptolemy, and in 274 he launched an invasion. On the surface this might seem to be a joint move, consequent on the marriage the year before, but Antiochos was clearly not prepared at that point for an Egyptian war, since he was in Sardis when it began, and had to move quickly into Syria when Ptolemy II's reply was an invasion of that country.[4]

Magas' invasion failed when a Libyan native uprising broke out in his rear and he had to turn back to deal with it; Ptolemy in turn was unable to exploit this because he found that a force of Galatian mercenaries he had recruited were about to rebel. (Ptolemy emphasized the victory he gained over them as an equivalent to Antiochos' elephant victory, and used it as a way of distracting attention from Magas' rebellion.)[5] For Antiochos the Babylonian chronicler is quite explicit; Antiochos 'went to Aber-Nahara ('Beyond-the-River', that is, Syria, which from Babylonia is beyond the Euphrates), against the troops of Egypt which were encamped in Syria, and the troops of Egypt withdrew before him'.[6] This may indicate that Antiochos was reacting against a Ptolemaic invasion which had been provoked by Antiochos' intrigues, or it might mean that he had invaded Ptolemaic territory in Syria.

This is the beginning of the 'First Syrian War', of which there were to be nine over the next two centuries. The enmity between the dynasties originated, of course, in the quarrel between Ptolemy I and Seleukos I over which of them should take over Phoenicia and Palestine as booty from the destruction of the kingdom of Antigonos I, and this remained the excuse all along. It is arguable that this series of wars was a major element in the weakening and eventual collapse of the Seleukid kingdom (though there were other causes of that as well). But those two first kings did not resort to war, and it might have seemed that the dispute had faded away. Nevertheless they fortified their own parts of Syria. Ptolemy held a series of existing cities, mainly along the coast, from Tripolis to Gaza, refounded Ake as Ptolemais, and made it the viceroyalty's capital, and seized control of Tyre and Sidon when Demetrios' power collapsed. Seleukos developed the great series of cities in his part of Syria almost from scratch, but by the time he died they existed. When the First Syrian War began, therefore, both parts of Syria were well stocked with fortified cities. Both kings faced major difficulties if they wished to invade their enemy's part of Syria, never mind conquer it.

Little or nothing is known of the course of the war though it was evidently a difficult time in Antiochos' kingdom, at least according to the Babylonian chronicler. He recorded a mobilization of wealth – 'silver, cloth, goods, utensils' – by the satrap of Babylonia. The satrap of Baktria, a man presumably appointed by Antiochos when he had travelled west to take up his inheritance, sent twenty elephants as reinforcement; the troops in garrison in Babylonia were collected together and sent on to the king in Syria.[7]

There was apparently one more royal action. For the previous year's diary entry, the chronicler records that 'Antiochos and Seleukos' were kings.[8] This Seleukos was the eldest son of Antiochos and Stratonike. In 275, the year of the notice, he was in his early 'teens (his parents were married by 292). He may have been the second or third child – the already married Apama being perhaps the first. When Seleukos was made joint-king is not known. His appointment is noted in a prologue of Pompeius Trogus, without a date, but his position is also confirmed in a cylinder from Borsippa in Babylonia of 268.[9] Given the age of Seleukos he is unlikely to have been promoted as joint-king before his 'teens, and the emergency of the Egyptian war could be a suitable occasion. Antiochos I after all had been fighting wars ever since he returned to the west (and had been fighting in the east before). A king's death in battle was very possible, and an emergency royal replacement would be handy; the lesson of 281–280 was thus learned.

The course of military events in the war survives as only a few details. There is a certain incident, when Ptolemy and his queen had to move to Pelusion to prepare to meet an attack, though how far Antiochos had penetrated into Ptolemaic Syria is not known.[10] The war is so badly recorded that all sorts of bits and pieces have been enlisted to help explain it, but they are now largely discredited. So Antiochos did not capture Damascus,[11] and Ptolemy did not mount an expedition by way of the Persian Gulf.[12] It is best to admit we know little beyond the fact that there was a war.[13]

The war lasted perhaps four years (274–271). It seems to have been concluded with a formal treaty. This procedure would provide a deal of security to both kings, and would permit them to turn away from each other to deal with other problems, just as Seleukos I and Ptolemy I were able to do after Seleukos agreed he would not fight for Syria. It is likely that Antiochos returned to the issue of Asia Minor's troubles. The Babylonian diarist noted that he was in Syria in 270, but for the rest of the reign he provides no similar information.[14] Asia Minor, however, did still require much royal attention.

Above all the Galatians continued to be troublesome. It was in 269 or 268 that the captives whose ransom was organized by Akhaios were taken; they were released next year, it seems.[15] Other raids are noted in the succeeding years, though they were not nearly as numerous as before. On the other hand, the Galatians who had settled in the central region which became known as Galatia were certainly active in a different direction.

Galatia was a thinly populated area partly in Kappadokia and partly an area claimed by Antiochos but hardly occupied by him or by his father, on the borders of Pontos and Paphlagonia. It was an ideal place to plant such an awkward and restless group as the warlike Kelts. For one thing their arrival produced instant enmity from some of their new neighbours, thus giving allies to Antiochos, though no doubt they complained about his arrogant assumption that their land was available. It is possible that Mithradates of Pontos saw it the other way about, and he may have helped them settle in Kappadokia as a shield against Seleukid attack. They are recorded as joining Mithradates in repelling a Ptolemaic landing on the Black Sea coast.[16] This has been dated to perhaps 266 as part of Ptolemy II's ambitious naval expeditions – which included fighting the Khremonidean war in the Aegean.[17]

Meanwhile Antiochos was more or less left in peace. He used the time to develop the urban defences of his territories in the west of Asia Minor and along the Royal Road. He was also concerned to intensify the authority of his kingship in the region by developing a system of government, and by bringing the existing cities into a dependent relationship with the royal government.

The Seleukid governing system was, of course, based on that which had been inherited from the Akhaimenid Empire, modified by being staffed, at least in the upper ranks, by Greeks and Macedonians. In 276 the Babylonian diarist mentioned the existence of satraps in both Baktria and Babylonia, who clearly from their actions had some military authority. But he also recorded the presence of a vice-general and of a general.[18] A certain hierarchy may thus be presumed; the satraps as governors, with the general (who collected the garrisons of Babylonia together and marched them to the west in 276) in charge of military affairs. On the other hand, the diarist credits the Baktrian satrap with sending the elephant reinforcements. There is not really a contradiction here, only the habit of allocating authority and action to a distant satrap.

He also refers to 'the satrap of Babylonia and the appointees', who all went off to Sardis to meet the king. The appointees are presumably officials of some sort, though their absence from Babylonia for several months also implies that their tasks were handed over to their deputies without any administrative disruption. Much of the satrap's responsibilities involved religious ceremonies, where he stood in for the king. In his time as joint-king Antiochos himself had frequently performed the ceremonies (he is referred to as 'Antiochos the crown prince').[19] There is one indication of a lower level of officials with specific geographical areas of action in the reference to 'Seleukos the district official' who appears to be involved with maintaining a canal.[20] In fact this can be associated with the brief reference by Diodoros to the subordinate official disciplined by Seleukos in 315, but who was then supported by Antigonos.[21] There is, of course, nothing particularly sophisticated in a satrap having authority over a large province and supervising subordinates who governed sections of his satrapy; it is what one would expect.

This administrative apparatus was inherited from the Akhaimenid system. Babylonia was a well-populated and productive land and imperial governments were always keen to extract taxation from it (though the system does not seem to have been as oppressive as that imposed on Egypt by the Ptolemies, who also, of course, inherited an ancient administrative scheme, which they tightened up and made even more efficient – that is, more oppressive). The denser the population the more numerous the officials who were required to extract the taxes. In other areas, however, there are signs of innovation. The territories east of Babylonia were eventually grouped into the 'Upper Satrapies', which included Media, Parthia, and Baktria (and sometimes seeming to include Babylonia). In fact these were all separate provinces until Baktria broke away and Parthia was seized by the invading army – it was as satraps that Diodotos II carried through his usurpation – after which the importance of Media grew, for it became the frontier province of the east. To the west there was probably a satrap in Mesopotamia (the land between the middle Tigris and the middle Euphrates), as there had been at times under Antigonos, for it was a crucial transit region between Syria and Babylonia and Iran.

There is, however, never any reference to a satrap in the Seleukis, North Syria. In Asia Minor there may be a reference to a satrap in the comment by the Babylonian diarist that when Antiochos went to Syria to fight the Egyptian army he left in Sardis the queen and 'a famous official'. The man is not identified otherwise, but one thinks of a man of the status of Patrokles. There seems little point in mentioning him unless he was given responsibility for governing the region during Antiochos' absence. Certainly later on Asia Minor was treated as a unit; it became a separate kingdom for Antiochos Hierax. Before him his cousin Alexander was governor of Lydia, and afterwards Zeuxis was viceroy there for twenty years. Its problems were such that a single authority for the large territory was clearly the optimum method of administration; this was also, it seems, the preferred solution to the problems in Baktria, where Sogdiana was added to that satrapy.

So it would seem that the original system of provincial satrapies inherited from Alexander and ultimately from the Akhaimenids, fairly quickly developed, under the pressure of events, into one of viceroys controlling large groups of provinces – the Upper Satrapies, Babylonia, Asia Minor – with the smaller, less geopolitically important areas (such as Mesopotamia), left under the old system. But these large viceroyalties were dangerous, for their rulers had major armed forces under their control, and any king was inevitably suspicious of them; and both Baktria and Asia Minor broke away under their satraps. In Babylonia the old sub-provinces seem to have survived as 'districts', and eventually at least one re-emerged as a separate satrapy, though this does not seem to have occurred elsewhere.

The North Syrian region is the major exception to this system. There is never any record of a satrap or a viceroy there. This is not definitive, of course, but compared to other areas Syria is well recorded, and a satrap would be expected to be mentioned, particularly in such times as the early years of Antiochos III, where Polybios has a detailed account of events. In fact, it is possible to account for this absence. First, for two decades after 301 this was a region under the direct control of the king; so far as can be seen, once he acquired Syria Seleukos I did not leave it until he marched into Asia Minor to confront Lysimachos, except to visit Babylonia, but we have evidence that Antiochos was there as 'crown prince' and as king. Seleukos stayed in Syria, of course, because he felt it to be under threat. He was also very busy setting up, building, and populating the cities he developed, and such a large task required his attention and his presence. So Seleukos would appear to have been his own Syrian satrap, a position all the more necessary as this was the real military power-house of the kingdom. By building the cities, Seleukos had built his army, but this was also a tool which could be used by a usurper.

The cities were in two broad groups. The four main cities were those named for his own family; Seleukeia, Antioch, Laodikeia, Apameia. They were planted careful distances apart, in such a way as to dominate the lower Orontes Valley and the coast between Kilikia and the land of the Phoenician city of Arados. It has been possible, by plotting the occurrences of inscriptions which record the cities to which a series of villages belong to map the boundary between Apameia and Antioch. (This is for the early Roman period, but there is no reason to suppose the boundary had changed.)[22] Seleukeia and Antioch were sufficiently close to each other – 20km – to imply they also had a joint boundary. The whole of the land in North Syria was thus divided among these four cities and Arados. The six cities in the region between Antioch and the Euphrates are sufficiently thickly grouped to imply that their territories also occupied the whole region. The distances between them vary from 30km to nearly 100, but they each had a smaller territory than the 4 great cities. This means that the whole of the area acquired in Syria by Seleukos in 301 became city land. Combined with the constant presence of the king in the area for 20 years, this would imply that there was no need for a local governor for the region. On the other hand, the king did need to ensure that the cities remained under his control, and here he had to operate with care.

The populations of the new cities came largely from Greece. There was a basic population of Syrians, as the incorporated village at Beroia and the temple-town at Hierapolis show; it may be presumed that this was the case in every city. Antioch received some Athenians and some Cypriots. The incomers were also partly Macedonian, probably survivors of the armies of Alexander and Antigonos and Seleukos, and partly Greek. The wars which ravaged Greece and Macedon generated plenty of refugees looking for better conditions of life. We know that much later a set of men who were present in Laodikeia had Macedonian names, and some of the institutions of local government were similarly Macedonian, but the majority of immigrants were probably Greek. Greece was more populous than Macedon, and Macedonian military emigration (and casualties) was certainly greater. Greece also had a substantial population willing to emigrate, a factor which had been common in Greece for centuries. Only a few of these immigrant groups are known – Athenians and Cypriots in Antioch – but in all likelihood the majority of emigrants into Syria under Seleukos I were from Greek cities.[23]

The native Syrians survived, if marginalized. Inscriptions and other sources, principally from the Roman period, show that the majority of the population spoke and wrote Aramaic. When the Seleukid grip on the land slackened, large areas came under the authority of Aramaic-speaking rulers. Particularly this was so in the mountainous regions, which had not been the target of the Greek settlers. But it is not necessary to wait until the Roman period to see this, for Arados was a Syrian city, autonomous all along. The Greco-Macedonians remained a Greek-speaking crust over the Aramaic-speaking mass. Eventually, of course, the Greek-speakers left at the time of the Muslim conquest; the Aramaic-speakers still survived, as they always had, and largely shifted into Arabic, as they had never taken to Greek.

The new immigrants, with the authority of the Greek-speaking king, implied and produced a new political dispensation. These Greeks arrived with the basic assumption that a city was a self-governing institution, and it is unlikely that they could have been induced to emigrate except on the understanding that they would be established in one. And indeed the cities were all equipped with the normal government system already developed in Greece – or rather Macedon, since the cities' autonomy was limited. There was a *boule* and an *ekklesia*, a council and an assembly of the citizens, where such necessary officials as the market supervisor, judges, and so on, were elected. The structure was superficially democratic, and in local issues the city was fully operational, but in practice local power was restricted to a wealthy oligarchy. And this local government was also subjected to two forms of supervision.

Each city was laid out on a similar plan. It included an area of land, usually on a river to be close to a water supply and which was more or less level; this was where the main part of the population lived and worked. This settlement was surrounded by a wall and in that wall was incorporated a citadel, the acropolis, which held a garrison of royal troops. This acropolis was always on the edge of the city, with access both into the city and to the outside. It therefore was not vulnerable to a civic insurrection, and could be accessed by reinforcements if attacked. No doubt the garrisons were composed of men from other places. (This condition, of course, is yet another argument against the rebellion in 281 being by the Greco-Macedonian civic populations.)

The second method of control was much more subtle. The king appointed a man as his representative with the city council. Usually, but not necessarily, he was from the city itself. He was not a governor, and it is unlikely that he ever interfered seriously in the city's affairs in local matters. But, because he was linked both to the city, as a citizen, and to the king, as one of his Friends, this official, called an *epistates*, could guarantee that information, complaints, even instructions, flowed both ways. The city therefore had easy access to the king; the king was able to communicate comfortably with the cities.

This system, simple and direct, worked. There are very few instances of cities rebelling in the Seleukid kingdom, and indeed very few records of disputes between the king and the cities, not that that means a great deal, given the poor sources. Any wish by the cities for greater autonomy, or even independence, was thus stifled because the city rulers were threatened by the existence of the garrison in the acropolis, and anyway they could make any discontent quickly known to the king. But there was a further influence, which was probably not articulated, though it was a constant background influence.

The king was the city-founder, the *ktistes*. This gave him and his heirs a privileged position of quasi-religious authority. The oligarchs who ruled inside the cities were emplaced there by courtesy of the king, who had allotted them the land whose rents they lived on, and who could clearly take that land back if he so wished. That is, the king and the cities depended on each other, each supporting the other in a dyarchic system which was designed both to exclude other groups – Syrians mainly – from access to power and wealth, and to supply the royal government with both tax revenues and recruits to the army. It was a system which operated successfully for at least a century and a half, helped by a generally more or less fair tax regime.

Like all governments, the Seleukid kings were greedy for cash and generally ingenious in persuading or compelling their subjects to supply it. Unlike the Ptolemies they seem to have been careful not to squeeze too hard. It appears, for example, that the tax on a peasants' product was a percentage rather than a set quantity, so that in a time of bad harvest the government's take fell in proportion. On the other hand, there were plenty of other imposts, such as a land tax, customs duties both at the external boundaries and at internal provincial boundaries, sales taxes, and so on. The burden on the peasants was substantial, as it was no doubt also on the lower classes in the cities.[24]

Mints were established in most of the major cities. In Syria Seleukos I minted coins in Seleukeia and Antioch, which were the main producers, and on a lesser scale in Apameia and Laodikeia. Kilikia was served from Tarsos. Western Asia Minor cities often had their own mints. Under Seleukos there were three of these, under his son five, and this rose to fifteen or twenty under Antiochos II. In Syria, however, the Apameia mint ceased, while Seleukeia was lost in 246; Antioch produced for the whole region, except for a small production at Laodikeia, and a local minting at Arados. (There were also all along a number of other mints, whose location the numismatists describe as 'uncertain'; they may have been mobile, or ephemeral.) In the rest of the empire each satrapy capital had a mint for local issues, though again there were lots of 'unlocated' ones. Many small mints were local, producing local issues for local needs, but they did so by royal permission, even if that permission was only assumed, rather than explicitly granted.[25]

A second state burden, but one which was felt mainly by the wealthier groups, and almost entirely by the Greek and Macedonian population, was the conscription of young men into the army. As with every Greek community, men aged eighteen or so were expected to undergo military training, and then to serve for a year or two with the regular army. On discharge they could return home, where they formed a militia which could be called upon to serve in the event of a major military emergency, or they could stay on in the army as professional soldiers. So the kings had a regular army, and a substantial trained reserve. It seems that originally some of the settlers took on their land with an obligation to serve in the army – cleruchic land that is – but this faded away in time, though the terms of the land ownership were always remembered. There was little point in establishing cleruchs with a specific military obligation when an obligation to serve was effectively universal.

The royal army was reinforced with mercenaries, usually specialist troops such as light cavalry and archers, even charioteers, but the essential basis was always the embodied citizen subjects, normally fighting as infantry in the phalanx. By the time of Antiochos III, when we have some numbers, the regular army was about 35,000 strong, and this could be expanded to double that by calling out the reserve.[26] This, however, was a recourse which had to be used only sparingly, since the disruption caused by calling out the reserve was substantial. It happened under Antiochos III only three times in a thirty-five year reign which was marked by military campaigns every year.

The basic principle of the kingdom's government was therefore to devolve power to the local level, to the cities, and even villages, and to the satraps of the provinces. The king himself had a fairly rudimentary central administration, which was kept small because of this devolution. He regularly consulted with his Friends in a council, which was fairly informal, so far as we know, and most kings paid heed to arguments in council.

The administration has been characterized as 'inefficient and rudimentary'.[27] It is revealed in a few inscriptions, one from Hellespontine Phrygia, one from Palestine, which consist of sequences of letters, by which successive governors and officials pass on royal decisions. It looks clumsy, and no doubt it was (but what government system is not clumsy?). But it was also fairly simple, and it was obviously the result of the distribution of power to various levels. It did result in most people being left to themselves, without the constant interferences which later governments sought to impose – all except for tax collections, of course. And many of the cities were very busy in their citizens' lives, which would be quite enough without the royal officials joining in. In effect the kings left the administration they found in any particular area in place, only developing a new scheme where none existed. Their one particular innovation seems to have been the *epistatai* in the Syrian cities.

The Seleukid state therefore was constructed in different ways in different regions, with a fairly light central administration. Syria was a collection of cities; Babylonia was governed just as autonomously and on Babylonian terms, as the powers of the priests show, as does the purely Babylonian institutions in the city of Uruk. Asia Minor was different again. The region under Antiochos I's control was a long narrow section along the Royal Road, bounded on the north by the lands of the Galatians and the Kappadokians, on the south by the Pisidian Hills which were inhabited by an independent and hostile people backed by the Ptolemaic-dominated south coast. At the western end of the road the Seleukid area widened out to south and north, but rarely reached any of the coasts. Mainly the region's cities were and remained autonomous, the king exerting pressure when necessary in a relatively polite and diplomatic way, with the whole supervised by a notably powerful viceroy. In the north the Bithynians and the several cities held the Black Sea coast and that of the Straits in complete independence, though that status was always precarious; on the west coast the line of ancient Greek cities occupied the whole region in proud and equally precarious independence, which was assured only because the kings refrained from interfering; in the south there were more cities largely ignored by the Seleukid kings; the Ptolemaic fleet dominated the Aegean Sea and the eastern Mediterranean.

The task for the king in Asia Minor therefore was to expand Seleukid power and control gradually. It would be all too easy to push too strongly and provoke an awkward counter-alliance, such as that between Bithynia and the Northern League of cities which had effectively frustrated expansion by Seleukos and Antiochos. Any expansion of central power had to be by means of influence, individual agreements, and opportune advances. It was therefore slow and piecemeal, and each step forward was liable to be undone by local catastrophes, such as the Galatian invasions; after a century it was still incomplete. The instruments of domination were decrees by the cities in honour of the king, or gifts by the king to the cities, both of which bound the two together. They reveal that the Seleukid government system operated with no reference to the cities as a group, each of which had its own individual relationship with the king.

The city of Ilion in the Troad, for example, voted honours for Metrodoros, Antiochos I's doctor.[28] Metrodoros was in fact a Macedonian, the son of a man from Amphipolis in Macedon. The city was seizing on an incident – Metrodoros' healing of a wound the king received in 'the battle' – to establish contact with a man they assumed had some influence with the king. In effect the city was choosing him to be a local version of the Syrian *epistates*, though he was presumably living at the king's court. What this was, of course, was less a matter of being generous to Metrodoros and more a way of fending off any pressure the king might wish to exert on the city. At the same time the relationship would obviously assist the city if it came under attack. (Ilion was occupied and looted by the Galatians; no doubt Antiochos was called on to help its recovery.) On a larger scale the League of the Ionians, a group of cities strung along the western Asia Minor coast, honoured the king on his birthday at some point in the 260s.[29] Erythrai, along the same coast, sent three envoys to present a golden crown to the king (either Antiochos I or Antiochos II); it could be taken as an acknowledgment of his suzerainty if the king felt so inclined; in the city it was probably a means of fending him off.[30]

Some cities were too strategically important to be allowed to get away with such an informal relationship. In the Thracian Chersonese, the city of Lysimacheia had been badly damaged in the Galatian wars (and by a preceding earthquake). When the pressure subsided Antiochos II reoccupied the peninsula, but also made a treaty with the city, which no doubt he had helped to revive and which was once more functioning. He guaranteed the city's constitution, and agreed to defend it against attack; in exchange he gained the use of bases at the city's harbours. This gave him a defendable base on the Hellespont to complement others on the Asian side, from which he was able to expand into Thrace. The text of the treaty appears to describe a relationship of equals, with reciprocal obligations, but the use of Lysimacheia's harbours by Antiochos' forces gives away the real relationship.[31] The king was expanding his power into Europe.

Within the region under Antiochos' direct rule, it was in the period after the defeat of the Galatians that the dynasts such as Dokimos and Lysias were able to develop their cities. Other Seleukid courtiers were granted estates only a little less ambitious. Akhaios was one of these; another was a man called Aristodikides of Assos, who was granted an estate of 800 hectares or so which was to be attached to the city of Ilion as part of the city's territory, which was a means to render the gift irrevocable. It also made him instantly both rich and a major figure in Ilion's affairs, and enhanced the wealth of the city.[32]

It is this grant which demonstrates some of the bureaucratic practices of the Seleukid government at this period. It is clear that the royal administration knew little or nothing about the estate being granted, and if its method of delivering it seems clumsy, it was nevertheless effective. It was clearly expected that it would be permanent, and the inscription of the various documents involved in stone was intended to be evidence of the grant for the future. This would suggest that it was also expected that the possession of the estate by Aristodikides and his heirs would be challenged in the future. That is, possession was not actually guaranteed by any applicable legal system. (This remained the case throughout the Hellenistic and Roman periods; it is not unknown to this day, of course.)

The complicated but effective government system in existence in the reign of Antiochos I in Asia Minor was probably an inheritance from the past. It is unlikely to have been set up as new since Seleukos I's conquest only a few years before, especially since the grant was awarded during or shortly after the Galatian wars. So it was a system which had been operated by Lysimachos and probably by Antigonos over the previous forty years, and was originally in all probability an Akhaimenid system, though Antigonos is perhaps more likely to have elaborated it. Since it was in operation in all its baroque complication by c.275, Antiochos would have had to develop it in the process of four or five years while engaged in several wars and while combatting the Galatian invasion, which seems unlikely.

On the other hand, it was a system which, complex and inefficient as it may have been, clearly worked, and was one which was particular to Asia Minor. There is no sign of it in Syria, or in Babylonia, both of which had different administrative systems inherited from the past, or were developed for their particular needs. (A version of it was apparently applied in Palestine in the next century, but this was a formerly Ptolemaic region, and it was probably originally a Ptolemaic system.) So, as with its political arrangements, Asia Minor was a region with its own complex administration, run by its own bureaucrats with its own system.

All this variety, of course, merely reflected the several stages by which the Seleukid kingdom had been built. It suggests that neither Seleukos I nor Antiochos I was much interested in the details of this administration, so long as it worked. The system of cities and *epistatai* in Syria was the one element of administrative originality in the kingdom, and that was not applied with any consistency anywhere else; it was, of course, essentially very simple, the sort of system which could well have developed out of the process of city-founding and building in Syria.

The central government was similarly fairly informal and rudimentary. The king was the engine of the whole system, but being only one man he could do relatively little. He had a court of men, referred to as his *philoi* ('Friends') who could be used for a variety of tasks. There was little specialization among these men, who could be used as governors, or diplomats, or military commanders as needed, or simply as royal advisers (whether or not they had the relevant experience). This put the onus of detailed administration on the provincial governors.

The purposes of government were thus simply the basics of tax collection and military command, and the administration was essentially limited to maintaining internal order. There was little in the form of a professional bureaucracy, though clerks were obviously employed, and so there was no possibility of developing a recognized and respected system of administration. Legal procedures were entangled in the administration, and as far as can be seen there was no development of case law or precedent. Cities and satraps were juries and judges, and the king was the final court of appeal, if he could be reached. There were cases of appellants trudging in the wake of the court for miles and days hoping to gain an interview, but, as with Seleukos I and the Herakleian envoy, it was always possible to catch the king in a bad humour. It cannot be said that the system was in any way efficient, but that probably did not much matter given its restricted responsibility.

Little changed in this system between the time of Seleukos I and the end of the Seleukid state. Lack of resources, and failure to see that anything needed to be done to change it, made for an acceptance of the whole business. In this of course the Seleukids were no different from other comparative states. At the civic level it was possible to be more elaborate, but most cities relied on unpaid officials elected for a year, and on slave clerks to keep the records – more administration on the cheap. Only the Ptolemies had a more detailed administration, which relied above all on the densely populated and geographically restricted inhabited area of Egypt to enforce the system – and even then the central government relied largely on the co-operation of the village headmen to get at the tax take. It is only with the Roman Empire, and even then only after a century or more, that a professional bureaucracy and a developed legal system emerged – and only after several centuries did anyone get round to attempting to codify the various legal decisions.

The Seleukid government system therefore was one which suited the time and place. Criticisms based on the modern experience of government are entirely misplaced. It is only with the vastly increased wealth and population in the last couple of centuries that government has grown to its present elaboration. The Seleukid system was one in a country of a relatively small population, mostly living close to subsistence. Anything more elaborate was impossible to sustain. The kings had the example of Egypt before them, and they could have imposed a similar system, though it is unlikely to have been very effective, given the size of the kingdom. That they clearly did not do so presumes that they recognized the limits of their reach. They used their inheritance from earlier regimes, even though this produced somewhat different systems in the several sections of the kingdom, and added in several sets of self-governing cities, which lightened the load on the king. It was a system developed – if such an activist term is permissible – by Seleukos I and his son, though in fact, apart from founding cities and appointing officials, the kings had little to do to bring the system into existence. But it did rely on a determined king to make it work. Antiochos I, even more than his father, was that sort of king. By the end of the war waged by Antiochos I against Ptolemy II the kingdom was operating in a way which continued on into the future.

Chapter Twelve

Creeping Imperialism

In 271 Antiochos I and Ptolemy II made peace, ending the First Syrian War. So far as we know, no territory changed hands as a result. In the diplomatic practice of the time, this treaty, sworn by public oaths by both kings, would last until the death of one of the kings. This did not always work, but it did on a surprising number of occasions, at least in treaties between kings; republican regimes had to be dealt with differently. This is the necessary diplomatic background to the actions of both rulers for the next ten years. Ptolemy became involved in war in Greece and the Aegean by 267 (the Khremonideian War); Antiochos took advantage of the preoccupation of the other powers to make careful, often subtle advances inside Asia Minor.

All was not well in the royal family, however. It is possible that Antiochos had taken a second wife, Nysa.[1] The evidence for her is poor, but is certainly suggestive, and it may be one of the factors in what evidently became a serious dynastic crisis. In about 267 Antiochos I had his eldest son and joint-king Seleukos executed.[2] The reason is not known, but can hardly be anything less than because Seleukos had aimed to remove his father from the kingship and take power to himself. Seleukos had been born some time after his parents' marriage, which took place in about 294. He was thus, in 267, in his early twenties and possibly even younger. He had been joint-king for a dozen years (the same length of time as his father had been Seleukos I's colleague), but there is no indication that he was ever given any political or military responsibility – not that this is in any way conclusive, since the sources are so poor. His father had commanded the cavalry in battle at the age of 20, and was ruler of Baktria by 30. Perhaps Seleukos was bored; certainly it would seem he was impatient.

Given his prominence and his position, his ambition to succeed his father as soon as possible is only to be expected. By 267 the dynasty could be described as well-founded, and Seleukos would be the third generation to rule. Antiochos continued the year-count initiated by his father, so 267 was 'year 45'. Normally kings had counted their own years starting in 'year 1' with the new reign, but the twelve years when he was joint-king no doubt habituated him to a continuous count; it was also a good propaganda point, implying a greater continuity than with individual reigns. Seleukos had been promoted as joint-king in the emergency of the constant warfare of his father in Asia Minor, and the First Syrian War with Egypt, and so had been referred to as king since adolescence. The reason for appointing a joint-king was always to ensure as orderly a succession as possible, and perhaps to deter usurpations. But the drawback of such an appointment was exactly the same as appointing any other heir; in some it provided an assurance that they had been chosen and would eventually succeed, in others it made them more impatient to be given sole power – that is, it might trigger a usurpation from within the dynasty, rather than prevent one from outside. Seleukos I had solved the matter by giving Antiochos major responsibilities far away, thereby providing Antiochos with experience and himself with safety. Ptolemy I had waited until almost the end before appointing Ptolemy II; until then he seems to have played the field, since there were several contenders among his children (among them, Ptolemy Keraunos, of course). There was no obvious method which would be successful in allowing the old king to live out his days and thus ensuring a peaceful succession; whatever choice was made almost invariably brought trouble.

Seleukos' death brought promotion for his younger brother Antiochos, who is recorded as joint-king only in the very late and compressed set of 'prologues' by Pompeius Trogus, which may simply be his assumption that a new joint-king would replace Seleukos.[3] Certainly Antiochos became the heir to the throne (and eventually succeeded) – he was now the only son of the king – but there is no contemporary or near-contemporary record naming him as joint-king or as heir. (But then there is almost no contemporary evidence at all.) The surest record would be the Babylonian diarist, who wrote up his records every month, but the tablets for the 260s are almost entirely missing; nor are there any Babylonian documents of their time naming these kings for dating purposes. The new joint-king was, it seems, already married; his wife was the daughter of Akhaios, whose family was now, if not earlier, decisively linked with the dynasty.

One reason for the lack of sources from this time is that attention was mainly directed at events in the Aegean, where Ptolemy II and Antigonos II and much of Greece were involved in the complex war named after the Athenian politician Khremonides, whose intrigues had brought it on. The main result of the war was that Antigonos Gonatas re-established Macedonian control over Athens and much of Greece, while Ptolemy did the same in the Aegean, and along parts of Asia Minor coast. Khremonides' aim of freeing Athens from Macedonian domination failed.

Antiochos kept out of the fighting, but the war's proximity and length – six years (267–261) – meant that he had to concentrate on affairs in the western part of his kingdom, if only to keep an eye on what was going on. It also enabled him to expand his control there. He was certainly in Babylon in 268 where he founded (or re-founded) the Ezida temple at Borsippa and oversaw the restoration of Esagila, the major temple in Babylon.[4] This last was an ongoing, never-ending, task. It is not known if he went further east at this time, but it seems unlikely given the crisis of the Khremonidian war, or the continuing, if reduced, Galatian problem in Asia Minor.

In the decade 271–261, between the end of his Egyptian war and his death, Antiochos oversaw the major work in Asia Minor of planting new cities and refounding and enlarging others, a work equal in scale and importance to his father's in Syria. Of the eighteen places in Asia Minor which have been suggested as his work, less than half were newly founded, four were synoecisms, and six were essentially cities and towns reinforced and renamed and so probably reorganized.

Two or three of these places were no more than forts. In Pamphylia a Seleukeia existed for a very short time, probably emplaced to break up the Ptolemaic domination of the region.[5] In the Sea of Marmara one of the islands near the Bosporos received the name of Antioch, and was probably a base used by Antiochos I's fleet in operations in the area in the 270s during his war with Bithynia; it is unlikely to have lasted long.[6] Near Magnesia-by-Sipylon in Ionia was Palaimagnesia, a fort held by Seleukid troops, who eventually in the 240s became integrated with the main city.[7] These places were not cities, and probably none of them remained in use for very long; but their essentially military purposes emphasize that this aspect of city-founding was often the paramount aim. It can be stated unequivocally that every new or reorganized city was planted or developed because it was in a strategic position or was otherwise militarily important. Defence and control were the primary purposes.

There were also more directly political reasons in some cases. Antiochos moved the population of Kelainai to a new site which he called Apameia. Kelainai had been an important centre for several centuries, established at the junction of the Royal Road with other routes to the north and south. Antiochos moved it to a new site at the junction of the Maiandros and Marsyas Rivers. The site may have been marginally more convenient and perhaps roomier, but it was scarcely a better military location. The strong associations with the Akhaimenids – there was a palace used by Cyrus in the city – and with Alexander and Antigonos (who made it a quasi-capital of his state), probably persuaded Antiochos to move the population, and so attempt to break those connections. Although he gave it the name of his mother, the local name of Kelainai continued in use.[8]

It is evident that a variety of methods were used to invigorate and expand the urban landscape of interior Asia Minor. Those cities which received new dynastic names but whose original name survived (such as Apameia-Kelainai), were presumably reinforced with new settlers and perhaps new buildings, and a new constitution. Some certainly received new infusions of people.[9] Hyrkanis, originally a settlement of colonists from Hyrkania planted there by the Akhaimenids, was reinforced by a contingent of Macedonians, who presumably then formed the governing crust of the city, so dominating the original ruling set;[10] Magnesia-by-Sipylos, as noted, acquired the group of Seleukid soldiers from Palaimagnesia; Alabanda became Antioch, no new settlers being attested, so the change must imply some action by Antiochos I (or perhaps by his son, since it is only after Antiochos I's death that the new name is recorded).[11]

The selection of places to reinforce or to honour depended on the king's geographical requirements in terms of defence. They were also a means of extending his authority, in particular in order to restrict that of Ptolemy. Antioch-Alabanda is one of the cities in the interior of Karia which Antiochos I (or II) renamed as Antioch. It was on the Marsyas River, a tributary of the Maiandros, which was a frontier region where the king carefully operated to extend his power. North of Alabanda two other places in the valley of the Maiandros were founded or re-founded; Antiochos I seems to have been responsible for founding Nysa and for renaming Tralleis as Seleukeia.[12] (Nysa appears to have been named for a member of the royal family; this is a helpful indication of the existence of a second wife, or she may be a daughter, of Antiochos I.) These cities established his control of the route along the Maiandros Valley, which led from the interior towards Ephesos on the Aegean coast. Ephesos was held for much of the third century by the Ptolemies and was obviously a major source of influence; Nysa and Tralleis therefore boxed in that influence. Thirty kilometres south of Alabanda along the Marsyas Valley, Antiochos I founded Stratonikeia, named for his wife, near the headwaters of the river. An inscription from the site shows that it had been Ptolemaic territory some time earlier. Its territory included two locally important temples, including the sanctuary of Zeus Chrysaoreus, which was the centre for a local religious league of cities, and 'the common possession on all Karians'.[13] Karia was a region repeatedly contested between the Seleukids and the Ptolemies (and it had been the base for the Macedonian dynast Eupolemos earlier). Establishing some measure of control over the sanctuary sensibly expanded the king's or dynast's influence, even control.

This series of cities, from Nysa and Tralleis to Stratonikeia, were therefore founded in a diplomatic and urbanizing campaign where the intention was first to restrict the Ptolemaic reach and influence emanating from the coast, and then to establish a Seleukid presence in its place. This was a largely quiet process, done with a certain amount of stealth, which was helped by Ptolemy's concentration elsewhere, but also by persuading the local communities to accept Seleukid sponsorship. Thus the area where Stratonikeia was founded had been Ptolemaic in some way in and after 282, but the organization of a new city trumped that Ptolemaic probe.

This sort of activity was partly forced on Antiochos by the need to keep the peace with Ptolemy, but it was also part of his political inheritance. It was only the Seleukid dynasty which used the mass foundation of cities in this way, and it was Seleukos who had originated the practice. Antigonos had founded several cities, usually for strategic purposes, along the Asian coast of the Hellespont, and he and the other new kings founded their dynastic cities – Kassandreia, Lysimacheia, and so on – as part of their mutual contest and their need for power and prestige. Seleukos himself had done that with Seleukeia-on-the-Tigris. But it was his response to the problem of controlling and defending North Syria by converting it into the Seleukis which Antiochos was drawing on for his inspiration in Asia Minor.

The example of the Marsyas Valley was replicated elsewhere in the peninsula. A similar strategic initiative perhaps lay behind two other new cities in the north. One of the dynasts who were part of Antigonos I's inheritance was Philetairos of Pergamon, guardian of part of Lysimachos' treasure. He had earned Antiochos' gratitude by his treason to Lysimachos and by rescuing the murdered body of Seleukos I, but he was also, as these deeds show, an independent character, and Antiochos planted two cities to restrict him. Philetairos did not make any overt move to make himself independent, but he developed his city of Pergamon into a well-defended centre of his power. From there he deliberately extended his influence through the surrounding regions. Thirty kilometres from Pergamon was the centre of a cult of Meter, to which several local communities were attached; Philetairos made offerings, and enlarged the temple; it was a means to influence these places.[14] (This was a similar influence to that which was used by the Seleukids in the south where the role of Meter was taken by Zeus Chrysaoreus.) Philetairos helped Kyzikos when that city was badly damaged in the Galatian wars.[15] His aim was apparently to establish a predominant influence within north-west Anatolia, from the Kaikos River (near which Pergamon stands), north as far as Kyzikos and the Sea of Marmara.

In view of this two of Antiochos' foundations can be seen to have been sited with a view to restricting Philetairos. At the headwaters of the Kaikos River was established the city of Stratonikeia; the name provides the dating, which is confirmed by its appearance on coins of the 190s; it is also on a major north-south route from the major centres of Seleukid power in Lydia towards the Sea of Marmara, thereby blocking Philetairos' expansion eastwards, and guarding a rival route to the north.[16] The second of Antiochos' anti-Pergamene operations in that region was at the town of Kebren, in the inland part of the Troad, north of Mount Ida. Kebren had been somewhat battered by Antiochos' predecessors. It had been included by Antigonos in a synoecism which produced his new city of Antigoneia, whose name was later changed by Lysimachos to Alexandria Troas. Evidently this synoecism did not entail Kebren's physical destruction, nor did it meet with the approval of the citizens, who still existed as a distinct community when Antiochos I allowed the Kebrenites to secede from Alexandria. He brought it and a neighbouring town, Birytis, into a new Antioch, distinguished as Antioch-Kebren to mark it out from all the others.[17]

This city became an island of Seleukid influence in a region of varied influences, of which that of Philetairos approached overland from the south and whoever was powerful at sea was just as important. It was clearly worth gaining local support with the new foundation, and by detaching Kebren from Alexandria Troas he was probably bidding for such support, and checking the expansion of Pergamene influence. Antiochos also established close relations with Alexandria Troas itself, and with Ilion north along the coast, and he had a treaty with Lysimacheia across the Hellespont.[18] Here was a region where several political authorities contended in a more or less polite way, and in which the pieces on the board were the local cities whose support was purchasable, at least temporarily, with favours.

The importance of the Royal Road for Seleukid authority in Asia Minor has been mentioned more than once in this study. With the establishment of

Galatian power in north-central Anatolia parts of the road had become much more vulnerable to interruption than before, notably the central section. To the south were the Pisidian Hills, whose inhabitants were a thorn in the side of every ruling power in Asia Minor throughout ancient times. They and the Galatians approached the road from both directions, so that it ran along a corridor only a few tens of miles wide, winding between hills and lakes and rivers. There is no evidence that the Pisidians and Galatians ever co-operated in their raids (except for a multi-party enterprise in Lykia), but both were close enough to the road to cut it if and when they wished.

It was in this pinch point that a series of cities was founded or refounded in the time of Antiochos I, clearly, once again, from strategic necessity, to ensure the Seleukid grip on the essential road connecting Syria and western Asia Minor. Apamea-Kelainai might be counted as one of these cities, a major base at the start of the difficult section; an Apollonia was founded a short distance to the east; and south of this was Seleukeia (later sallied Sidera, 'the iron') planted squarely in the gap between two of the lakes. Apollonia may have claimed Seleukos as founder, and Apollo was the chosen god of the Seleukid dynasty; there were many Macedonian names among those of the citizens of Metropolis (though this might imply that the city had been founded at any time since Alexander)[19]. Lysias and Philomelion were the foundations of Lysias the dynast, who probably came to Asia Minor with Seleukos (though one would suppose the cities could have been founded in the reign of his son). Dominating the territory between two of the great lakes of the region was Antioch-near-Pisidia, with Neapolis somewhat to the south. Antioch's name guarantees that it was a Seleukid foundation, and it was probably Antiochos I who planted it. The founding colonists apparently came from Magnesia-on-Maiandros, but another group seem to have been Thracians;[20] Thracians were also among the settlers at Neapolis, which could date the origin to Antiochos' reign.[21] The invasion and ravaging of Thrace by the Galatians could have sent refugees into Asia, and there were Thracian units in the Seleukid army. (In the raids into Lykia later there were Thracians along with Galatians and Pisidians, so not all contingents settled down peacefully in cities.)[22]

These cities were reinforced by those founded by Dokimos (Dokimeion, to the north of the road), whose original base was the old Phrygian town of Synnada halfway between Lysias and Dokimeion. Further east at some point the city of Laodikeia Katakekaumene ('the Burnt') was planted square on the road. The date of this foundation is not clear. So far as is known

Antiochos I did not use that name in his foundations, but this is hardly a good argument for denying his authorship, even if the earliest note of the city's existence is in the Roman period.[23] The position of the city has to be seen in relation to the other places on and near the Royal Road, and in that case it is clearly part of a system developed to control the road and to deter raids upon it. So if it was not founded by Antiochos I it was in all likelihood part of his original scheme. Antiochos I's son, Antiochos II, did found at least one other city called Laodikeia, named after his wife, though the name had also been used by Seleukos I; he could thus have been responsible for the last of the road cities.

Finally there was a group of cities in the area between those planted to protect the great road, and those forming part of Ptolemaic sea power along the Ionian and Karian coasts. In the Maiandros Valley there were several places in addition to those already mentioned which had already existed as towns or even cities before the Seleukid times, and which were founded or refounded, or perhaps just garrisoned and renamed, in order to assert Seleukid control. Antioch-on-the-Maiandros was formed, it seems, by the union of two places, Symmaethos and Kranaos, probably under the guidance of Antiochos I. It reinforced control of the valley, and was situated where the Royal Road crossed the Maiandros by a bridge.[24] A little to the south lay two further cities attributed to Antiochos I, Herakleia and Apollonia, both surnamed 'Salbake' from a nearby mountain. The latter seems to have had a cult temple of Seleukos I, but his time in Asia Minor was so brief it seems unlikely he could found the city in such a relatively out-of-the-way spot; if the founding was the work of Antiochos I then the cult may also have been his work.[25] On the other hand here is Apollo again, and it is quite possible that Seleukos was, in later generations, viewed as the founder by the citizens by association. Hierapolis, near the Lykos River, can be more securely attributed to the work of Antiochos I. It included, at least later, men who claimed to be Macedonian (as did the Seleukid kings, of course), and several of the city tribes were named for Seleukid kings and queens.[26] East along the road from Antioch was Laodikeia-on-the-Lykos, probably a foundation of Antiochos II named for his first wife, whom he put aside in 253. As he was fully occupied with a war from the time of his accession until then, it seems likely that the foundation of a city at this place was planned by his father. Its institutions laid considerable emphasis on its Seleukid origin, with the tribal names, a festival called the Antiocheia, and worship of Apollo. The site was a new urban one, though it incorporated two villages, Diospolis and Rhoas.

Its plan shows the characteristic Seleukid layout of a fortified city planted on a minor plateau with valleys all round and an acropolis on a higher hill in one corner.[27] This group of cities was a tight set of Seleukid foundations in a relatively small area – it is only 100km from Nysa to Laodikeia – so the process established a distinctly Seleukid mark on this urban landscape.

To the north in the valley of the Hermos there is much less evidence of Seleukid work. The main centre here was Sardis, the city used by the Seleukids as their administrative capital. The shift from Apameia-Kelainai, which performed that function under Antigonos, to Sardis, was a mark of the shift from the administration of Anatolia to its defence against Ptolemy. Antigonos did not have to concern himself with threats from the Aegean, but Antiochos I and his son did.

There is plenty of evidence in this area to show that there were settlements of Macedonians. Most of these do not seem ever to have been cities; perhaps it was the preference of some Macedonians to live a rural life. But the result was that this central part of the old Lydian kingdom was thickly planted with Macedonian settlers, as it had been earlier with Iranians. This was always the heart of power in western Anatolia until the rise of Constantinople, and settling Macedonians – probably the work of Antigonos and Lysimachos – was a sensible political move.[28]

The location of the cities in the Maiandros Valley and along the Royal Road makes it clear that the overall purpose of founding and developing them was both to defend and to control the population, native and immigrant. The cities surrounding the Pisidians were designed to prevent them from raiding into the lower, richer lands, though they were also useful as bases from which the Seleukid forces themselves could mount attacks into the hills if this was thought necessary.

All this apparent defensiveness may have been uncharacteristic for a Hellenistic king, but perhaps it did not really go against the general tendency of specifically Seleukid methods. Seleukos I had only advanced to the attack on anyone when he was sure that his opponent was beatable. This method was evident all through his career from the battle of Gaza through to Koroupedion. He had waited twenty years before seeking his revenge on Lysimachos for the short change he had received from the booty of Antigonos' destruction. Ptolemy I was also cautious, but Seleukos' version was different. Ptolemy I from the start aimed to hold Egypt, and then identified his defensive needs as the supplementary control of Palestine and Cyrenaica, taking over those lands early on. When ejected he returned to them when he could, in a policy he pursued tenaciously from 320 until his death. Seleukos by contrast was always interested in expansion, and if defeated, as he may have been in India, he cut his losses and went elsewhere – just as he had when challenged by Antigonos in Babylon in 315.

Antiochos I's policy in Asia Minor had plenty of subtle aggressiveness within it, even if it appears defensive. The series of cities in the Maiandros and Marsyas Valleys – Tralleis, Nysa, Alabanda, Stratonikeia – was certainly designed to block Ptolemaic expansion from the coast, but he also, particularly at Stratonikeia, took over areas which Ptolemy II had earlier sought to control; the whole set of places appears defensive, but the advance to Stratonikeia was surely an opportunity he created by developing or founding the other cities. On a small scale, it was reminiscent of his father.

This was the exception in a generally defensive and controlling pattern. Antiochos had begun by following his father's policy of attempting to establish his control over the whole peninsula, excepting only the cities on the Ptolemaic-dominated western coast, since neither he nor his father wished to be involved in a Ptolemaic war. But after the Galatian and Egyptian wars were over it seems clear that Antiochos became concerned to hold what he had gained and to consolidate his grip. The several minor states along the north coast were left alone; indeed, the settlement of the Galatians in the north of Kappadokia increased their number. Evidently Antiochos did not feel strong enough to tackle them with a view to conquest; even Philetairos was treated with suspicion, but no more.

The Galatian settlement appears to have been encouraged, or perhaps even supervised, by Mithradates of Pontos. He will have been quite pleased to be able to place them across his southern boundary where they could act as a defence for his kingdom against any further Seleukid pressure. For the moment the Kappadokians clearly bore the brunt of the Galatian presence. The Galatians were anything but peaceful, operating in 266 against the Ptolemaic landing at Amisos, and in the late 250s intervening again in another succession dispute in Bithynia, and raiding in Lykia. They were in a sense still nomadic for a time, but their future political centres of Ankyra and Tavium, and their respect for the sanctuary of Kybele at Pessinos, operated in all likelihood from the start. They subdued the local population, and the size of their later armies suggests that they were fairly quickly integrated.[29] In effect their settlement was much the same in its social results as that of the Greeks and Macedonians planted throughout the Middle East and since Alexander's time; a caste of immigrants over a subjugated native population.

The Seleukid kingdom in Asia Minor was considerably reduced by the loss of resources caused by the Galatian war – mainly manpower, of course – but there is also evidently a shift in policy from military campaigns of conquest and towards expanding the king's territory by founding or acquiring cities. This, of course, as in Syria, would also eventually solve the manpower problem by generating a new citizenry whose young men were liable for military service. This is one explanation for the lack of aggressiveness after about 275, but other factors may have been at work also; Antiochos by 270 was in his fifties, and the necessity (as he surely saw it) of executing his son in 267 may have sapped his will. On the other hand, the quiet, careful, chess-like expansion against the Ptolemaic lands in the west is quite clear. He could not afford to be too obvious in his advances, since he was bound by the peace treaty which ended the fighting in 271, and any overt aggression might bring on a new war. But a constant diplomatic intrigue to deprive Ptolemy of marginal territories and influence was clearly permissible and was not seen as a reason for war. Similarly it is clear that the Galatians accepted the principle that a peace treaty lasted until the death of one of the parties, and so most Galatian attention was directed northwards, and raids elsewhere could be ascribed to dissident bands. Antiochos could assume he was free of attacks by the main Galatian bands he had defeated for several years at least, and of an attack by Ptolemy until one of them died.

In the last ten years of his reign therefore Antiochos was able to concentrate on consolidating his hold on the central areas of Asia Minor and securing full control of the Royal Road, and on setting up the organization and fortification of his territories to block any future Ptolemaic advances. He did not seriously challenge the Ptolemaic position, except marginally, but at the same time Philetairos of Pergamon was steadily developing a policy of increasing independence and influence, using Seleukid methods against Antiochos. The situation was in fact unstable, and was only held in check by Ptolemy's preoccupation with the Khremonideian war (until c.261) and by the peace treaty of 271.

The first break came in 263, when Philetairos died. He left his wealth, his position, and his territories to his nephew Eumenes, who at once asserted his position without reference to Antiochos, technically his suzerain, who should have been consulted on any changes. (Maybe he was consulted, we don't know, but Eumenes clearly did not seek his agreement.) Eumenes, in other words, was making himself a wholly independent ruler.

Strabo called Philetairos the 'master of Pergamon', but Eumenes was a 'dynast of the surrounding country'.[30] Antiochos had no choice but to object to Eumenes' self-promotion, and to the removal of Pergamon from his kingdom, which is what Eumenes was doing. To enforce his authority, he prepared to launch an attack. Eumenes evidently had prepared for this, and a battle was fought between their forces near Sardis, in which the Seleukid forces were defeated. This was Antiochos' local capital, so Eumenes had invaded Antiochos' territory rather than waiting to be attacked, and had probably caught Antiochos by surprise and without the full levy of troops from the region.[31]

A single defeat would not normally be more than a spur to further activity for a Seleukid king, especially when inflicted by a minor ruler such as Eumenes – referred to, note, by Strabo as a 'dynast', the equivalent of Lysias and the others. But in this case it appears that Antiochos quickly made peace, thereby in effect recognizing Eumenes' independence. It may have helped that Eumenes did not use his victory to claim the title of king, which would have humiliated Antiochos into taking further action. Perhaps, though, the main reason for Antiochos' restraint was his age; he died two years later, in June 261, aged over 60, so perhaps he was already ill and weary.

Antiochos' death happened at about the same time as the end of the Khremonideian war; indeed that war may have ended in part because of Antiochos' death, since the peace treaty of 271 now no longer operated, and Ptolemy II was free to consider a new Syrian war, or was concerned that he might be attacked by the new king. Antiochos' successor was his son Antiochos II, his joint-king for the past several years. The new king was married to Laodike, the daughter of Akhaios (after whom he named the two cities Laodikeia Katakekumene and Laodikeia-on-the-Lykos). They already had children, though they were still young, the eldest son being about 20-years-old in 246, and so he was born in or before 266 and the marriage had happened before that. Laodike must have been at least 15-years-old when she married, and so her birth took place before 284 or 283, perhaps several years before. They had thus been married since before Antiochos became joint-king. They had three sons and two daughters, all born before 253, when the parents separated. (If Akhaios was the son of Seleukos I, Antiochos II was married to his cousin, hardly a surprise in any royal family of the time.)

Antiochos I's careful expansion at Ptolemy's expense in a series of small areas of Asia Minor was not answered by Ptolemy II until he was both free of the Khremonideian war and Antiochos I was dead. By then Ptolemy could contemplate a new Syrian war without the possibility of having to fight in Greece at the same time. In 260 he installed his son Ptolemy Epigonos, 'the Son', as ruler of Ephesos; at about the same time he put his stepson Ptolemy son of Lysimachos into control of the Lykian city of Telmessos.

These were actions similar to those which had been taken by Antiochos I in Asia Minor but more destabilizing, especially when the new and recent independence of Eumenes of Pergamon is added into the account. Ptolemy Lysimachou was the son of Arsinoe II, the widow of Lysimachos and the wife of Ptolemy II until her death in 270. He had been in Egypt since he and his mother had fled for refuge there from Ptolemy Keraunos in 280. Even then he had been old enough to voice his suspicions of Keraunos' motives, and so in his 'teens, by 260 he was in his thirties. Yet he was now suddenly produced and installed close to the land which his father had ruled until twenty years before. His principality was small, only a single city, but it was his presence in Anatolia which was potent; he could not be seen by Antiochos II as anything but a threat.[32]

The installation of Ptolemy the Son at Ephesos was similarly an indication that Ptolemy II was thinking aggressively. The Son seems to have been his eldest son, and had been joint-king since 267.[33] Therefore he had been groomed for the succession, and sending him to Ephesos was a way of giving him experience in ruling without direct supervision, just as Seleukos I had successfully trained Antiochos. But the scheme went wrong. The Son rebelled, almost as soon as he was put in place, in alliance with an Aitolian mercenary commander, Timarchos, who commanded the garrison at Miletos. Timarchos made himself tyrant at Miletos, seized control of Samos, and then, having moved into Ephesos in agreement with the Son, had him killed; Timarchos had thus made himself a dynast, and controlled a neat little principality. This did not last long. By 258 Ptolemy II was back in control of Ephesos, and meanwhile Antiochos II had both removed Timarchos from Miletos and gained control of that city; Samos reverted to Ptolemaic control.[34]

But Antiochos' move meant that Miletos had shifted from the Ptolemaic to the Seleukid sphere. In a way this was no more than what Antiochos I had been doing in places such as Stratonikeia, but this was a major city and seaport, and it was the first city along the Asia Minor coast to have fallen into firm Seleukid control. No matter how or why this had happened, Ptolemy II could only see it as an attack on his position in the whole region, and a move which was no longer semi-clandestine and which could be ignored, as had been the case at Stratonikeia, or the installation of Ptolemy Lysimachou at Telmessos. This is in fact the first move in the 'Second Syrian War'.

The war thus begun would be fought elsewhere than in Ionia. In the Aegean Ptolemy's power depended on his fleet, which was of little use in waging war against a Seleukid inland empire, which consisted by now largely of an archipelago of well-fortified cities. Further, the city of Rhodes, normally a staunch Ptolemaic friend, took the Seleukid side in this war, though we do not know why. The lack of the opportunity for gaining territory or for campaigning in Asia Minor, and the hostility of Rhodes, may be why Ptolemy shifted the focus of the war to Syria. The work of Antiochos I in constructing a formidable fortified defence in Asia Minor may thus be said to have been effective. It may also help to explain the installation of Ptolemy Lysimachou at Telmessos, close to Rhodes, perhaps as a local agent, and to ensure continuing Ptolemaic influence in the Lykian mainland. So the war which began with a dispute over Miletos became a truly Syrian war.

Chapter Thirteen

Antiochos II

The effects of the war which began about 259, the 'Second Syrian War', bade fair to destroy the Seleukid kingdom.[1] It had begun, of course, with a relatively minor dispute over control of two Ionian cities, but Ptolemy II deliberately moved the action eastwards to Syria. There is, just as with the First War, little or no record of any of the events of the fighting, but scraps of evidence from archaeology, and a sign of trouble at one of the cities, allows some inferences to be made.

Ptolemy's army, in invading Seleukid Syria, faced formidable problems. The area was now dotted with walled cities, garrisoned and prepared, and populated by citizens loyal to the new king. The succession of Antiochos II had been, so far as we know, quietly accepted there, though there was a disturbance in Babylon, where Antiochos I was when he died. A man called Seleukos, not the king's son of that name, caused some trouble. The tablets on which the diarist recorded what happened are fragmentary so details are lost, but someone was killed by impaling, usually a sign of a conviction for treason; there was trouble with the guard in a fortress, probably in Babylon; later, valuables were stored in the royal palace at Babylon against an enemy.[2] The problem is that the enemy, unless it was the troublesome Seleukos, is not identified. (One wonders if the 'Seleukos' was an imposter, claiming to be the dead prince.) It is possible the trouble was bad enough to bring Antiochos II to Babylon.

If this last was so, then, combined with the disturbances at Miletos and Ephesos, it is hardly surprising that Ptolemy II took advantage of Antiochos' difficulties. The evidence for his military incursion into Syria is indirect, though difficult to account for except by warfare. A hoard of Ptolemaic gold coins was found near Antioch.[3] All the coins date to between 261 and 259, and since Ptolemaic coins did not circulate in the Seleukid kingdom, they can only have been brought to Syria by a Ptolemaic official – one imagines him to be a military paymaster, or a quartermaster. This would imply a Ptolemaic military campaign in the region of Antioch and Seleukeia in 259 or 258.

In Kilikia next door, where the cities were less densely sown, another Ptolemaic coin hoard, again of gold coins, has been found at the ancient city site of Kelenderis in Rough Kilikia.[4] This is a region where Ptolemy II had probably had a presence, at least along the coast, before the war, as one or more of a string of Ptolemaic naval bases maintained along the south Anatolian coast. The burial of the hoard, as with that near Antioch, suggests that there was fighting in the area. There was also fighting in the Seleukid part of the country, Smooth Kilikia, where the mint in the city of Tarsos, which had been producing coins for Antiochos II from the start of his reign, switched to the production of Ptolemaic coins not long after Antiochos' accession. This fighting lasted for two or three years, that is, say 259 to 257, for all these events were concentrated in that brief period.[5] It seems reasonable to conclude that this was a time when a Ptolemaic military force operated against the cities of Syria and Kilikia. At least one city, Tarsos, was apparently captured, but the invaders had no success in Syria. Possibly the defeated Ptolemaic forces were pursued as far as Kelenderis. It may be assumed that the Ptolemaic forces were expelled in 258 from Syria and from Tarsos and Kilikia a little later.

It was exactly in that brief period that a major change took place in the relationship of the city of Arados and the Seleukid king. Arados was the only Phoenician city to be part of the Seleukid section of Syria. It was built on an island a short distance from the coast – just as Tyre had been before Alexander's assault-mole linked it to the mainland. It also controlled, or aspired to control, a stretch of the adjacent mainland, its *peraia*, where there were a string of towns and villages. This was perhaps 70km of coast, from the mouth of the Eleutheros River northwards. The river formed the boundary between the Ptolemaic and Seleukid parts of Syria, and the city's territory also stretched inland for some way along the river. Arados therefore dominated this strategic region of the coast and the lower river valley of the Eleutheros, both of which regions were useful routes by which a Ptolemaic army could invade Syria. The river valley in particular was a very useful route connecting the coast with the interior, between the Lebanon and the Bargylos mountain ranges; Apameia had been built just to prevent a Ptolemaic invasion reaching much farther inland.[6]

In 259 Arados' calendrical era was changed. The city abandoned the Seleukid era and began to use a new one, with 259 as the new Year 1. The evidence for this is in the coins the city produced, but the precise details of any change in the status of the city other than its coinage are not known, though it is significant that the local monarchy now disappears.[7] It is reasonable to assume that the replacement of the Seleukid era by one applying to the city alone implies a change in the governing regime in the city. That this took place just at the time when the kingdom was plunged into a new war can hardly be a coincidence. The regime change was sufficient to keep Arados on the Seleukid side in the war, perhaps by the removal of the king and the installation of a friendlier city government. It was not the last time the city would be involved in this way.

The Second Syrian War lasted until 253 or 252, and ended with a negotiated peace treaty. But in that period other changes besides that at Arados took place. The conflict over Ephesos continued until perhaps 258, when the city fell to a combined attack by Rhodian ships and the Seleukid army, apparently under Antiochos' own command.[8] In the Troad meanwhile the alliance of the Seleukid king with Ilion and Alexandria Troas evolved into Seleukid near-control of those cities, the city coinages being replaced by royal control of the mints, implying a much closer supervision by Seleukid officials of both the mint and the city itself.[9] No doubt the threat of a Ptolemaic naval attack upon these cities of the coast was instanced as the reason.

Elsewhere in Asia Minor, however, there were clear signs that Seleukid authority had ebbed during the conflict. In Bithynia the king had founded a new city in 264. It was named Nikomedia for himself, and it was an action which, like the founding of the Seleukid cities in Asia Minor and Syria, rendered his kingdom more defensible. It was populated by the people of Astakos nearby, who were shifted to the new site. It became the king's 'royal city'.[10]

In Pergamon Eumenes had trouble with a band of mercenaries he had recruited. They had to be conciliated with a formal treaty by which they were settled in two new settlements, Philetairia and Attalcia. The first is distinguished as 'under Mount Ida', and is suggested to have been east of that mountain, since the land to the west is thought to have already belonged to other cities, including Antioch-Kebren and Alexandria Troas. Attaleia was placed to the east of Pergamon in a most carefully chosen position, at the headwaters of a tributary of the Hermos River, only a few miles from the Stratonikeia founded not long before by Antiochos II.[11] Attaleia therefore was placed so as to block or control the same north-south route which Stratonikeia had been founded to control. These two bases, named for Eumenes' uncle and his father, were thus planted in order to extend

Eumenes' territory, converting an area under Philetairos' influence into one under Eumenes' control. It is also probably in this region that he gained control of the seaport of Elaia; never large, this was a town and port capable of development into an important naval base.[12] Eumenes very carefully kept clear of the Syrian war being waged all around him, but he used the distraction to which his more powerful neighbours were subjected to reach out and extend his territory and to make it better defended; like Philetairos he was using Seleukid methods against the Seleukid king.

Something similar happened in the interior. The Galatians had been blocked from attacking Seleukid territory by the victories of Antiochos I and by his vigorous policy of fortifying his defences, but they had fought elsewhere in Asia Minor. They had been settled, hardly by chance, at the intersection of Pontos and Kappadokia, with Bithynia and Armenia not very far off, so their raids and relationships were with these lands. Their friendship with Mithradates of Pontos appears to have continued with his son Ariobarzanes, as it had with Nikomedes of Bithynia, but both of these kings died in about 255, and this appears – the sources are, as usual, few and difficult – to have triggered a series of changes in the region.[13]

The deaths of the kings were greeted by the Galatians in contrasting ways. The Galatian-Bithynian connection was demonstrated again in the 250s. The death of Nikomedes I, the Galatians' ally, opened up another dispute over the succession. Nikomedes had married twice, and named his son by his second wife, Zipoetes, as his heir. This was disputed by the son of the first wife, Ziaelas, who was in exile in Armenia. Ziaelas allied with the Tolistobogian Galatians and campaigned to secure the throne. In the event he succeeded, but more by a solution negotiated by Herakleia Pontike than by conquest. Deprived of the loot they had expected to gather in the campaign, the Galatians blamed Herakleia for their 'loss' and raided the city's lands as a recompense.[14]

At about the same time one of the lords of Kappadokia, Ariarathes 'III', made himself king, again about 255. It is perhaps inevitable to assume that all these changes in the north had something to do with the Syrian War being fought at the time. It is certainly true that both the great kingdoms came under serious pressure during the war, but there is no obvious link with events in the north of Anatolia. The several kings appear, for example, to have died naturally. The case of Kappadokia may be said to emphasize this lack of connection. Ariarathes III was the latest of a family of Iranian aristocrats to have power in the country, though his recent predecessors are almost invisible in the records, and the extent of their sway is not known. One might guess that they emerged from a crowd of lords as the most effective defenders against Galatian raids. The event of 255 here was that Ariarathes took the title of king.[15] Normally a self-promotion such as this took place as the result of a military victory, and it is noticeable that the Ariarathid family, though they had ruled in some way in Kappadokia since before Alexander, only now did so. No doubt the country had suffered repeated raids and invasions in the previous decades, first by the Macedonians and now by the Galatians. Seleukos I seems to have conquered part of Kappadokia as booty from the Antigonid kingdom, since there is a region called Seleukid Kappadokia. Since Ariarathes III made himself king in 255 it seems likely he had won a battle – or yet another battle – probably against the Galatians. It is worth noting that Ariarathes was not a new ruler when he took the title. If he won a battle he will have been in power for some years. At the same time it is likely that he had not been long in control, since a war with the Galatians in all probability came soon after his accession.

He took his new title perhaps by winning his battle and by agreement with Antiochos II. Any Galatian defeat would be welcome, and Ariarathes was no threat to Antiochos. Indeed Antiochos provided him with a royal wife, his daughter Stratonike, to be his queen, just at this time. This certainly indicates the Seleukid acceptance of the new kingship, and it is possible that Antiochos handed over Seleukid Kappadokia to his son-in-law as a dowry, or as a wedding present. (Another possibility is that Ariarathes' status was raised in order to make him eligible for his royal wife.) The political result was to make Kappadokia a Seleukid sub-kingdom, one which was presumably now sufficiently organized to be a viable state.

There was therefore by this date a line of well-established kingdoms along the north of Anatolia – Bithynia, Pontos, and now Kappadokia – and a less well-organized region of Galatian settlement in the interior. This was still divided among the three original tribes, the Trocmi, Tolistobogii and Tectosages, who occupied separate and contiguous parts of Galatia. The Trocmi were the furthest east, making a centre at Tavium near the old Hittite capital of Boghazkoy; the Tectosages were to their west, with Ankyra, still only a village, as their centre and probably with the Halys River as their boundary with the Trocmi; the Tolistobogii were further west again, in the area of the old Phrygian centre of Gordion and the valley of the Sangarius River, which was presumably why Ziaelas who had hired them in pursuit of his claim to the kingship; they were the closest to Bithynia. Being a disunited group the Galatians as a whole were unpredictable; any of the tribes, or indeed any section of a tribe, could set off on a raid alone. One of the better ways of reducing this capability was by recruiting their young manhood as mercenaries – so long as they could be kept under control.[16]

East again was the kingdom of Armenia, under yet another surviving Iranian aristocratic family. In their mountains they seem to have kept well clear of any entanglements with Seleukid affairs, as did their eastern neighbour, the kingdom of Media Atropatene. All this meant that the Seleukid kings had to be constantly vigilant in order to ensure that these potential enemies – actual enemies, in some cases – were deterred from interfering. The marriage of Stratonike to Ariarathes suggests that Antiochos II had his own ideas about policy towards these kings.

The difficult beginning of the Second Syrian War, and Antiochos' concentration on events in Syria and Asia Minor, meant that the eastern satrapies received little attention from Antiochos II, and in fact had probably not been visited by Antiochos I once he had succeeded his father in 281. Satraps were of course appointed, though we know of none for a couple of decades. Antiochos II was presumably responsible for the appointment of Diodotos as satrap of Baktria some time in the 250s, and he held this post all through the rest of that king's reign. No doubt he did so because he was successful. At least one serious enemy is recorded as having been defeated by him and driven out of Baktria, though this cannot have been an unusual occurrence.[17]

Their distance from the events of the Second Syrian War meant that Parthia and Baktria were less than wholly subject to Antiochos II's authority. Diodotos I did move towards independence, but this was not achieved until the next reign. This slow separation was, of course, a function of the isolation of Baktria from events in the west, and Diodotos' necessary concentration on local affairs.

An attempt was made by Justin to link events in the west and east, but it is unconvincing.[18] He has the name of a Roman consul wrong, and all the other events we know of are clearly to be dated to the time of Seleukos II. It may be that something happened in about 256 – Justin's apparent date – in the east, perhaps a major nomad raid into Baktria, but it appears to have had no wider consequences other than to introduce enough confusion to keep historians puzzled.

These events in the east would seem, therefore, to have had little or nothing to do with the progress or otherwise of the war in the west, though the lack of Seleukid response to the events in Media and Baktria was certainly a consequence of that war. Antiochos II, involved in Asia Minor and with the threat of another invasion of Syria, could not attend to any eastern problems. It may be that Diodotos was enlisted to respond, if he needed to be gingered up, and it may be that he did so, but the net result was clear evidence of a serious weakening of the imperial system, with a clear potential for the separation of east and west.

In addition, there was more trouble in Babylonia. It is frustrating that the fragments of the Babylonian diarist's work are so discontinuous. There had certainly been a major problem at the time of Antiochos II's accession in 261, when a man was impaled and the royal palace served as a refuge for the local wealth. At that time the satrap is named as 'Terunu', which is a Babylonian version of a Greek name (possibly Theron). That however is all that we can glean from the diary for 260. There follows a gap in the record until 255, when another fragment comments that someone 'entered Babylon'. This could be Antiochos, on one of his fairly regular visits. The next sentence, however, claims that the troubles of 261 still continued, or had returned: 'the people of the land ... in ... in battle in the district of Eridu opposite Esangil.'[19]

The diary rarely uses the word 'battle', so in this case it would seem that a fairly substantial encounter had taken place. 'Esangil' is the name of the great temple of Bel-Marduk in Babylon. 'Eridu' was, as he says, a 'district', but more to the point it is a distinct walled area within Babylon city, right in the centre, with Esangil a short distance south of it. That is, the battle took place in the very centre of the city. The temptation is to link the fighting with whoever 'entered Babylon' in the previous sentence, but whatever was happening, it was clearly serious, and the king would have to take note. This took place in all probability as a consequence of the strain of the war with Ptolemy. But the sheer geographical range of the issues the king had to attend to is an indication of his difficulties.

Antiochos II's conduct of the Second Syrian War had been generally successful. He had seen off Ptolemy's invasion of Syria and Kilikia. He had more than held his own among the cities of the Aegean coast. He had obviously had to concentrate attention and forces on these areas, so that events in other areas, perhaps even in Babylon, had had to be left to local satraps, or deferred for later attention. But in addition he had laid considerable emphasis on diplomacy as a means of frustrating whatever intentions Ptolemy had. He had neutralized any hostility from Kappadokia by recognizing Ariarathes as king and giving him a daughter; he had induced Rhodes to join him in fighting against Ptolemy for the only time in Rhodian history – at least one may assume Antiochos was the persuader; any trouble from the Galatians was obviated when they became involved in the succession war in Bithynia; this was probably not Antiochos' doing, but he certainly did nothing to stop it, and was no doubt happy to profit by it. He arranged the marriage of his other sister, another Stratonike, to the heir to the Macedonian kingship, who became Demetrios II in 239 on the death of Antigonos II Gonatas.[20]

It is not clear when the marriage took place. Demetrios was the son of Antigonos and Phila, who was Antiochos' half-sister. Stratonike was presumably the youngest child of Antiochos I and Stratonike the daughter of Demetrios I, and since the elder daughter (Apama) was already married to Magas of Cyrenaica in 275, and Phila to Antigonos Gonatas in 276, the marriage cannot have taken place until Phila's son was fairly adult – which would be about 250 at the earliest. So the marriage was arranged perhaps in the interval between the end of the Khremonideian War (in which Antigonos fought Ptolemy), and the beginning of the Syrian War (in which Antiochos fought Ptolemy), or possibly during that last war, but in any case it would become a major signal to Ptolemy that he just might have to fight both kings. It seems that Demetrios was some years younger than his wife, which may explain some later events.

The diplomatic expertise exercised by Antiochos II is directly relevant to the peace agreement which he secured with Ptolemy to end their war. Their mutual invasions had involved little transfer of territory; Ptolemaic attacks in Syria and Kilikia had been repelled; the Seleukid attacks in Asia Minor had been marginally successful, in that Miletos had become Seleukid, and a tighter grip had been established in other cities. For a seven-year-long war these were meagre results indeed.

Meanwhile both kings had problems. Antiochos' diplomacy may have shored up his position in the west, but there was clearly a serious continuing problem in Babylonia, specifically at Babylon city. The long period of Diodotos' government in Baktria was probably unusual, and suggests that Antiochos may have found it difficult to remove him, or simply neglected to. Ptolemy's problem seems to have been mainly financial. He had not suffered invasion so far as we know, but he was the only one of the great powers to maintain both a major fleet and a large army. Antiochos had no fleet worth considering, though his father had inherited ships which had been Lysimachos'. By 260 many of these will have reached the end of their lives (twenty-five years was the usual life of a Hellenistic galley).[21] Antigonos had an efficient fleet, and could call up a useful army, but his financial resources were much less than those of either of his rivals, and his forces were usually disbanded in peacetime.

Ptolemy used his fleet to maintain his empire. He had acquired permanent bases in the Aegean, at Itanos in Crete, on the island of Thera, and at Methana on the Greek mainland; he had control of the Island League of the Kyklades; he also had to maintain squadrons in Cyprus and in Egypt. One calculation suggests he had 4,000 ships in service, though the effective warship strength was probably a tenth of that.[22] In addition to this he had to maintain a substantial army, principally on the defensive in Syria facing a possible Seleukid attack, but he also had other armed forces with his fleets in Cyprus and in the Aegean. Since all these forces were permanently mobilized, and were mainly composed of mercenaries, in contrast to the Antigonid citizen forces, the whole military and naval establishment was extremely expensive.

In 258 Ptolemy launched a new survey to uncover untapped potential tax possibilities.[23] This, given the relentless squeeze already exerted on the peasantry of Egypt, suggests that the barely fought Second Syrian War had strained his resources to the breaking point as early as the second or third year of the fighting. No doubt his investigations were successful in finding new wealth to tax, but this was not an exercise which could be indulged in very often.

So by 255, if not before, both sides will have been searching for a way to make peace. Neither of course could admit the necessity, so such negotiations as there were will have been slow. Agreement, however, was reached in 253. Only one of what were probably several clauses of the agreement is known precisely; the delivery of Ptolemy's daughter Berenike to Antiochos as his new wife.

Antiochos was, of course, already married. His first wife was Laodike, the daughter of Akhaios, a marriage which ancient sources claim was a love match, but they only do so in the context of this second marriage, which in fact ended disastrously, and they are therefore retrospective judgments. Such judgments are unreliable, whether ancient or modern. (The marriage had taken place before Antiochos became joint-king, so the possibility of a love-match is heightened.) It is also the judgment of historians, particularly moderns, that this treaty was a Ptolemaic triumph, that he was inserting an asp into the Seleukid kingdom, to poison and destroy it. This is an interpretation which is open to doubt.

Certainly Ptolemy made a great fuss over the marriage. He sent Berenike north through Palestine and Phoenicia, travelling by land, when it would have been much easier to go by sea. She was accompanied by Apollonios the *dioiketes*, one of Ptolemy's senior ministers, was attended by a great suite of diplomats and servants and slaves and guards, and accompanied by rich gifts.[24] The marriage took place, very probably, in Antioch, and Ptolemy was assiduous in keeping contact with his daughter, even sending her water from the Nile, which was supposed to be a certain help in achieving pregnancy.[25] In short the marriage was given great publicity.

The marriage agreement may have included an item which required Antiochos to repudiate Laodike in some way, and it may have included one by which any son of Berenike's would become Antiochos' heir. Certainly this would explain a good deal of what happened later. It is also said that the dowry consisted of Koile Syria, the Ptolemaic lands of Palestine and Phoenicia. If this last idea was so, it would mean the transfer into Antiochos' control all the Ptolemaic lands from the Eleutheros River to Gaza. This would obviously count as a major diplomatic defeat for Ptolemy, so major in fact that it implies that Ptolemy had suffered a great military defeat in the war, and that the peace terms were being dictated by Antiochos. There is, however, no sign of such a clause being implemented. This simple fact cuts the ground from under the most extravagant interpretations. In particular the idea that Koile Syria was in some way delivered into Seleukid hands, or even that its tax product formed part of the dowry, is clear nonsense. No Ptolemaic king would ever deliver that land to the Seleukid enemy without a long and bitter fight, and no Seleukid king, having got hold of it, would let it go without another major fight. This element in the agreement cannot be admitted.

Similarly it does not seem to be required that Antiochos need repudiate his first wife. Nor in fact did he. Having two (or more) wives was hardly unusual in this time particularly among kings, just as marrying one's sister or niece was not in any way an unusual royal practice. It may not have been common among the general population, but royalty was always different. Ptolemy II had been married to his sister, who had been married earlier to her half-brother. Antigonos II had married his niece (Phila) and their son married the daughter of her father's sister. The great Macedonians, Philip II and Alexander the Great, had had multiple wives, as had Antigonos' father Demetrios; it is at least arguable that both Seleukos I and Antiochos I had had two wives simultaneously, even if the evidence is poor. There was no need for Antiochos to put away Laodike, though it seems he was careful to keep the two wives apart, Laodike in Ephesos, and Berenike in Antioch. The 'repudiation' which is supposed to have happened seems based on the absence of the royal title in the inscription which recorded the gift of an estate by Antiochos to Laodike. But Seleukid practice was inconsistent in this, and the gift is nowhere said to be a divorce settlement, as is sometimes assumed.[26]

Once Berenike was delivered and married, of course, there was little Ptolemy could do to enforce such a silly detail as insisting that Antiochos repudiate Laodike. On the other hand, it is possible that the death of Queen Stratonike, Antiochos' mother, may have had some effect on the situation. She died in 253, the year of the peace agreement, and the year before the marriage to Berenike. Stratonike was a prominent person in her own right, in Babylonia where she is noted in a building inscription from Borsippa, in Syria where she is associated with the development of the Atargatis temple at Hierapolis-Bambyke, in Asia Minor where she was honoured by the Ionian League, at Delos where she made numerous gifts to Apollo (as did her brother Antigonos Gonatas), at Sardis where she gave gifts to Artemis.[27] This last example gives a clue to the reason for her prominence, for she is there described as 'daughter of Demetrios, granddaughter of Antigonos', to which everyone could add wife of Seleukos I, wife of Antiochos I, and by the time of her death, mother of Antiochos II and of the Queens of Kappadokia and Cyrenaica. The Babylonian diaries noted in 274 that when Antiochos went to fight the Egyptians he left Queen Stratonike in Sardis, and twenty years later he noted that she had died, also at Sardis.[28]

Such a prominent and well-regarded woman would obviously have considerable influence at the royal court. The coincidence of her death and the peace treaty might suggest that it was her death which opened the way for the peace agreement to be made, and that she had been hostile to the new marriage. Her long apparent residence in Sardis will have made her a centre of power in Asia Minor, as would her ancestry and fame, and her gifts to the various deities made her influential elsewhere. Her association with Atargatis at Hierapolis-Bambyke in Syria involved the story of one of her courtiers castrating himself because his desire for her was so great. We do not have to believe the tale, but it goes along with the story of her being handed on to Antiochos I by his father, to suggest that she became the subject of male sexual innuendo and fantasy.[29] If so, it only emphasizes her importance.

The marriage of Antiochos with Berenike did not apparently immediately lead to a pregnancy. One of the assumed elements in the marriage agreement was that any son born to Berenike would become Antiochos' heir, displacing the two sons the king already had with Laodike. How Ptolemy imagined he or his successor could enforce this is impossible to imagine, and its impossibility is perhaps the reason Antiochos might have accepted it. The ages of the two kings will have entered into their calculations; Ptolemy was 55-years-old at the time of the peace, Antiochos was almost twenty years younger; it would be assumed on both sides that Ptolemy would die first, and almost certainly well before any child born to Berenike was adult. This is another alleged detail in the peace agreement which is assumed but which makes little sense and might well be best abandoned.[30]

There is another element in this marriage which is strange. Berenike was the only Ptolemaic princess to marry outside the Ptolemaic family in the first century and a half of the dynasty. Seleukid princesses were married out regularly – Phila to Antigonos, Stratonike to Ariarathes, and her aunt to Demetrios II, a Laodike later married Mithradates of Pontos, and so on. This had been the practice of Ptolemy I also, but from the time of his son onwards, the only marriages permitted to Ptolemaic princesses were to members of their own family. So that of Berenike is unique until the marriage of Kleopatra Thea to Alexander I Balas in 150. The reason these women were retained within the Ptolemaic family is that in royal theory they carried with them a claim to the Ptolemaic kingship. Therefore, since Berenike was Ptolemy II's daughter, she was a potentially valuable dynastic property. Yet she was now married to an enemy king who, in default of a male heir from Ptolemy II, might be able to claim the Egyptian kingship, and any son that they had might do the same – and Ptolemy had already lost one son. In fact Ptolemy had two sons still alive even after the death of his chosen heir (Ptolemy 'the Son'), so the issue probably did not arise except as a distant possibility, though it must have been in both kings' minds. The unusual nature of the marriage suggests that it was enforced on Ptolemy, not a ploy by him to subvert the Seleukid dynasty (even if that is what actually happened).

The conclusion to be reached from this is that the peace treaty was more in favour of Antiochos than of Ptolemy, and therefore that the marriage to Berenike was Antiochos' price for agreeing to the peace. If this is so, then the alternative would have been a continuation of the war. This in turn would suggest that Ptolemy's internal problems of finance were more pressing than the disturbances in the east and in Babylonia were for Antiochos. Both kings wished for peace, in other words, so as to be able to deal with their internal difficulties, but Antiochos knew that he could solve his – or ignore them – more easily than Ptolemy could his. The publicity Ptolemy used for the marriage was therefore a means of disguising his diplomatic and military defeat. He made a special visit to Memphis to celebrate the peace and there he distributed lands to soldiers who were settling in the Fayum region.[31] One wonders how many were fooled when it was clear that Antiochos had gained and kept control of Ephesos and Miletos.

The conclusion of the treaty did guarantee peace between the kings until one of them died, but it did not prevent both of them from intriguing to improve his diplomatic and military position in preparation for the next war. In this Antiochos, perhaps because of the example of his father, was particularly successful. He visited Babylonia in 250, no doubt to deal with any lingering problems from the previous troubles, and to attend to his religious duties; it may be he was also there two years later, though the record is not specific.[32]

The real diplomatic contest was at the western end of his kingdom and its borders, and there Antiochos made a treaty (or rather renewed one his father had made), with the Cretan city of Lyttos. This was a neighbour of the Ptolemaic naval base at Itanos, so this treaty could only be viewed as a threat to that base.[33] Most significantly he led or dispatched expeditions across the Hellespont into Thrace. His treaty with Lysimacheia, and his domination of the Asian coast of the Hellespont gave him access, and peace with Ptolemy rendered Ptolemaic naval power neutral. He campaigned as far as Byzantion and captured Kypsela after a siege.[34] He minted coins at Lysimacheia, and at a series of cities on the Asian side of the Straits.[35] This was a region which Seleukos I had claimed and which Antiochos I had had to abandon when the Galatians invaded Asia. It was one of the regions which were always liable to be attacked by a Seleukid king if he could reach it. Such a repeated claim and Antiochos' campaigning – reminiscent of Ptolemy I's repeated grasps at Palestine – was a clear warning to anyone that no Seleukid claim to territory was ever abandoned. The only area not so treated was Macedon, which Seleukos I had been about to take over when he was killed, but several royal marriages linking the Antigonid and Seleukid families rendered Macedon almost a part of the Seleukid kingdom.

Meanwhile the connection with Cyrenaica, which had been quiescent since the First Syrian War and the reconciliation of Magas and Ptolemy

II, was finally broken in 250 when Magas, his widow, Antiochos II's sister Apama, imported the Antigonid prince Demetrios the Fair, as a husband for her daughter Berenike (II). The story devolved into a titillating bedroom farce, ending in Demetrios' death apparently at Berenike's hands, Apama's disgrace, and Berenike's marriage to Ptolemy's son and heir. The result was that Cyrenaica was once more firmly attached to the parent Ptolemaic state. There is no sign that Antiochos II became involved, nor, for that matter, did Antigonos Gonatas intervene, though we might assume a strong interest by both kings; they were, it seems, outmanoeuvred by Ptolemy, who in fact held all the best cards.[36]

In 248 or thereabouts Antiochos II's Berenike gave birth at last to a son, named, unimaginatively, Antiochos. We learn the name from a letter from the Ptolemaic governor of Lykia to the small city of Kildara; the Ptolemaic interest in the new baby is evident even in this obscure region.[37] Antiochos the king already had two or three sons from Laodike, Seleukos, Antiochos, and 'Apammu'. This third name is only recorded by the Babylonian diarist; other sources only regard the first two as worth mentioning. 'Apammu' may be the Babylonian version of Apames, though such a male name is not recorded otherwise; it may also have been a female name, and so another royal daughter. He or she in fact dropped from the story at once.[38]

Antiochos continued to regard Laodike as his wife, or one of them, and she is so referred to by the Babylonian diarist (who never refers to Berenike), in 247.[39] It is hardly surprising that strained relations existed within the royal family, particularly between the two women, who probably never actually met. These became worse when Berenike's baby was safely delivered and proved to be a son. Until then there can have been no question that the eldest son of Antiochos and Laodike was the presumed heir to the kingship. The eldest son, Seleukos, was not made joint-king during his father's lifetime, but the arrival of the new child clearly set up a future problem. This problem became active when in 246, unexpectedly, Antiochos II died while on a visit to his first wife at Ephesos.

Chapter Fourteen

War, Collapse, and Fragmentation

W hen he died, Antiochos II was something over forty years old, and the presumption of domestic discord has inclined historians to the suspicion that he was poisoned by his (first) wife.[1] But of evidence for this there is none. He died in a Mediterranean seaport at the height of summer – this should be enough to account for his illness and death. It does seem that he named his son Seleukos as his successor as he was dying, and this may well be the result of wifely presence. Even if he did not do so, it was obvious that Seleukos would succeed, and he was so proclaimed by Laodike.[2] He was the eldest son, his brother Antiochos (soon to have the surname Hierax bestowed on him), was some years younger, and his half-brother Antiochos (in Antioch with his mother Laodike), was an infant. In rational, political terms, this was no contest.

Antiochos died in July; his rival Ptolemy II had died in January.[3] The way was now open for a new Syrian war though Antiochos shows no signs of having intended to begin one, and it may be that he was already ill. On the other hand, the new Egyptian king, Ptolemy III Euergetes, the husband of the Cyrenaican Queen Berenike (II), was well-prepared and was on campaign by late 246, so he had spent the first months of his reign in preparations. But it was Antiochos' death which was the trigger for the war, since Ptolemy's first move was into Syria to contact his sister Berenike.

It seems probable therefore that Ptolemy Euergetes intended attacking the Seleukid kingdom even before Antiochos II died. If Antiochos was ill for some time before his death this would provide a good opportunity; that he died made the attack all the easier. However, from the sequence of events in Antioch Ptolemy's invasion did not happen until some time after Antiochos' death.

There were also other factors besides the death of the king which operated in Ptolemy's favour. In the Aegean and Greece Antigonos Gonatas was involved in another crisis, this time concerning the rebellion of his governor in Corinth. It may be that his campaign to recover control included a collision between his fleet and a Ptolemaic squadron near Andros. The date of this battle is one of the more difficult problems of Hellenistic history, and 246 is only one possibility, though even if the battle took place in 246 it had no obvious wider consequences. Antigonos did not follow up his victory and turned to deal with Corinth. Ptolemy did not pursue the issue (as he could have) and so was relieved of the need to do anything in the Aegean in response.

One other reason Ptolemy did nothing for some months may be that he was involved in his own negotiations over Cyrenaica. The career of Magas had shown the need to at least neutralize any threat from his western flank, if Ptolemy was to fight in Syria. Magas was now dead and Cyrenaica was ruled by Apama, Antiochos II's sister, and her daughter Berenike (who had earlier rejected Demetrios the Fair). Apama was either dead or disgraced soon after, and the marriage of Berenike to Ptolemy III had been negotiated in the period since the *coup* which killed Demetrios and sidelined Apama. The citizens of Cyrene had not been pleased with the royal family, and for a short time had attempted to rid themselves of it; by 246, with his marriage to Berenike II, Ptolemy II had mastered the situation, though Cyrenaica was confirmed to be treated as a separate state under Berenike as queen, minting a separate set of coins, for instance (produced by a master artist).[4] The marriage took place about the time of Ptolemy's accession; as a result Cyrenaica ceased to be a threat.

During 246, therefore, Ptolemy III found that all the obstacles to a war with the Seleukid kingdom were dissolved; he was king in place of his aged father; Cyrenaica was his, and a new wife; Antigonos Gonatas' troubles in Greece meant that any possibility of his interference, either in Asia or in Cyrenaica, was removed; Antiochos II was (probably) incapacitated by illness, and then died. And as a further result of Antiochos' death, Ptolemy's sister had an arguable claim to have her infant son made king of the Seleukid kingdom, with herself as regent ruling in his name.

Laodike, however, held more cards in this situation that her rival, and perhaps ignored, or refused to acknowledge, the possibility of a Ptolemaic war. She was present when Antiochos II died; she had on hand her eldest son, Seleukos, who was at once proclaimed king; and she had time to arrange for her rival to be removed. Berenike will not have heard of her husband's death for some time, but when she did she also acted with decision. She had her infant son proclaimed king, and he was accepted in Antioch, in Seleukeia, and possibly in other cities in Syria as well. She gained control of at least some of the army, and she sent a force by sea (so she had control of the Seleukid ships at Seleukeia), into Kilikia where at Soloi a treasure was seized and brought to Antioch. The Kilikian governor, Aribazos, escaped but was killed by mountain brigands on his flight.[5] Berenike had thus gained control of Syria and Kilikia. In the midst of all this she also sent an appeal to her brother for assistance, presumably realizing that any further progress was uncertain, as was the depth of support she could count on locally. She must have realized that Laodike and Seleukos would be making preparations to dislodge her.

Ptolemy answered her appeal promptly, which rather suggests he was already prepared for a new Syrian war. An officer, Andriskos, arrived off the coast with a squadron of Ptolemaic ships. He could have come from Cyprus, or from any of the Ptolemaic ports in Phoenicia. He captured a city, though which one is not known – Seleukeia-in-Pieria is the most likely; any Seleukid forces, land or sea, were no doubt ordered not to oppose him. Ptolemy himself arrived with another naval force not long after and paused at Poseidion, an old Greek town between Laodikeia and Seleukeia, until preparations had been made at Seleukeia for his landing and his welcome. It seems clear that he hoped to be able to continue without any fighting. The cover story was that Ptolemy was visiting his sister.[6] This meant of course that he could not bring much force with him, no more than a ceremonial guard.

Some time elapsed while this was happening. The news of Antiochos' death may have taken a week or two to reach Antioch, perhaps as long or longer to reach Alexandria, and perhaps another two to four weeks must be allowed for Berenike's and Ptolemy's actions. (The Babylonian diarist received the news of Antiochos' death in August, but dated Seleukos' accession in July – the news thus took over a month to reach Babylon.)[7] It was in that interval that Laodike and Seleukos were able to organize their reverse *coup* in Syria. Berenike's local support was limited, and there were plenty of Seleukos' supporters still in Syria. Berenike's actions had brought her to power and given her a precarious control, but once it was known that Seleukos had been proclaimed king in Asia Minor, his supporters in Syria could act. Instructions reached some of Antioch's prominent citizens, apparently from Laodike; two men, Ikadion and Gennaios, acted. They killed Berenike's child, and Berenike was killed by her Galatian guard.[8]

These deaths were concealed, since both groups feared that the other would carry out a violent purge. (The news of the accession of 'King Antiochos' reached at least to Kildara in Lykia – Ptolemaic territory – but not, it seems, to Babylon, where the Babylonian diarist moves directly from Antiochos II to Seleukos II.)[9] Both Antiochene groups, of course, were also waiting for support from their principals. In this Ptolemy was nearest, and was able to arrange a ceremonial welcome into Seleukeia. The cover story of a fraternal visit ensured another absence of resistance when he reached Antioch. He received another ceremonial welcome, much to his surprise; but then at the palace he found that his sister was dead.[10]

Ptolemy's speedy arrival was, of course, due to his presence nearby; Seleukos had relied on his local supporters, since he was unable to move quickly enough to reach Antioch first – though it is not clear how much he knew of Ptolemy's movements. It seems likely that Seleukos – or Laodike, who is given credit for these actions in the ancient sources – relied on the Antiochenes to remove Berenike and the child and maybe assumed that this would be enough to bring Syria back to loyalty. The intrusion of Ptolemy upset such plans.

Ptolemy had arrived in Syria with only a small force, in keeping with his ostensible purpose in visiting his sister. How far this reason was accepted by his Syrian hosts is unclear, but once he and they knew that Berenike and the child Antiochos were dead he needed to produce a new reason for his occupation. In this he was aided by the continued concealment of their deaths which will have given him time to bring up more troops close to Syria. He had permanent existing garrisons in Phoenicia and in Cyprus, and in some of the small coastal cities of Rough Kilikia, so he would not have needed long to bring more troops in. The news of the deaths of Berenike and her son were no doubt revealed fairly soon – it was now in the interests of the party of Seleukos and Laodike to reveal it – but by then Ptolemy had won this race as well.

Ptolemy was assisted in maintaining his position in Syria by the fact that the civic officials had surrendered to him – 'satraps and other officers and priests [and] the boards of magistrates', is the description in the Ptolemaic account of events. These were thus compromised, and if not reliable (from Ptolemy's point of view), were probably imprisoned. The acropoleis in the cities will have been occupied by Ptolemaic troops, and the taxes collected for Ptolemy's use, the Seleukid troops no doubt disarmed and dismissed. Some will have got away to join Seleukos, but it was obviously going to take even more time for him to gather up his forces in sufficient numbers to be able to return in force to Syria.

Without much fighting, Ptolemy thus gained control of North Syria as far as the Euphrates and the Taurus Mountains; his sister's control of parts of Kilikia was expanded. He captured the Seleukid elephant park at Apameia, with which he supplemented his own force of African elephants, and ships of the Seleukid fleet, such as those used by Berenike, also fell to him. Arados was taken over, perhaps very early, and its mint produced coins on the Ptolemaic standard for a time.[11] Later it was claimed, in an inscription exhibited at Adulis on the Red Sea coast in Eritrea, that he crossed the Euphrates and subdued Mesopotamia, Babylonia, Susiana, Persis, Media, and as far as Baktria.[12] This is clearly Ptolemaic propaganda and not to be taken seriously. It is just possible that he personally could have got as far as Babylon, but that was several weeks' journey from Syria, putting him well out of touch with Egypt, and leaving his Syrian base wide open to an attack by Seleukos, who was in Asia Minor.[13] He certainly did not reach Media or Baktria, and it is highly unlikely that the satraps of those regions gave him any submission. Well before he could reach Babylon, the news that Seleukos was active and that Berenike and son were dead, will have reached the east – the Babylonians went directly from Antiochos II to Seleukos II; there could be no point in submitting, even merely formally, to Ptolemy, even if he did reach Babylon.

Ptolemy remained in and about Syria during the winter of 246–245, though he had not apparently yet decided what he was to do with his expanded authority. It must have become clear that when the passes were opened in the spring, he would face an attack. He was probably not able any longer to rely on the populations of the Syrian cities, and he faced the danger of having much of his army distributed among the hostile cities as controlling garrisons, leaving his reduced field army vulnerable to Seleukos' attack. As it happens Seleukos had launched an expedition by sea, using a fleet gathered from the various ports he controlled, but it was wrecked by a storm on the coast of southern Asia Minor, with considerable loss of life.[14]

For Ptolemy, saved for the moment by Seleukos' failure, it must have been tempting to annex Syria and Kilikia. They will have looked defensible behind barriers of the sea, the mountains, and the rivers, except that the people of the cities were hostile. He was rescued from his dilemma by trouble in Egypt, where there were disturbances ('seditio'). It is usually assumed that this was a peasant rebellion occasioned by heavy taxation. It was certainly serious enough to call the king home – unless he simply wanted to find an excuse to leave.[15]

His decision for Syria was to hold on to it. He appointed governors, Xanthippos for Mesopotamia, and Antiochos for Kilikia – but not for anywhere further east – and gathered up all the portable wealth his forces could find in the Syrian cities, including the elephants and the warships. When he returned to Egypt he boasted about how much he had stolen, mentioning the sum of 40,000 talents, and claimed to have liberated many of the captured gods and statues taken by the Persians before Alexander – '2,500' of them, he claimed.[16] This evidence of new wealth may have helped pacify whoever was in rebellion, but it was no doubt quickly distributed among Ptolemy's courtiers and soldiers. A portion of the army was left in North Syria, but it was evidently not expected to hold everything there for very long. The governor of Mesopotamia did not therefore have a permanent appointment. This was a delaying action, not an annexation.

Seleukos II had had to make considerable new arrangements before attempting to recover the territories Ptolemy had taken. His first priority, once he had decisively lost the race for Syria, was to shore up his base in Asia Minor, which must have been shaken by the rival king's existence and then by the wreck of his fleet. It was at this point, it seems, that his sister Laodike (I) was married to Mithradates II of Pontos; his other sister Stratonike was already married to Ariarathes of Kappadokia.[17] Seleukos himself, now or earlier, was married to Laodike (II), the daughter of Andromachos, who was another of his mother's brothers (she was Seleukos' first cousin, therefore).[18] Laodike I, Laodike II, and Andromachos were all descendants of Akhaios, whose family was now fully integrated as part of the dynasty. The Seleukid family was now in effect another of the dynastic families of Asia Minor. To cap the system Seleukos appointed his younger brother Antiochos Hierax as his viceroy for Asia Minor, an action which suggests he knew he was going to be effectively cut off from communicating with the region during the reconquering expedition he now began. Since Antiochos was several years younger than the king, their mother, the formidable Laodike I, seems to have exercised much influence.

Seleukos evidently had a clear plan. First he secured Asia Minor by the marriages and by planting his brother as his viceroy (just as Antiochos I had sent Patrokles to take control in 281–280). His next move, in 245, was to secure Babylonia, to which he went in that year. According to a near contemporary inscription from Smyrna, Seleukos 'crossed into Seleukis', thereby attacking the heart of the Ptolemaic position.[19] This would at once cut off any Ptolemaic forces under Xanthippos in Mesopotamia, and would confirm Seleukos' authority there and in Babylonia and the east. Xanthippos' tenure as governor was perhaps even briefer than Ptolemy intended. We may assume that Seleukos had established his full control over both Mesopotamia and Babylonia by mid-245, by about the time Ptolemy returned to Egypt.

The Seleukid kingdom had been broken into several parts; Seleukos II controlled Babylonia and Mesopotamia, and was mounting his attack on Syria, which was controlled by Ptolemy III's forces, though Ptolemy himself was on his way back to Egypt; Asia Minor was under the control of Antiochos Hierax and Laodike I, and for the present it was loyal to Seleukos; east of Babylonia the Persian regions were largely loyal to Seleukos, though he probably had little influence in Baktria, where Diodotos I had ruled as satrap for a decade and more. Therefore at this point Seleukos' primary object was now to regain control of Syria, which in many ways was the heart of the kingdom.

As ever in these wars, the details of the recovery of Syria by Seleukos are largely lost, though it is fairly clear that he had gained Antioch by 244, where the mint produced coins in his name.[20] When peace was made three years later he had also recovered most of the other cities. There are some fragments of information which seem relevant. Arados, for example, coined Ptolemaic coins from 245, and so was in some way subject to Ptolemy, though, this being Arados, it is all but certain that the city fathers negotiated an advantageous deal, and eventually, when it was equally advantageous, they negotiated a return to the Seleukid kingdom. This seems to have been about 242, by another calculation of the coins and the eras they record.[21] A certain permanence of Ptolemaic control over several years is suggested by a stele found near Laodikeia on the coast, on which a list of soldiers' names and their home cities are inscribed, probably as some sort of a religious dedication. The names and origins strongly imply that these were mercenaries in the Ptolemaic service. Their origins were either within Ptolemy's lands (Cyrene, Philoteria, Salamis in Cyprus), or Pisidia, along a region of recruitment by the Ptolemaic kings (Etenna, Pisidia), or old Greece (Phokis, Boiotia, Athens and others). There are no men from the Seleukid lands. Although undated, the only time such a group of men could set up such a memorial so close to a major Seleukid city is in the late 240s. We may take it as evidence of Ptolemy's control of the coastlands for some years.[22]

The recovery of Arados (and at some point, Apameia), opened the way for a Seleukid invasion of Phoenicia. Seleukos captured Orthosia, just south of the Eleutheros River boundary, and having thereby penetrated into the

Bekaa Valley he was apparently able to reach as far as Damascus.[23] Neither place was held, but the point was thereby made, that Seleukos, even if parts of the Seleukis were still in enemy hands, was quite able to commit severe damage to Ptolemaic parts of Syria. This would probably encourage the evacuation of Ptolemaic troops from the rest of the Seleukis.

Ptolemy seems to have simply let his forces fight a slowly retreating battle in Syria until he was able to make peace. Meanwhile he was more active in the Aegean, where he could use his fleet. During the 240s his forces gained control of Ephesos (where another *coup* had taken place which ended with a Ptolemaic takeover),[24] though Miletos had hastened to demonstrate its Seleukid loyalty, with an embassy to the king, carrying gifts.[25] He also gained control of some of the cities on both sides of the Hellespont. Several places close to Lysimacheia in Thrace had become Ptolemaic by 240, and to the west the cities of Ainos and Maroneia were under Ptolemaic control by 243 and had a Spartan as governor for Ptolemy in the 230s and 220s.[26] Lysimacheia had minted coins for Antiochos II and then did so for Antiochos Hierax; the gap between c.246 and c.230 was therefore probably due to a Ptolemaic occupation.[27] On the Asia Minor side of the Hellespont the town of Larisa was taken over and renamed Ptolemais during Ptolemy III's reign, giving him control of both shores.[28]

The fighting in Syria reached a stalemate by 241, or so we must assume. Seleukos had recovered the cities of the interior, from Seleukeia-Zeugma on the Euphrates to Apameia and the posts along the Orontes at Larisa and Arethousa. He had recovered Laodikeia-ad-Mare and had re-established his suzerainty over Arados. It is evident that he was unable to recapture Seleukeia-in-Pieria, for when the peace was made Ptolemy held it still.[29] This was a city which had probably been intended by the founder Seleukos I to be the heart of the kingdom, its major opening to the western sea. It was a major port, well fortified (as Ptolemy's forces proved by what one must assume was a successful defence), it commanded an important route to the interior, and held the tombs of the early kings in a temple on the acropolis. Seleukos will have wanted to recover this city perhaps more than any other in Syria, though he was clearly unable to do so.

Despite this the peace, at least so far as can be seen from later dispositions, included a restitution of the old mutual boundary along the Eleutheros River, with Arados on the Seleukid side. The only exception to the restoration was Seleukeia. The area of Smooth Kilikia was also recovered, though Ptolemy still held posts along the coast of Rough Kilikia further west. Both kings had abandoned any interest in Pamphylia, which, behind its mountains, was only a cul-de-sac. (The archaeological evidence implies that Phaselis had been relinquished by about 250 or so.)[30] Ptolemy however had acquired control over an indeterminate part of the Aegean coast, certainly including Ephesos, which became a major Ptolemaic control centre for the next half century. In the north of the Aegean the Hellespont and the coast to the west was under Ptolemaic control, which meant that Seleukos (or perhaps Antiochos Hierax) had been expelled from Thrace. The peace is said, by the only source to mention it, to have been for ten years, but this is unlikely; no other Seleukid-Ptolemaic peace had such a time-limit (so far as we know); both kings ignored the supposed expiry date of 231; it is best to assume that Justin was wrong and that the normal condition, that the peace would last until the death of one of the kings, applies.[31]

The restoration of peace drew attention to other problems in the Seleukid kingdom which had developed during the conflict. The loss of territory, particularly at the Hellespont and Seleukeia-in-Pieria, was also a serious loss of prestige for the dynasty. So, although Seleukos II could claim to have won back most of Syria, he had in fact suffered defeat in the war as a whole. For a dynasty which relied on its military expertise as the main prop for its authority, this was a serious diminution. And in order to concentrate on recovering Syria he had been compelled to cede virtually independent authority in Asia Minor to his brother, and perhaps tacitly to the long-standing Baktrian governor Diodotos.

With peace, of course, Seleukos was bound to attempt to re-assert his control over the semi-independent fragments of his empire. This turned out to be something to which the rulers of those areas were averse. Antiochos Hierax was particularly unwilling to knuckle under. At some point he had taken or had been given the royal title.[32] It is probable that he needed the title to be able to exert some real control over his Asia Minor territory. Also, since Seleukos was busy fighting all the time from 246 to 241, Antiochos was presumably regarded as Seleukos' heir, at least until Seleukos' children had survived the first years of their lives. But when Seleukos had won his war the independence of Hierax was threatened. He resisted his demotion. Seleukos brought his army into Asia Minor.

Hierax recruited an army largely made up of Galatian mercenaries. He had the alliance of Mithradates of Pontos, his brother-in-law, and was supported by his mother's family, including her brother Alexander, who had been made governor in Lydia. Seleukos made this area the target for his invasion, and was able to reach Lydia before meeting Hierax' forces, which he defeated. He was, however, unable to take any of the cities Antiochos held, which included the viceregal city of Sardis.[33]

The aim of Seleukos in this campaign is obvious – to recover control of Asia Minor. The aim of Hierax is less clear. He does not seem at this stage to have laid claim to the whole kingdom, but he did wish to hold onto his position as king in Asia Minor. It is possible he was in this a prisoner of his advisers, the family of Akhaios, above all his mother, who may have aimed at the definitive separation of Anatolia from the Seleukid kingdom, thereby forming a new state, with the family of Akhaios supplying the kings. Such a situation would clearly suit both Mithradates and the Galatians, who would thereby gain a greater freedom of manoeuvre when they did not have to face the power of the whole united Seleukid kingdom.

After the war had lasted two years or so, during which we have no information on its progress, Seleukos was defeated in a great battle against the united forces of Mithradates, Hierax, and the Galatians near Ankyra, perhaps in 237. He was evidently invading Galatian territory. For a time it was thought that Seleukos had perished along with '20,000' of his soldiers. Antiochos theatrically put on mourning, but he must have also appreciated that this made him the sole king, and that his next task would be to establish his authority in other parts of the kingdom. But it turned out that Seleukos had survived, having escaped the battlefield in disguise. (His concubine Mysta was captured and sold to a Rhodian; she was recognized and returned to Seleukos at once; other prisoners were less lucky.) Hierax publicly rejoiced that his brother was alive, but he was never again to have the opportunity to rise to greater power.[34]

Antiochos had to be content with being king in Asia Minor; Seleukos apparently withdrew to Syria; there was perhaps a tacit agreement to divide the kingdom. By this time Seleukos had married and had at least two sons (the younger was about 18 in 225), whereas Hierax, still probably less than 20, had not yet married. Any position he had held as heir or joint-king was now eliminated. Seleukos went off on campaign elsewhere so it would seem that some arrangement between the brothers was made to return to the situation which had obtained before their war, in effect dividing the kingdom between them, Antiochos to have Asia Minor, Seleukos the rest. This is not recorded in any of the sources, but it is evident that they managed to ignore each other for several years. Seleukos turned to deal with the situation which had developed in the east. One element here was probably the long tenure of Diodotos as Baktrian governor, but it is also likely that the condition of Parthia was involved.

The written sources name three men who were satraps of Parthia, Pherekles, Agathokles and Andragoras, all involved in some way in the invasion of that satrapy by nomads from the north led by a chief called Arsakes. Of the three men Andragoras is named on a small number of coins, which show a man wearing satrapal gear; it is possible the two Andragorai were the same man; it is a reasonably rare name, and two men, with that name, in that area, and at much the same time, is extremely unlikely.[35] It does not seem likely that all three men were one and the same – the differences in their names are really too great for mere copying mistakes – so we may assume that all three at some point were acting as Parthian satraps. It is not unreasonable to assume that all three of them faced nomad attacks, nor is it unreasonable to assume that Andragoras began leading the Parthian satrapy into a sort of independence, which is what his minting of coins might imply. But none of this can be proved from the evidence which survives.

Further east, in Baktria, a more subtle political development was going on. Antiochos II was the first Seleukid king without direct experience of the eastern section of the kingdom. He certainly travelled more than once as far as Babylon, but there is no indication that he went further, and Seleukos II had not been able to do so either. So no Seleukid king had visited the east since 281. Clearly these men had quite enough to do in the west, but they presumably appointed satraps when necessary. Diodotos was one; he was Antiochos II's appointee in the 250s. Similarly whoever was in office in Parthia, Pherekles or Agathokles or Andragoras, was Antiochos' man. Satraps' terms in office were not fixed, but Diodotos held his post for perhaps two decades, which is probably not normal. Given the preoccupation of Antiochos II with western problems, if Diodotos was seen to be competent it was probably thought best to leave him there.

Whoever was in office in Parthia in the mid-250s is not known, though the most popular candidate is Andragoras, named by Justin. It is better to leave aside the name for the present, though Justin does describe a reasonable sequence of events, and is supported in general terms by Strabo.[36] The background is the situation of Parthia and Baktria in a time when the Seleukid kings were inevitably mainly occupied by the events in the west. The eastern satraps were compelled to take matters into their own hands, being much occupied with the defence of their provinces.

The story which emerges is that Diodotos had to fight an enemy called Arsakes, who gathered support from the nomads outside Baktria.[37] Diodotos was successful in driving Arsakes away from Baktria, but the invader then recovered, gathered a new army among the nomads and attacked Parthia, which was a small and weak target. In this he killed the satrap and succeeded in occupying at least part of the satrapy. It is possible that the satrap ('Andragoras') had moved into independence beforehand, but it seems just as likely he was left to fight alone, though Arsakes is said to have feared both Diodotos (who had already defeated him), and the Seleukid king (whose territory he had invaded). This is, however, not a sign that his enemies were combining against him.

The dating of all this is controversial, largely because of attempts by the ancient sources to provide chronological links to known events in the west. It is clear that such links do count – the Seleukid kingdom was the connection, and it is incontestable that events in the west, which was the power centre of the kingdom, had their effects in the east. The Ptolemaic invasion of Syria and the effective collapse of the kingdom as a result cannot have failed to have its effect in the rest of the state. The dating of the invasion of Parthia by Arsakes and his nomads, the Parni or Aparni, is the crucial matter, for such an attack called for a reply. Diodotos had already repelled Arsakes from Baktria, but he could not operate outside his satrapy without incurring, at the very least, hostile suspicion from the king. The invasion, especially one which killed the satrap, demanded a royal response. If it took place in Antiochos II's reign, as one supposed date (256) suggests, Antiochos II would have had the responsibility of combating it, probably once he was clear of the Second Syrian War in 253. But he did not do anything in the east, and was clearly quite content to go on campaign in the west (it was in this period that he campaigned in Thrace).

So the better alternative time for the eastern events is the reign of Seleukos II. Here the beginning of the Arsakid era is relevant. This is put at 247, but only, it seems, by a back-calculation made some years, or even decades, later. It may or may not be accurate, but it is clearly at least approximately correct, which is to say that something of importance to the Parthians took place about that time. A new era was begun because some notable event had happened, and for the Parthians the notable event was the occupation and conquest of the Parthian satrapy, which became their kingdom for a century. This therefore took place about 247, or perhaps a year or so later. (Maybe the year was chosen in order to imply that the invasion was directed against a united kingdom rather than taking advantage of its temporary collapse.) It was not, however, until some years later that they were able to count themselves secure in the new conquest, and for Arsakes to take the royal title. In the Hellenistic world such a self-promotion occurred as a result of winning a battle, or a war, against another king. The Parthian victory was not over Antiochos II, who ignored them; it was therefore a victory over Seleukos II.

The collapse of the Seleukid state in 246 was thus the trigger for its division, and for one of its enemies to cut off a slice for himself. Arsakes, at some point in the later 240s seized control of part of the Parthian satrapy, killing the satrap in the process. Seleukos could not do anything about the situation until after the war with Ptolemy was over and the new war with his brother had been brought to a temporary end. If the battle of Ankyra is dated to 237, Seleukos was free to attend to the east from 236 onwards.

The one reasonably reliable chronological link between east and west, because it is integral to the Seleukid kingdom, is the comment by Justin that it was the news of the defeat of Seleukos at Ankyra which brought Arsakes to invade the Parthian satrapy.[38] This would mean that the earlier attack had only succeeded in part, and that the news of Ankyra permitted him to seize the rest of the region. Quite probably Seleukos had had to call up the satrapal forces to fight in the west, leaving the satrapy without proper defences. Arsakes feared a reaction from both Seleukos II and the Baktrian satrap Diodotos (who was probably still loyal at this point). He built up a strong force in preparation. But then – in this order – Diodotos I died, Arsakes made a treaty with his son Diodotos II, and Arsakes defeated Seleukos II's attack.

In addition to all this, in 237 there was further trouble in Babylon. The diarist there reports that there was fighting around the palace, and that the guard of the palace came out and fought with the soldiers of the king. (There was a locust plague at the time as well.)[39] This was clearly a very serious outbreak, in effect a civil war between two parts of the king's army. We do not know what was the cause of the repeated outbreaks of fighting in the city – in 255, 237, 234, and 229 – but such an event inevitably demanded royal attention, perhaps even more so than a foreign invasion of a distant satrapy.

One of the suggested dates for the collision between Arsakes and Seleukos is precisely 237, though the actual fight was probably later. Justin says this was a defeat for Seleukos, though he refrains from describing it as a battle. A fairly convincing linking may therefore be made between Arsakes' relief at the death of Diodotos I, which seems to have taken place in the mid-230s, followed by his treaty with Diodotos II, who wished to make himself king and did not need a war with Arsakes, but did need to be free of any threat from Seleukos, who was now separated from Baktria by independent Parthia. When Seleukos marched east to deal with Arsakes therefore he did so not long after the defeat at Ankyra, which had been Arsakes' inspiration. And when he did so Seleukos found he could get no help from Diodotos, and had to fight Arsakes alone.

The dating of all this is, it must be admitted, vague. Given that these events took place in the 230s, and that a reasonable sequence can be deduced, it is nevertheless impossible to pin down the date of any one particular incident. If it was possible, this might allow the rest to be fitted into place. But one must also always recall that great distances are involved – it is several thousands of kilometres from Ankyra to Baktra, in a straight line – so precise correlations between eastern and western events are equally difficult. Nevertheless the fact that all this took place in the Seleukid kingdom makes them all problems for the king to deal with, and such was the condition of the government of the kingdom, he had to do so in person. Leaving large tasks to powerful subordinates was exactly what had got Seleukos into his multiple difficulties.

The losses at Ankyra will have weakened Seleukos' field army, and the troubles in Babylon will have led him to leave at least some of his forces there; others were probably forming a frontier guard against anything Hierax might do. He therefore marched through Media against the Parthians with less than the full Seleukid field army he would normally have taken with him. It is possible he expected help from Diodotos, which failed to materialize because Diodotos I died. Hence his defeat, which may have been no more than the realization that he was unable to face Arsakes' forces. He therefore retreated and turned to deal with Babylon instead.

Chapter Fifteen

Failure

Seleukos II's reign, having started badly, continued in the same way. About 235 the new governor of Baktria, Diodotos II, declared himself king, an event which the local coinage marked by replacing coins in the name of King Antiochos with those in the name of King Diodotos. The portrait is that of the younger of the two Diodotoi, though on some coins this portrait had already been used on those of Antiochos II. There are no coins of Seleukos II from Baktrian mints. So the gradual shift into independence is demonstrated by the coinage, with Diodotos II's earliest coins naming Antiochos as king; only after several coinings did his own name as king appear.[1]

By this time Arsakes the invader of Parthia had also claimed the royal title, and the two usurping kings were allies, or at least friendly, facing as they did the presumed enmity of the Seleukid king. They may also have felt threatened by the Indian Mauryan Empire, where the powerful emperor Asoka ruled until about 230. He was certainly active at Kandahar in Arachosia, where one of his edicts has been found, written in both Greek and Aramaic, the first showing that there were Greeks in the city, the second for the surviving Akhaimenid population.[2] The Baktrian kingdom was also probably threatened by nomad attack. It seems that Sogdiana, the northern region, beyond the mountains separating the Oxus and the Iaxartes valleys, had been abandoned. No doubt this was the area Arsakes had originally operated from. His transfer westwards allowed him to join with the organized kingdom of the nomads in the area east of the Caspian Sea, which had been producing coins since about 300.[3] This coinage is generally identified with the kingdom of the Dahai, and Arsakes' people, the Parni, are also referred to as Dahai.

Arsakes had taken over a region south of the territory of the Dahai; probably the first area he controlled was the northern slopes of the Kopet Dagh, the mountain range running east-west which formed the northern edge of the Iranian plateau. The first capital of the Parthian kingdom was in this area, at Nisa or Asaak.[4] Later conquests, perhaps as a result of the news of Ankyra and Seleukos II's defeat, were to penetrate the mountain range and so gain access to the higher plateau-lands to the south, the Parthian satrapy proper. The capture of the city of Hekatompylos was the definitive conquest of Parthia. The city was probably the satrapal capital, and lay astride the Royal Road which ran from Babylon and Seleukeia-on-the-Tigris to Baktria and India at a junction of several routes   the city's name, after all, means 'Eight Gates'.[5] Cutting the Royal Road meant the Parthians now had some control over the traffic along it. They were able to levy customs duties on the goods being transported, but they were also able to intercept any diplomatic traffic between the Seleukid and Baktrian kings. Cutting the road was also a useful defence for Baktria if the Seleukid king should try to suppress its independence.

Arsakes also gained control over the eastern part of Hyrkania. This is the land between the Caspian Sea and Elburz Mountains (the Kopet Dagh is an eastward extension of the Elburz). Hyrkania (modern Mazanderan) is an agriculturally rich region, and it contained some small Greek cities. Arsakes had to fight to conquer the area, and seems only to have controlled the eastern part, round the south-eastern corner of the Caspian, at least for the present.

His kingdom had quickly become a facsimile of all Hellenistic states, the population including Greco-Macedonians (in the cities), Iranians, and his nomads. In this it was much like the Baktrian state further east and the mixture of populations justifies the adoption of the geographical name Parthian for the kingdom as a whole. On the other hand, ruling caste were the Parni, though they did not interfere with the Greeks in the cities.[6]

The other major detached fragment of the original Seleukid state was, of course, Asia Minor. Here Antiochos Hierax was technically king, but he did not have full control. Without the backing of the Seleukid state and its armed force, his part of Anatolia was not powerful enough to dominate the rest of the peninsula. The victory of Hierax over his brother at Ankyra was also a victory for the Galatians. Their numbers had substantially increased since their original settlement, partly no doubt by continued Galatian immigration and partly by the assimilation of the local population. Their victory gave them confidence in their prowess and perhaps convinced them to become more united in fighting than their well-attested division into three major tribes might suggest. They were also allies of Ziaelas in Bithynia and, through Hierax, with Mithradates II of Pontos, so with these and Antiochos' territories closed to them, their targets had to be Kappadokia to the east and/or the Greek cities of the western coast. For Kappadokia we have no information, but its king was married to Stratonike, the sister of both Seleukos II and Antiochos Hierax, and so he may have received help in resisting any attacks. To the west, the Galatians came up against the new dynast of Pergamon, Attalos I.

Attalos was another member of the extended family descended from Akhaios (I), being the son of a cousin of Eumenes I and Antiochis, the daughter of Akhaios (see Table B).[7] This made Attalos another brother-in-law of Hierax (and of Seleukos II). Attalos was Eumenes' cousin, who had been adopted by him as his heir in default of any closer male relations. He inherited the state when Eumenes I died in 241, just when Hierax was about to make himself independent, and just before the renewed outburst of Galatian aggression which the breakup of the Seleukid kingdom encouraged.

The Attalid state was about the same size as the other native Anatolian kingdoms, though smaller than Hierax' share of the Seleukid state. Based at the well-fortified city of Pergamon, Eumenes had extended the area under his direct rule to the sea at Eleia, north to Mount Ida, and south and east to the watershed between the Kaikos (Pergamon's river) and the Hermos River. He had also gained wider influence, especially in the Troad beyond Mount Ida, and by careful diplomacy and well-publicized gifts to Delos and Delphi he had established the reputation of his dynasty for friendship with and generosity towards Greek cities.

This geographical and ethical position put Attalos between the Galatians and their prey, those many rich Greek cities which Attalos and his family had cultivated with their friendship. There was no other enemy the Galatians could attack, with any profit, without either breaking a treaty or provoking a heavy response. No doubt they were by no means averse to raiding Pergamon as well. It took the Galatians no time at all, after Ankyra, to appreciate that they now had the initiative. Antiochos Hierax was compelled to pay them tribute and they remained allies.[8] The one power which stood against them was Attalos, perhaps not by choice, since he ruled the land which was coveted by Hierax (and Seleukos) as estranged Seleukid territory, and by the Galatians for its potential loot.

The war which resulted is, as usual, poorly known. The main evidence comes from a much broken inscription found at Pergamon, in which Attalos listed his victories in a dedication to Athena. At least they may be assumed to be victories since he lists them in his thank-offering; he does not therefore list his defeats, of which there were surely some. There are six battles listed in the dedication, but it is not clear if they happened in the order they are shown.[9]

Further, although Attalos took the title of king as a result of at least one victory over the Galatians, it is not known when this was, though some time in the 230s is probable. He is said to have reigned for forty-four years, dying in 197, but this is not evidence that he took the royal title in 241; 'reigning' and being king are not necessarily synonymous.[10] In the list of his victories, only two are said to be over Galatian forces, whereas four were over the forces of Hierax (one being over both Hierax and the Galatians), and one was over the forces of Seleukos II, but which were commanded by his generals.

It is, perhaps, this last which is the clue to Attalos' activity. It is a victory against 'Lysias and the generals of Seleukos'. It is listed fourth in the arrangement of the dedication, but this is not necessarily its place in the order of events. Nevertheless the fact that it is listed along with the other battles is a clear indication of Attalos' purpose in fighting these wars. It was not just a war against the Galatians, though the great victory monument in Pergamon showing the deaths of Galatians in battle tends to emphasize that aspect. The battle was against two forces fighting in alliance: 'Lysias' and 'the generals of Seleukos'. Such a battle was one which was fought for the domination of all Anatolia. The 'Lysias' was the current representative of the family of the dynasts established in their cities along the Royal Road. It would seem they were operating as semi-independent allies of Seleukos, certainly against Attalos, and so probably against Hierax as well, though his earlier rule was probably more acceptable than that of Attalos. Attalos' aim was to capitalize on the weakening of the Seleukid position in Anatolia which happened as a result of the split between the brothers, and to replace Hierax as king.

Such an ambition necessarily required the defeat of Hierax, whose alliance with the Galatians was clearly as opportunistic as was Attalos' own new ambition. The record as compiled by Attalos therefore organizes events into four wars; one against the Hierax-Galatian alliance, one against the Galatians alone, one against Hierax alone, and one against the forces of Seleukos II and Lysias. Since the Hierax-Galatian alliance was a hangover from their joint victory over Seleukos at Ankyra it would make sense to put that war first, followed by the breaking of the alliance, perhaps as a result of the defeat mentioned in the second battle, at the Aphrodision just outside the walls of the Pergamon city, a battle clearly the result of aggression by the allies.

The war with the Galatians alone perhaps came next. Two of the tribes had taken part with Hierax, but only the Tolistobogii were involved in the contest with the Galatians alone, where the battle was fought at the springs of the Kaikos River. This is about 60km east of Pergamon, in the area of both the cities of Stratonikeia founded by Antiochos II and Attaleia where Eumenes had settled his mercenaries once their quarrel had been patched up. A battle there implies that Attalos had good warning of the Galatians' approach and was able to meet them at his convenience and on his borders, and by defeating them there he effectively protected his own lands.

This victory was also decisive in that it resulted in a peace agreement, whereby the Galatians (or perhaps only the Tolistobogii), agreed to keep clear of the Pergamene territory in the future.[11] This was presumably succeeded by a period of Galatian restraint throughout Anatolia, since they were by this time either allied with or at peace with every power in the region.

The war against Antiochos Hierax, however, probably followed the defeat of the Galatians. He had, of course, earned Attalos' enmity by participating in the attack which was defeated at the Aphrodision. How active this conflict with Hierax was during the fighting with the Galatians is not clear, but it is evident that their alliance no longer operated. The battles recorded against Hierax were spread all over western Asia Minor. One took place in Hellespontine Phrygia in the northwest, a second at the Harpasos River in Karia, and a third at Koloe in Lydia.

The distribution of these battles is instructive. It seems clear from the numismatic evidence that the major part of Hierax' strength lay in the northwest, in Hellespontine Phrygia and the Troad, which is exactly the region in which Eumenes and Philetairos before him had made serious efforts to gain influence, but also where Antiochos II had expanded his power in the period after 253.[12] It would seem therefore that Hierax had seized this area – he had mints at five cities along the Hellespont, one at Lysimacheia, and one at Skepsis in Mysia. This is a greater density of mints in this area than for any other Seleukid king. His other mints were in Lydia, but many of these seem to have produced relatively few coins, or were closed down when Ptolemy's fleet gained control over many of the coastal cities in the 240s. The weight of Hierax' coinings lay in the Troad cities, where he continued to coin in the 230s.

The control of Mysia and Hellespontine Phrygia was therefore one of the elements in the contest between Hierax and Attalos. But while the Troadic mints suggest that Antiochos was particularly active there, the true centre of power in Asia Minor was always Lydia, and the war was fought there as well; Koloe is a station on the Royal Road between Seleukeia-Tralleis and Nysa, in the Maiandros Valley, and the Harpasos River is a tributary of the Maiandros south of Laodikeia-ad-Lykos.

In fact the Koloe battle is said by Pausanias to have been the last fight between Hierax and Attalos, and after his defeat there Hierax fled to Armenia where the king briefly gave him refuge.[13] It is probably at this point that Attalos had to fight Lysias and the Seleukid generals, since, if Hierax had left Seleukid territory, Seleukos would surely attempt to regain control, but Attalos was victorious again. This was a clear warning that he would need to fight yet again; Seleukos would scarcely give up after one defeat.

Antiochos' refuge in Armenia was only temporary, and he left rapidly when he suspected a plot to eliminate him. Either before he went there or after, he made an attempt to invade Seleukos' territory; a brief minting from a place in eastern Kilikia might be a record of this invasion, though he is also noted as having attempted to invade Mesopotamia.[14] There he fought a force commanded by Andromachos, who had earlier invaded Armenia, presumably in pursuit of Hierax. Andromachos was Hierax' uncle (his mother's brother); he had been beaten in the Armenian invasion, but succeeded in defeating Hierax' own invasion of Mesopotamia.[15]

Hierax fled again, this time to Thrace. He had by this time lost control of any part of Asia Minor, and Thrace had slipped from his grip as well. Ptolemy III had acquired Lysimacheia and posts on the eastern shore, and Hierax' arrival inevitably made him Ptolemy's enemy. Since he now had no friends he was vulnerable. He was captured by a Ptolemaic patrol, but escaped. His captivity was evidently fairly comfortable, even relaxed, since he was able to escape with the help of a courtesan. He was picked up by a group of local Galatians, described in conventional terms as brigands. (There was a Galatian kingdom, the kingdom of Tylis, established in interior Thrace.) Probably when his value as a prisoner or hostage turned out to be minimal – no-one wanted him – they killed him. Just to add to the romantic aspect of the 'king in the heather', his horse is said to have avenged him by killing a Galatian chieftain.[16]

By this time Attalos, having for the moment defeated all his local enemies, had extended his control all through what had been Seleukid Asia Minor along the Royal Road as far as the northern side of the Taurus Mountains, taking control of many of the Seleukid cities on the road. But the intrusion of Seleukos into the fighting, and the participation of Lysias as a partisan of Seleukos, makes it obvious that his hold on the conquered region was precarious. In addition there had been a split within the ranks of the family of Akhaios. The generation of Queen Laodike, Antiochos II's widow, seems largely to have taken Hierax' side, but several of the next generation were with Seleukos. Andromachos, Laodike's brother had joined Seleukos, and of his two children, his daughter Laodike had married Seleukos II, and his son Akhaios (II) also joined Seleukos. (Just to complicate matters even further, Akhaios (II) eventually married the daughter of Antiochos Hierax, though since Hierax was only married in 230, this daughter cannot have been old enough to be married before about 216; she was called, almost inevitably, Laodike.)

Seleukos II was thus defeated in his attempts to recover Parthia and perhaps Baktria, where Arsakes and Diodotos made themselves kings and he was also unable to intervene decisively either against or in support of his brother in Asia Minor, with the result that another man, Attalos, had also made himself king, and had seized control of the Seleukid territories. The reason Seleukos was unable to act successfully in either direction, was that he had plenty of problems in the remaining territories he still controlled. But it began to seem as though the disintegration of the Seleukid kingdom was becoming a permanent condition.

This condition of disunity and civil war was no doubt of much interest to Ptolemy III, as was the success of Attalos in conquering Seleukid Asia Minor, though there was no need for him to intervene for most of his reign. He did assist Antiochos Hierax early on, about 241, to suppress a mutiny of his Galatian mercenaries at Magnesia, but this may be counted as both self-preservation and as a public benefaction.[17] He had, however, clearly established friendly contact with Hierax, and at the end, when his men captured him, it seems he was to be kept as a political pawn (before he escaped). Any interest Ptolemy took in him was, of course, entirely on his own behalf.

The first and most fundamental problem for Seleukos was perhaps the number of troops at his disposal. He had lost a large part of his army at Ankyra – 20,000, so we are told, but this is probably an exaggeration. He had lost more men in whatever fighting had taken place in the east, and this was on top of the losses incurred in the Third Syrian War. He had certainly lost his elephants, which had been so important to Antiochos I's victory over the Galatians, and he had lost his warships as well, the elephants taken by Ptolemy when he captured Apameia, the ships lost in Seleukos' shipwreck.

Much of what forces he still had were needed to hold his remaining territories. The cities of Syria had fallen all too easily to Ptolemy in 246 and required garrisons, perhaps stronger than before; forces were needed to prevent any further advances by the Parthians, which meant increased garrisons in Media; the domination of Asia Minor by Hierax and then by Attalos required that some of his forces were needed to block the passes out of Asia Minor; the frontier with Ptolemaic Syria required a constant watch – and all this with fewer human resources.

The losses of territory, in the east, in Asia Minor, and at Seleukeia-in-Pieria, also had very damaging financial effects on the kingdom. This may be stated with confidence, although the precise extent of these losses cannot be stated. But Asia Minor was one of the wealthiest parts of the kingdom, and while the resources of Parthia and Baktria are not known, and they may well have been largely absorbed in the east, the loss of the land was replaced by the need to develop defences against their hostility. The Ptolemaic control of Seleukeia-in-Pieria meant that trade between Syria and the Mediterranean world had to either go through a foreign-controlled city, or had to be channelled by way of the two remaining Syrian ports (Laodikeia and Arados) or had to go by way of the Kilikian cities, all of which would increase merchants' costs.

So Seleukos' task after his defeat in the east and west was to hold onto the kingdom which remained, build up his resources, and plan to recover his losses. This, given his obviously weakened political situation, was not going to be easy. Two regions, Babylonia and Syria, were crucial to the recovery of his finances. Syria, however, had been comprehensively looted by the Ptolemaic army in the 240s as it retreated, to the benefit of Ptolemy III's treasury and his courtiers. Damage repair in the cities would no doubt absorb a good deal of the local resources for some time. Yet it is noticeable, despite further political problems at home that Seleukos was able to send an army, however ineffectually, into Asia Minor in the early 220s, and his son was able to mount a major invasion in 224 and 223. In other words, the power of the kings in the heart of the kingdom had been largely recovered by about 228.

This was in the face of continuing problems in both Babylonia and Syria. It has long been understood, from a comment by Justin, that Seleukos' war with Arsakes in the 230s was interrupted because he had to attend to more urgent matters in the west.[18] It is often assumed that this was caused by Hierax, but they had a peace agreement and both seem to have kept to it.

Another explanation has been trouble in Syria. In fact, the transcription and publication of the Babylonian Astronomical Diaries makes it clear that the trouble was in Babylonia.

Until these appeared in full Babylonia had been thought to be quiet, a convenient and productive tax producer, loyal to the Seleukid dynasty and a dependable support for it. Some of this appears correct, in that such evidence as there is does support the notion that the region was generally loyal. Its tax production naturally will have varied with the harvest and with commercial activity, and both were inevitably affected by such extraneous events as locust plagues and floods. The kings, moreover, were generally assiduous in performing their religious duties, and this was a good way to retain Babylonian loyalty. So far as can be seen the normal and traditional systems of law and commerce continued. There are, for example, several records of contracts from the reign of Seleukos II, apparently unaffected by the wars and other distractions.[19]

These 'other distractions', by the records of the diarist, were frequent, but they were concentrated in Babylon. At least the diarist tended to concentrate on affairs of the city, but he was also in touch with events in other Babylonian cities, and received news from the wider kingdom which he reported if it was of political moment, such as the death of the king, or, in the case of Stratonike, of a queen. One of the ways the population was kept loyal, or at least informed, was the dispatch of royal messages, marked by the diarist by the phrase 'a message on the leather scroll to the Babylonians'.[20] This was a message which was sent to the governors, who then had it proclaimed publicly. One of these was pronounced in 241, no doubt announcing the end of the war with Ptolemy.

The troubles in Babylonia in 237 which interrupted Seleukos' Parthian war have been mentioned already. It is worth emphasizing that it was fighting between the palace guards and the army which the diarist records, not a rebellion by the people of Babylon. We do not know the cause, or even the results, of the fighting. But it was clearly a deep-seated problem, for it happened again in 234. Again the surviving parts of the diarist's notice do little more than indicate that fighting was taking place, but it was once more between the different parts of the royal forces 'in the palace which had rebelled against King Seleukos'.[21]

It is quite possible that this was in part a result of trouble in Syria the year before which had been caused by Stratonike, the sister of Antiochos II who had married Demetrios the son of Antigonos Gonatas. She had left her husband some time before – he had taken another wife – and had returned to Syria. This seems to have happened before Demetrios' accession in 239, and Stratonike had apparently lived in Antioch ever since. At some point in the 230s – 235 is the most popular guess – she proposed that she should marry the king her nephew, a plan he rejected.[22] (This has been one of the presumed 'western problems' or problems in Syria which have been assigned as the cause of Seleukos breaking off his Parthian war.)

Stratonike, rejected and no doubt infuriated, raised a rebellion in Antioch against the king. It is often assumed that she was acting in alliance with Antiochos Hierax, but of this there is no evidence. It must be said that the cause of the city's rebellion is unconvincing – why should the Antiochenes care? Since it did happen, more must be involved than Stratonike's rejection. One might suggest taxation, and it is perhaps significant that Seleukos II is credited with organizing an expansion of the city, no doubt in the second half of his reign.[23] (He was, after all, particularly busy in the first half.) The loss of Seleukeia-in-Pieria to Ptolemaic control had some, though an unknown, effect on Antioch, possibly by receiving refugees, certainly by disrupting its trade. The status of capital which had been Seleukeia's was now Antioch's, meaning that the city had a greater population of wealthy courtiers and their hangers-on, and this increase in numbers no doubt put pressure on the accommodation in the city. All this was disruptive. It is said that Seleukos had to besiege Antioch to recover it from his aunt, and that she then fled towards Seleukeia-in-Pieria, but was captured before she got there; Seleukos had her executed.

How much of this is to be believed is difficult to decide. The sources are confused, the motivation for Stratonike is crude and barely convincing, and her proposal is very likely to be mere assumption by the sources; the connection of her revolt with Hierax is without any ancient evidence. But what is certain is that there was trouble in Antioch, and that Seleukos II had to deal with it, to the extent of waging war and executing a close relative. It is worth noting that Stratonike fled towards Seleukeia, which was in Ptolemaic hands at the time; but once again, any connection beforehand between her and Ptolemy lacks any evidence. The connection with the fighting in Babylon is also unproven, but given the apparent sensitivity of the situation in Babylon it seems likely that the news of a dynastic crisis and a revolt at Antioch could well have set off more fighting in that city.

The Babylonian diarist mentions troops in the city in 230, but not what they did.[24] They may be assumed, however, to have done something, and in

Babylon. Next year more of his text survives, and he refers to 'fights', and to 'the palace of the king' in the next line. A slightly later reference, but still within the same month, mentions 'the general over the four generals' (the diarist's term for the Babylonian viceroy or satrap, who had supporting *strategoi* in the major cities), being 'against' something, and that King Seleukos and his sons were 'on the left of the Euphrates'.[25]

This is, of course, a good deal less than clear, except that there was trouble in the city, involving the palace, and that both the satrap of Babylonia and the king and his family were also involved in it in some way. And this was the third time in eight years that such disturbances had occurred in Babylon. This happened along with one or possibly two invasions by Hierax (in Kilikia and in Mesopotamia) and the revolt at Antioch, so this seems quite enough to account for Seleukos being unable to deal with the rebellions in Parthia and Asia Minor during these years.

The presence of King Seleukos at Babylon in 229 may well have marked the end of the troubles in that city. He had two sons, Alexander and Antiochos, and one daughter, Antiochis, none of them older than fourteen at the time. Later, Antiochos was stationed at Babylon, and this may have been the solution to the city's problems, for if a royal prince was in the city, so was a quasi-royal court, and the royal guards in the palace were thus under much closer control. Perhaps the troublesome units were posted away, since a royal prince might be too much of a potential hostage for disloyal guards to be near him. Their problems, whatever they were, could then be the more easily dealt with. This is mere speculation, since little survives concerning Babylonia for the two decades after 229, though Antiochos was certainly living in the city between 225 and 223.[26]

There is, however, one other relevant document, a tablet recording a set of offerings by King Seleukos III to Esangil. The ceremony was carried on in accordance with instructions earlier given by Seleukos II, and consisted of offerings for the gods Bel and Beltiia within the temple. The ceremony was carried out by the *shatammu*, a senior administrator of the temple. The king's offering consisted of shekels of silver (the number is missing but was certainly in the plural), and to this the *shatammu* added 'from his own house', 'eleven fat oxen, a hundred fat ewes, and eleven fat ducks'. It is apparent that the king was not present at the ceremony, but his generosity was marked. (One may assume that the animals were actually paid for by the king; the silver was in addition.)[27]

This has been interpreted as an early indication that there was a cult of the royal family in Babylon, in addition to the local, spontaneous, cults which had developed in several of the other cities of the kingdom. It may perhaps be better seen as one of a long sequence of royal gifts to Esangil, which the diarist records in various fragments of his tablets from the time of Seleukos I on. The king also paid regularly for repairs to the temple. In all this the Babylonians in the temples were effectively in control, and their procedures were followed, while at the same time the king, by providing the money was clearly able to keep the priests under political control – they had learned to do this from Seleukos I.

This was clearly one means of controlling Babylon, but it probably had little effect on the restless palace guards, who are likely to have been Greeks or Macedonians, or even Galatians. The fact was that as a major city Babylon was fading. The foundation of Seleukeia-on-the-Tigris by Seleukos I transferred the centre of government to a new site, and the alteration of the location of the government persuaded many Babylonian citizens to move. Seleukeia was now the 'royal city'. And it was a Greco-Macedonian city, where, so far as we know, the palace guards were not prone to rebel. But the riots or rebellions of the guards in Babylon, together with the assiduous royal attentions to the major temples (not just Esangil) imply that there was a considerable tension between the various groups in the city which is not otherwise visible, but which was perhaps exacerbated by the city's decline. The presence of a royal prince, or even better the king himself, together with his entourage and personal guards, was probably the best way of damping down these tensions.

In 227 comes the best indication that Seleukos had recovered control sufficiently to plan for an expedition to recover Asia Minor. In that year the arrangement by which Arados continued to control its *peraia* was changed. The change is visible only numismatically, but was decisive nevertheless. Arados continued to coin, but it was suddenly joined in this by a string of towns which had been in its *peraia*, and which, by producing coins themselves, were demonstrating that they were no longer under Arados' control. Marathos, directly opposite the island-city, Simyra, a little to the south, Karne, Balanaia and Gabala north along the coast, all coined. The only way this could have happened is if the king had imposed himself, removed the *peraia* from Arados' control, and then made these places into autonomous communities.

The *peraia* was an obvious weak link in Syria's defences. Arados' city had accepted Ptolemy as king in 246–242 and clearly regarded itself as only loosely attached to the Seleukid kingdom. The best interpretation of Aradian history is to see it as a community bent on gaining its full independence, and in the meantime expanding its autonomy. It had been autonomous until 227, but Seleukos II was apparently unable to accept this status. He was about to fight Attalos, who was a friend, at least, of Ptolemy, and it was best to secure his full authority in Syria (and Babylonia), before he set off.[28]

Seleukos II died suddenly, of a fall from his horse, in the Seleukid year 87, which is 225/224 BC.[29] His son Alexander succeeded him, taking the throne name Seleukos (III). Nicknamed Keraunos ('thunderer'), he may have been a noisy impatient sort, like the original Ptolemy Keraunos. He launched himself into a war with Attalos I in Asia Minor, a war originally planned by his father; indeed he may have been the Seleukos whose commanders joined with Lysias in the battle which Attalos recorded in the dedications listing his victories at Pergamon.[30] The fighting was unsuccessful, even with a full levy of the kingdom. After a reign of only three years (225/224 to 223/222– probably 225–222), he fell victim to a plot among his senior commanders.[31]

His situation had been difficult from the start. The death of his father meant it was possible that a new Ptolemaic war might begin at any moment, and it certainly freed Ptolemy III from any inhibitions about intervening in Seleukid affairs. It was surely among Seleukos' aims to attempt to recover the territories lost in his father's war with Ptolemy. But the death of Hierax the year before had given Attalos the opportunity to consolidate his hold on his conquests. Attalos was certainly vulnerable, but a war with Egypt was a much more difficult proposition. By the time Seleukos III was in power and settled (after perhaps a year) it may also have been known that Ptolemy III was involved in the developing crisis over the Spartan revolution of King Kleomenes in Greece, a most distracting business. A new attempt at the reconquest of Asia Minor, relying on the presumed residual loyalty of the Greco-Macedonian inhabitants towards the Seleukid dynasty felt by men such as Lysias, was probably the best option.

The details of Seleukos III's death are muddled. A Galatian, Apatourios, is blamed, as is Nikanor, one of Seleukos' officers. The means are said to have been poison. The two men are then said to have been immediately killed, though if poison was used it is difficult to know how their guilt was established; and with their immediate deaths their reasons, and the names of any of their collaborators, remained unknown. Speculation ranges widely, of course, and must include the aftermath of the problems in Babylon, but is ultimately futile without more evidence.

The deaths of two kings in three years dealt a further heavy blow to the Seleukid kingdom. It had broken in the previous generation into three large sections, Asia Minor, now seized by Attalos, Baktria, where the satrap Diodotos II had made himself king, but had recently been overthrown by a usurper, and the central section from Syria to Media. Reconquering either of the breakaway areas, both of them large, looked very difficult, and Seleukos II and Seleukos III had both failed in their attempts. Further, the dynasty seemed to be expiring. There was just one male representative left, Seleukos' younger brother Antiochos, who became the next king at the age of about 20 years. The time when kings could expect to live for sixty or seventy years (Seleukos I and Antiochos I) seemed to have passed – Antiochos II and Seleukos II died in their forties, Seleukos III in his twenties.

Seleukos III died just over a century after the death of Alexander the Great, the inspiration for most of the Seleukid kings. That had signalled the start of the disintegration of his empire. Now the deaths of two Seleukid kings in three years may well have signalled the continuing breakdown of the largest fragment of Alexander's empire. The parallel is not exact, of course, since the Seleukid kingdom was already disintegrating before the 220s, and the heir to the kingdom was a young man of 20 years. But Alexander's heir had been a young man (Philip Arrhidaios), and his managers (including Seleukos), were as capable as the ministers of the young Antiochos III. But as it turned out most of Antiochos' ministers were as avid to destroy the kingdom as those first inheritors. The Seleukid kingdom appeared in 222 to be as complete a political failure as Alexander's.

Notes and References

Introduction

1. E. R. Bevan, *The House of Seleucus*, 2 vols, (London 1902, reprinted 1966); A. Bouche-Leclercq, *Histoire des Seleucides*, 2 vols, (Paris 1913); Sherwin-White and Kuhrt, *Samarkhand to Sardis*.
2. E. Will, *Histoire politique du monde hellenistique*, 2 vols, 2nd ed., Nancy (1979–1982); Peter Green, *Alexander to Actium*, (California 1990). There is also, of course, the *Cambridge Ancient History*, vols VII and VIII, but it is particularly unsatisfactory for the Seleukid kingdom, and Will's chapters are essentially English versions of his own book.

Chapter 1

1. I have discussed Alexander's failure to provide for his empire and his inheritance in *Alexander the Great Failure, the Collapse of the Macedonian Empire*, (London 2008).
2. This is well documented, in Q. Curtius, book IX, and Arrian, *Ta meta Alexandrou* (*FGrH* 156) leading to several modern accounts, including R. M. Errington, 'From Babylon to Triparadisos, 323–320 BC', *JHS* 90, (1970), 49–77, E. Badian, 'The Struggle for the Succession to Alexander the Great', *Gnomon* 34, (1962), A. B. Bosworth, *The Legacy of Empire, Politics, Warfare and Propaganda under the Successors*, (Oxford 2002); in addition any general book on the period has an account of these events.
3. This was clearly done by pre-arrangement. The hijacking occurred at Damascus, which is not on the route from Babylon to Macedon, where Perdikkas wanted the burial to take place (Diodoros 18.28.2–3; Pausanias 1.6.3; Arrian, *FGrH* 156, 9, 2, 10; Strabo 17.1.8.
4. Cornelius Nepos, *Eumenes* 5.
5. Polyainos 4.6.4; Arrian *FGrH* 156, 1.33.
6. Arrian, *FGrH* 156, frag. 2.3.
7. Plutarch, *Eumenes* 13.3–4; Diodoros 18.60.1–62.1; Polyainos 4.8.2.
8. Billows, *Antigonos*, ch. 3.
9. Diodoros 18.43.2; P. Wheatley, 'Ptolemy Soter's Annexation of Syria, 320 BC', *Classical Quarterly* 45, (1995), 431–440.
10. Diodoros 19.15.6; Appian, *Syr* 52.
11. Pausanias 1.25.6.
12. Diodoros 19.12.2–3.
13. Diodoros 19.14.1–2.
14. Diodoros 19.12.4–13.9.
15. Diodoros 19.18.1, 3.5.
16. Xenophilos: Billows, Antigonos, app. 3, no. 119.
17. Deaths: Diodoros 19.44.1–2 (Eumenes); 46.1–4 (Peithon).
18. New satraps: Diodoros 19.48.1–3 (easterners).
19. Diodoros 19.5.1–2 (Peukestas), Billows, *Antigonos*, app. 3 no. 90; Peukestas and many other men who were apparently deposed by Antigonos continued in his service

afterwards, sometimes for many years; it would seem that they respected his position; they are listed with brief biographies in app. 3 of Billows, *Antigonos*.
20. Treasure: Diodoros 19.46.6 (Ekbatana); 48.6–7 (Susa).
21. Diodoros 19.55.1.
22. Diodoros 19.55.2–9; Appian, *Syr.* 53.

Chapter 2
1. It may in fact have been deliberate propaganda on Seleukos' part: Justin 15.4.2–10; there are two biographies: A. Mehl, *Seleukos Nikator und sein Reich*, (Louvain 1986) (Vol I, but the only one published) and my *Seleukos Nikator, Building a Hellenistic Kingdom*, (London 1990), which is rather briefer; the histories of Bevan and Bouche-Leclercq also deal with him.
2. Justin 15.4.2.
3. John Malalas 198, 202–203; also Eustathios 915; on the whole issue of Seleukos' family see also Ogden, *Polygamy*, 119–124.
4. Diodoros 19.56.1–2.
5. Diodoros 18.14.1 (Kleomenes; 43.2 (Laomedon); P. Wheatley, 'Ptolemy Soter's Annexation of Syria 320 B.C.', *Classical Quarterly* 45, (1995), 433–440.
6. The existence of these men suggests that either they were part of the fifty horsemen who accompanied him in his flight, or there were more men involved in the journey.
7. Diodoros 19.56.3.
8. Billows, *Antigonos*, app. 3, no. 88.
9. Diodoros 19.56.5.
10. Diodoros 19.56.4.
11. Diodoros 19.57.1.
12. Diodoros 19.57.2; Appian, *Syr.*, 53
13. Diodoros 19.57.4.
14. Diodoros 19.60.3–4.
15. Diodoros 19.58.5–6.
16. Diodoros 19.57.1; Arrian, *FGrH* 156, F 24.
17. Diodoros 19.59.2.
18. Diodoros 19.60.1 and 61.1; R. Hope Simpson, 'Antigonos, Polyperchon and the Macedonian Regency', *Historia* 6, (1957), 371–373.
19. Diodoros 19.61.1–3; E. Anson, 'The Evolution of the Macedonian Army Assembly (330–315 BC)', *Historia* 40, (1991), 230–247.
20. Diodoros 19.61.3; R. Hope Simpson, 'Antigonos the One-Eyed and the Greeks', *Historia* 8, (1859), 385–409; Billows, *Antigonos*, ch. 6.
21. Diodoros 19.62.1.
22. Diodoros 19.62.1–5.
23. Diodoros 19.62.6.
24. Diodoros 19.64.4–8.
25. Diodoros 19.62.7.
26. Diodoros 19.64.8.
27. Billow, *Antigonos*, 118, no. 45.
28. Diodoros 19.68.5–69.3; Billows, *Antigonos*, 120–121, and map 4.
29. Diodoros 19.75.6.
30. Diodoros 19.79.3–80.2.

31. P. Wheatley, 'The Besieger in Syria 314–312 B.C.: Historiographical and Chronological Notes', in P. Wheatley and R. Hannah (eds), *Alexander and his Successors: Essays from the Antipodes*, (Claremont, 2009), 323–333.
32. Mehl, *Seleukos Nikator*, 82–89.
33. Diodoros 19.80.3–85.4; A. M. Devine, 'Diodoros' Account of the Battle of Gaza', *Acta Classica* 27, (1984), 31–40; I. Kertesz, 'Ptolemy I and the Battle of Gaza', *Studia Aegyptica*, (1974), 231–241; Billows, *Antigonos*, 124–128.
34. Roger Bagnall, 'The Origins of Ptolemaic Cleruchs', *Bulletin of the American Society of Papyrologists* 21, (1984), 7–20.
35. Diodoros 19.85.5; Billows, Antigonos, app. 3, nos 9, 77, 88, 92.
36. Diodoros 19.86.1–2; 93.1–2.
37. Wheatley, 'Besieger in Syria'; J. K. Winniki, 'Militäroperationen von Ptolemaios I und Seleukos in Syrien in den Jahren 312–311 v. Chr', *Ancient Society* 20, (1989), 55–92 and 22, (1991), 147–227.
38. Diodoros 19.70.1.

Chapter 3

1. Diodoros 19.90.1.
2. Amelie Kuhrt, 'Akhaimenid Babylonia: Sources and Problems', in H. Sancisi-Weerdenburg and A. Kuhrt (eds), *Akhaimenid History* IV, (Leiden 1990), 177–194.
3. R. McC. Adams, *Heartland of Cities*, (Chicago 1981), 177–179; R. McC. Adams and H.J. Nissen, *The Uruk Countryside, the Natural Setting of Urban Societies*, (Chicago 1972), 55–57; Gilbert McEwan, 'Babylonia in the Hellenistic Period', *Klio* 70, (1988), 412–421.
4. Collections of cuneiform documents demonstrate this clearly; examples are, chosen almost at random: G. Kh. Sarkisian, 'New Cuneiform Texts from Uruk of the Seleukid period in the Staatsliche Museen zu Berlin', *Staatsliche Muzeen, Forschungen under Berichte* (1974), 15–58, and Paul-Alain Beaulieu, 'Textes Administratives inedits d'époque hellénistiques provenant des archives du Bit Res', *Revue Assyriologie* 32, (1989), 53–81; there are numerous others.
5. As an example, L. Timothy Doty, 'The Archive of the Nana-Iddin Family from Uruk', *Journal of Cuneiform Studies* 30, (1989), 65–91; the first of these documents dates from 8 SE/304 BC, the latest to 144 SE/168 BC; Doty distinguishes six generations of the family involved in producing the documents in the archive.
6. Martín A. Beek, *Atlas of Mesopotamia* (trans. D.R. Walsh, ed. H. H. Rowley) (London 1962), 139; R. J. van der Spek, 'The Babylonian Temple during the Macedonian and Parthian Domination', *Biblioteca Orientalia* 42, (1985), 542–562.
7. Diodoros 17.112.2–6; Arrian, *Anabasis*, 7.17.1–4.
8. Aperghis, *Economy*, 108.
9. Diodoros 19.90.1 and 91.1–2.
10. Diodoros 19.91.4.
11. *Astronomical Diaries*.
12. Grayson; those numbered from 10 are Hellenistic.
13. Aristotle, *de Caelo* 2.12.
14. Amelie Kuhrt, 'Berossos' *Babyloniaka* and Seleukid Rule in Babylonia', in A. Kuhrt and S.M. Sherwin-White (eds), *Hellenism in the East, the interaction of Greek and non-Greek civilizations from Syria to Central Asia after Alexander*, (London 1987), 32–56; an edition and translation of what remains is in Gerald P. Verbrugghe and John M. Withersham, *Berossos and Manetho*, (Ann Arbor 1996).

15. A large collection of these were published by M. M. Rostovtzeff, 'Seleucid Babylonia: bullae and seals of clay with Greek inscriptions', *Yale Classical Studies* 3, (1932), 1–114; they were mainly from the excavations at Seleukeia; others have been found at Uruk, on which see S. M. Sherwin-White, 'Seleucid Babylonia: a case study for the installation and development of Greek rule', in Kuhrt and Sherwin-White, *Hellenism in the East*, 1–31.

16. Sherwin-White and Kuhrt, *Samarkhand to Sardis*, 50–51.

17. Ibid, 149–150; among many articles on Uruk the following are notable: A. Aymard, 'Une ville de la Babylonie Seléucid d'après les contrats cunéiformes', *Revue des Etudes Anciennes* 40, (1938), 5–42; R. Wallenfels, 'Apkallu Sealings from Hellenistic Uruk', *Baghdader Mitteilungen*, 24, (1993), 309–333; Doty, Sarkisian and Beaulieu (notes 4 and 5 above); R. J. van der Spek, 'The Babylonian city', in Kuhrt and Sherwin-White, *Hellenism in the East*, 57–74.

18. Sherwin-White and Kuhrt, *Samarkhand to Sardis*, 155–158.

19. P. M. Fraser, *Cities of Alexander the Great*, (Oxford 1996).

20. Diodoros 19.52.2 (Kassandreia) Strabo 7, frags 21 and 23 (Thessaloníki); Cohen, *Hellenistic Settlements/Asia*, 95–99 and 101–105.

21. Holbl, *Ptolemaic Empire*, 26–27.

22. Antigonos' cities: Billows, *Antigonos*, 145; Diodoros 20.47.5 (Antigoneia in Syria); Lysimacheia: Diodoros 20.29.1; Cohen, *Hellenistic Settlements/Asia*, 145–148, 164–165, 391–392, 398–400, and 82–89.

23. Cohen, *Hellenistic Settlements/Asia*, 177–180.

24. R. A. Hadley, 'The Foundation Date of Seleucia-on-the-Tigris', *Historia* 27, 1978, 228–230, chose 300 as his preferred date.

25. Appian, *Syr.*, 58; also Pausanias 1.16.3 and Strabo 16.1.5.

26. The first group of excavations, by an American team, is summarized in Clark Hopkins (ed.), *Topography and Archaeology of Seleukeia on the Tigris*, (Ann Arbor 1972), with a curious interpretation of the plan on p. 2; later work, by an Italian team, is reported in successive volumes of Mesopotamia 1–8 (1966–1974); see also Antonio Invernizzi in *Sumer* 32, 1976, 167–175 and 'Seleuceia on the Tigris, Centre and Periphery in Seleukid Asia' in P. Bilde (ed.) *Centre and Periphery in the Hellenistic World*, (Aarhus 1997), 230–250; a summary plan is in Colin McEvedy, *Cities of the Classical world*, ed. Douglas Stuart Oles, (London 2011), 334–335.

27. Pausanias 1.16.3; *Astronomical Diaries*, – 274.

28. Adams, *Heartland of Cities* (note 3).

Chapter 4

1. Plutarch, *Demetrios* 6.1–2; Diodoros 19.93.1–3.

2. Billows, *Antigonos*, app. 3, no. 38.

3. Diodoros 19.90.1; Appian, *Syr.*, 54.

4. Appian, *Syr.*, 53.

5. Billows, *Antigonos*, 415–416.

6. P. Wheatley, 'The Besieger in Syria, 314–312 BC, Historiographical and Chronological Notes', in P. Wheatley and R. Hannah (eds), *Alexander and his Successors, Essays from the Antipodes*, (Claremont, 2009), 321–333.

7. Appian's word (*Syr.*, 54), though Diodoros is not so definite.

8. This name is actually not attested until later; this is a suggestion only.

9. Diodoros 19.91.1.

10. Diodoros 19.91.3; Billows, *Antigonos*, app. 3, no. 101.
11. Diodoros 9.91.3.
12. Grayson, 10; Diodoros 19.91.4.
13. Diodoros, 19.92.1.
14. Diodoros, 19.2.2–3.
15. Diodoros 19.92.3–5; Appian, *Syr.*, 55, says that Seleukos killed Nikanor, but this must have been in another fight in Media later.
16. Diodoros 19.105.1; *OGIS* 5 (Antigonos' account in a letter to the city of Skepsis).
17. *OGIS* 5.
18. Diodoros 19.100.3.
19. Grayson, 10, rev. 9–12.
20. Diodoros 19.100.5.
21. Diodoros 20.19.4.
22. Diodoros 20.19.5 and 27.1.
23. Diodoros 20.27.1–3.
24. Appian, *Syr.*, 55.
25. Diodoros 19.100.4–5.
26. See note 28.
27. Diodoros 19.100.5–6.
28. Arrian, *Indika*, 43 4–5; Billows, *Antigonos*, 139; L. Schober, *Untersuchungen zur Geschichte Babyloniens und der Oberen Satrapien zem 323–303 v. Chr.*, (Frankfurt 1981), 128–129 points out that Arrian's comparison with Kambyses' crossing of the Egyptian desert implies that Ptolemy sent a considerable force, not just a messenger or an ambassador.
29. Plutarch, *Demetrios* 7.2; Diodoros 19.100.6–7; Grayson, 10 rev. 24–25. Alexander's army marched from Thapsakos to the Tigris, 276 miles by the bematists' count (440km.); at the usual rate of 20km per day, Demetrios' march from Damascus to Babylon (twice the distance), would have taken at least fifty days, and possibly more: cf. Donald W. Engels, *Alexander the Great and the Logistics of the Macedonian Army*, (California 1978).
30. Plutarch, *Demetrios* 7.2–3; Diodoros 19.100.7; Grayson, Chronicle 10 rev. 25–31; Billows, *Antigonos*, app. 3, no. 14.
31. Plutarch, *Demetrios* 7.2.
32. Grayson, 10 rev. 34–41.
33. Polyainos 4.9.1.
34. P. Wheatley, 'Antigonos Monophthalamos in Babylonia, 310–308 BC', *Journal of Near Eastern Studies* 61, 2002, 39–47.

Chapter 5

1. Grayson 10, rev. 26–29.
2. Plutarch, *Demetrios* 17.2. – 18.1; E.S. Gruen, 'The Coronation of the Diadochoi', in J. Eadie and J. Ober, *The Craft of the Ancient Historian, Essays in Honor of Chester G. Starr*, (Lanham Md, 1985), 253–271; Billows, *Antigonos*, 157–158.
3. Diodoros 20.47.5.
4. I have argued this interpretation in *Seleukos Nikator*, 98.
5. Polybios 5.52.
6. N. M. Waggoner, 'The Early Alexander Coinage at Seleuceia on the Tigris', *American Numismatic Society Museum Notes* 15, (1969), 21–30; Houghton, *Seleucid Coins*, Seleucus I.

7. Diodoros 19.90.1–2; this, of course, may be Diodoros', or his source's, interpretation, or imagination; on the stories which follow see Samuel K. Eddy, *The King is Dead, Studies in Near Eastern Resistance to Hellenism, 334–31 BC*, (Lincoln, Nebraska 1961).
8. Grayson 10, rev. 5, 35–36.
9. Diodoros 19.90.4; Appian, *Syr.*, 56.
10. *OGIS* 213, 744, 745.
11. Diodoros 19.14.7–8.
12. Justin 15.4.12–13.
13. Hemchandra Raychaudhuri, *Political History of Ancient India*, (Oxford 1996), 234–256 and 591–601.
14. See Frank M. Holt, *Alexander the Great and Baktria*, (London 1989), 88–91.
15. Ibid, 87.
16. Romilla Thapar, *Asoka and the Decline of the Mauryas*, (Oxford 1997), 280; P. M. Fraser, *Cities of Alexander the Great*, (Oxford 1997), 132–140.
17. Justin 15.4.11.
18. Appian, *Syr.*, 55.
19. Justin 15.4.12–13.
20. Strabo 15.2.9.
21. This is a much-discussed issue; see Klaus Karttunen, *India and the Hellenistic World*, (Helsinki, 1997), 260–265.
22. W. W. Tarn, 'Two Notes on Seleucid History', *JHS*, 60, (1940), 84–94; there has been much scepticism over these elephant numbers, needlessly.
23. Plutarch, *Demetrios* 17.2. – 8.1.
24. Diodoros 19.105.2; Kassander ordered his jailer Glaukias to commit the murders, but he had in effect been given permission to have them killed by the others in the peace treaties of 311.
25. Diodoros 20.73.1–76.6.
26. Gruen, 'Coronation'.
27. For Seleukos: Plutarch, *Demetrios*, 18.3; for Antigonos: Diodoros 19.48.1 and 55.2.
28. Plutarch, *Demetrios*, 25.4; also in slightly different versions in Plutarch, *Moralia* 823 C – D, and Athenaios 6.261 B (from Phylarchos: *FGrH* 81 F 31); H. Hauben, 'A Royal toast in 302 BC', *Ancient Society* 5, (1974), 105–119.

Chapter 6

1. For this campaign see Billows, *Antigonos*, 169–173, who gives full references.
2. Diodoros 20.106.1–2.
3. Diodoros 20.106.3.
4. Diodoros 20.110.2–4.
5. Diodoros 20.110.4–6.
6. Diodoros 20.107.2–4.
7. Diodoros 20.107.4.
8. On Macedonian settlements in this region see Richard A. Billows, *Kings and Colonists, Aspects of Macedonian Imperialism*, (Leiden 1995), chapters 4 and 5; Cohen, *Hellenistic Settlements/Asia* 295–299 (Dokimeion).
9. Diodoros 20.107.2 and 4–5.
10. Diodoros 20.108.1.
11. Diodoros 20.108.2–6.
12. Diodoros 20.113.1.

13. A. Mehl, *Seleukos Nikator und sein Reich*, (Louvain 1986), 196–198, argues in favour of the raid to Babylon, but all the evidence he adduces is pre- or post-302/301; his argument is unconvincing.
14. Diodoros 20.113.4.
15. Diodoros 20.109.2–4.
16. Diodoros 20.112.1–4.
17. The sources for this campaign and the battle are Plutarch, *Demetrios*, 28–29, and Diodoros 21.1.1–4b; modern interpretations include B. Bar-Kochva, *The Seleucid Army*, (Cambridge 1979), 106–110, A. Mehl, *Seleukos Nikator*, 200–207; W. W. Tarn, *Hellenistic Military and Naval Developments*, (Cambridge 1930).
18. A point made by Diodoros in explaining why Demetrios withdrew so readily from Greece, 20.111.1.

Chapter 7

1. Xenophon, *Anabasis* 1.4.
2. I have summarized the condition of the country in *Cities of Seleukid Syria*, (Oxford 1990), ch. 1 and App. 3; for the Bekaa see Leon Marfoe, *Kamid el-Loz, 14, Settlement History of the Biqa up to the Iron Age*, (Bonn 1998).
3. See Ephraim Stern, *The Material Culture of the Land of the Bible in the Persian Period, 358–332 BC*, (Warminster 1982), which is immensely detailed, though these details effectively obscure the total picture. Even so, the general impression is of an impoverished population.
4. Cohen, *Hellenistic Settlements/Syria*, 76–79.
5. C. H. Kraeling (ed.), *Gerasa, City of the Decapolis*, (New Haven 1938); to be accurate, the city also claimed Alexander and Antigonos as founders; Cohen, *Hellenistic Settlements/Syria*, 248–253.
6. Cohen, *Hellenistic Settlements/Syria*, 155–156 (Doliche), 169–170 (Europos), 181–184 (Kyrrhos), 153–155 (Beroia), 94–101 (Pella-Apameia), 245–247 (Dion), 117–118 (Larisa), 101–102 (Arethousa).
7. Diodoros 21.1.5.
8. J. Seibert, *Historiche Beiträge zu den dynastischen Verbundungen in hellenistischer Zeit*, (Wiesbaden 1967), 95–96.
9. Plutarch, *Demetrios* 31.2.
10. Ibid.
11. Ibid 31.3–32.1.
12. Ibid, 31.3–32.2.
13. Ibid 32.2.
14. Ibid 32.4.
15. Eusebios, *Chronographia*, II, 119.
16. Plutarch, *Demetrios* 35.3.
17. The date at which Ptolemy took Tyre and Sidon is disputed: some say 295/294 (e.g., Holbl, *Ptolemaic Empire*, 23) but others 288. There is no definite evidence either way, but 288 seems to fit the wider situation best.
18. M. Launey, *Recherches sur les armées hellénistiques*, (Paris 1949–1950), discusses all aspects of soldiering; G. T. Griffith, *Mercenaries of the Hellenistic World*, (Cambridge 1935).
19. I have discussed this in *Cities of Seleukid Syria*, part 1, where full references are given.
20. Cohen, *Hellenistic Settlements/Syria*, 111–116 (Laodikeia-ad-Mare), 94–101 (Apameia), 126–135 (Seleukeia-in-Pieria), 80–93 (Antioch)).

21. J. Balty, L'Apamene antique et les limites de la Syria Secunda', in *La géographie administrative et politique d'Alexandre à Mahomet*, (Strasbourg, n.d.), 41–75.

22. Cohen, *Hellenistic Settlements/Syria*, 149–150 (Amphipolis-Thapsakos).

23. H. Seyrig, 'Le monnayage de Hierapolis de Syrie à l'époque d'Alexandre', *Revue Numismatique* 11, (1972), 11–12, expanded by Leo Mildenberg, 'A note on the coinage of Hierapolis-Bambyce', 273–283.

24. Lucian, *De dea Syria*, 18–25; G. Goossens, *Hierapolis de Syrie*, (Louvain 19430); Cohen, *Hellenistic Settlements/Syria*, 172–178.

25. Cohen, *Hellenistic Settlements/Syria*, 190–196.

26. Diodoros 33.4a.

27. It is now ar-Restan and as recently as 2013 stood a siege in the Syrian civil war.

28. *Corpus Inscriptionum Latinarum* III, 6687; cf. Franz Cumont, 'The Population of Syria', *Journal of Roman Studies* 26, (1936), 187–190.

29. John Malalas 201 – though this figure refers to Antigoneia and has been transferred to Antioch; this is a hazardous procedure based on a notoriously inaccurate writer.

30. Polybios 5.61.1.

31. J. Sauvaget, *Alep*, 2 vols, (Paris 1941), *planche* 52.

32. Colin McEvedy, *Cities of the Classical World*, ed. Douglas Stuart Oles, (London 2011); unfortunately he only considered one of the cities of Syria, Antioch, and his figures all seem rather low.

33. Aperghis, *Economy*, 13 -14, 35–36.

34. *OGIS* 213; *I. Didyma* 479 and 480.

35. Lucian, *De dea Syria*, 19–27.

36. An eventuality discussed by Ogden, *Polygamy,* 120–123, and Sherwin-White and Kuhrt, *Samarkhand to Sardis*, 24–25.

Chapter 8

1. Grayson 11.

2. Plutarch, *Demetrios* 35; Appian, *Syr.*, 59; K. Broderson 'Die Liebeskranke Konigssohn und die Seleukidische Herrshaftsauffassung', *Athenaeum* 63, (1985), and 459–469; A. B. Breebaart, 'King Seleucus I, Antiochus, and Stratonice', *Mnemosyne* 20, (1967), 154–164.

3. 292: A. T. Olmstead, 'Cuneiform Texts and Hellenistic Chronology', *Classical Philology* 32, (1932), 1–14 (at 6); 291: *Astronomical Diaries* -291.

4. A. J. Sachs and D. J. Wiseman, 'A Babylonian King List of the Hellenistic period', *Iraq* 16, (1954), 202–211.

5. As noted by Ogden, *Polygamy*, 122 and note 24.

6. *OGIS* 213 (Miletos); *I. Didyma* 480; L. Robert, 'Pline VI, 49. Demodamas de Milet et la reine Apame', *Bulletin de Correspondence Hellenique* 108, (1984), 468–474.

7. Strabo 11.7.1–3; Diodoros 19.100.5.

8. Strabo 2.14. 15.12 etc; Klaus Karttunen, *India and the Hellenistic World*, (Helsinki 1997), 69–76.

9. Strabo 2.68, 70, 76; Karttunen, *India*, 93–94.

10. P. M. Fraser, *Cities of Alexander the Great*, (Oxford 1996), 132–140.

11. Romilla Thapar, *Asoka and the Decline of the Mauryas*, (Oxford 1997), 21; Hemchandra Raychaudhuri, *Political History of Ancient India*, (Oxford 1996), 322–323.

12. Karttunen, *India* 292.

13. Pliny, *NH* 6.58; Strabo 11.7.1–3.

14. Michael Mitchiner, *The Early Coinage of Central Asia*, (London 1973), 19–25.
15. Sherwin-White and Kuhrt, *Samarkhand to Sardis*, 18–19.
16. Pliny NH 6.49; Frank L. Holt, *Thundering Zeus*, (California 1999), 27; Robert, 'Demodamas'.
17. Appian, *Syr*, 55, in fact claimed it as a foundation of Seleukos I.
18. W. W. Tarn and G. T. Griffith, *Hellenistic Civilisation*, 3rd ed., (London 1952); excavations at the site (now Khojent, formerly Leninabad) are said to have shown that the earliest deposits are of Seleukid date (so Sherwin-White and Kuhrt, *Samarkhand to Sardis*, 106.)
19. P. Bernard, 'Fouilles de la mission franco-sovietique a l'ancienne Samarkand (Afrasiab), 1989,' *(CRAI* 1990), 356–380, and 'Fouilles de la mission franco-ouzbeque a l'ancienne Samarkand, 1990–1991', *(CRAI* 1992), 275–311.
20. Sherwin-White and Kuhrt, *Samarkhand to Sardis*, 82–84.
21. Under the title *Fouilles d'Ai Khanoum*, Paris from 1973, and numerous studies in *CRAI* from 1966.
22. P. Bernard and H.-P. Francfort, *Etudes de géographie historique sur la plaine d'Ai Khanoum (Afghanistan)*, (Paris 1978).
23. Aperghis, *Economy*, 178 and 278.
24. Polybios 10.49.15 and 11.39.1–10; Strabo 11.8.9.
25. Sherwin-White and Kuhrt, *Samarkhand to Sardis*, 103–105.
26. For Greek epigraphy in the region, see the recent summary by Frank L. Holt, *Lost World of the Golden King*, (California 2012), ch. 6.
27. Ekbatana: Appian *Syr.*, 57, claiming that Seleukos I founded it, implying he had organized it as a Macedonian city; Strabo 16.1.27; Konkobar: cf, Sylvia Matheson, *Persia, an Archaeological Guide*, (London 1977), 124; Laodikeia-Nihavand: Strabo 11.13.6, Austin 153, L. Robert, 'Encore une inscription grécque d'Iran', *CRAI* 1967), 281–296.
28. Isidore of Charax, *Parthian Stations*, ed. W. W. Schoff, (London 1914), paras 7–8.
29. Founded by Atropates, hence the name; it was probably formally subject to Seleukos I, who marched through it on his way to Ipsos in 302.
30. P. Bernard, 'Herakles, les grottes de Karafto et le sanctuaire du mont Sambulos en Iran', *Studia Iranica* 9, (1980), 301–324.
31. Houghton, *Seleucid Coins*, Antiochos I.
32. *OGIS* 233.

Chapter 9
1. Outline plans of several of these cities, and a full discussion, are in my *Cities of Seleukid Syria*, (Oxford 1990).
2. As becomes clear in the burning of Antioch in 143: I Maccabees 2.47–48; Josephus, *Jewish Antiquities*, 13.139–140.
3. Cohen, *Hellenistic Settlements/Asia* 369–371.
4. Plutarch, *Demetrios* 43.
5. Ibid 44; Justin 16.2.1–2; Plutarch, *Pyrrhos* 11.
6. T. L. Shear, *Kallias of Sphettos and the Revolt of Athens in 286 BC*, (Princeton 1978); Christian Habicht, *Athens from Alexander to Anthony*, trans Deborah Lucas Schneider, (Cambridge, MA, 1997), 95–97.
7. H. Hauban, 'Philokles, king of the Sidonians and general of the Ptolemies', *Studia Phoenicia* 5, (1987), 413–427.
8. Plutarch, *Demetrios* 46.3–5.

9. Ibid, 46.3; he deserted her almost at once; she produced a son, Demetrios the Fair.
10. Ibid 47.1.
11. Ibid 47.2–4.
12. Ibid 48.1–4.
13. Ibid, 49.1.
14. Ibid 49.2.
15. Ibid 49.3–51.1.
16. Cohen, *Hellenistic Settlements/Syria*, 120–121, ignores the connection with Seleukos, which is stated on coins of the city.
17. Ibid 51.3.
18. Holbl, *Ptolemaic Empire* 24–25.
19. Justin 17.1.4–6; Pausanias 1.103.4; Strabo 13.4.1; Memnon *FGrH* 434 F 5–6.
20. Helen S. Lund, *Lysimachos, a Study in Hellenistic Kingship*, (London 1992).
21. Ptolemy II's coronation took place on 7 January 282; Holbl, *Ptolemaic Empire*, 35.
22. Plutarch, *Demetrios* 52.3–53.3.
23. Appian, *Syr.*, 62; Memnon *FGrH* 434, F 5–6.
24. Appian, *Syr.*, 62, 64; Justin 17.18–2.2; Memnon *FGrH* 434, F 7; Pausanias 1.10.5.
25. Polyainos 8.57; she dressed a maid of honour in her own robes, and herself in beggar's clothing. She got away; the maid was murdered.
26. Appian, *Syr.*, 62; Strabo 13.4.1; Pausanias 1.16.2.

Chapter 10
1. A. J. Sachs and D. J. Wiseman, 'A Babylonian King List of the Hellenistic Period', *Iraq*, 16, (1954), 202–211.
2. Memnon *FGrH* 434 F 11 8.1.
3. William M. Brashear, 'A New Fragment on Seleucid History', *Atti del XVII Congresso Internazionale de Papirologia*, (Naples 1984), 345–350; the fragment deals with a process of honouring a king after his accession, and seems to apply to Antiochos' succession; it is brief and not really all that informative, except that such ceremonies probably happened whenever the news of a new succession arrived.
4. Ptolemy and Pyrrhos: Justin 17.2.1; Herakleia: Memnon, *FGrH* 434 F 11 8.
5. *OGIS* 219 = Austin 162.
6. The Seleukid policy towards these cities is detailed in John Ma, *Antiochos III and the Cities of Western Asia Minor*, (Oxford 1999), which spreads itself wider than its title claims.
7. Richard A. Billows, *Kings and Colonists, Aspects of Macedonian Imperialism*, (Leiden 1994), ch. 4.
8. Strabo 13.4.1; Appian, *Syr.*, 63.
9. Justin 17.2.4–8; 24.2–3.
10. *OGIS* 55; Ma, *Antiochos III and the Cities*, 94.
11. J. M. Cook, *The Persian Empire*, (London 1983), 176–182 and fig. 12.
12. Cohen, *Hellenistic Settlements/Asia* 145–149 (Apameia-Kelainai), 177–180 (Ephesos).
13. Allen, *Attalid Kingdom*, 12–15, and 183–185; Billows, *Antigonos*, app. 3, no. 91.
14. Billows, *Kings and Colonists*, 104; Jones, 49; Mitchell, *Anatolia*, 85; Cohen, *Hellenistic Settlements/Asia* 295–299.
15. Billows, *Kings and Colonists*, 99–100; Billows does not include Lysias the regent.
16. Cohen, *Hellenistic Settlements/Asia*, 311–313, 319–321; the exact locations of these places are not known.

17. Ibid, 96–99; Ogden, *Polygamy*, 120, does not accept the relationship (see also next note).
18. M. Worrle, 'Antiochos I, Akhaios der Altere und die Galater', *Chiron*, 5, (1975), 59–87 (= Austin 168).
19. The town of Herakleia-in-Media (actually in Areia) was refounded as Achaia in the time of Antiochos I (Pliny *NH* 6.48); if it was renamed for Akhaios this is a further indication of the man's royal connections – no Seleukid city was named after a non-royal person after Seleukos I.
20. Diodoros 19.12 and 20.50; Athenaios 7.289 and 10.438d; Jones, *Cities*, 49–50; Cohen, *Hellenistic Settlements/Asia*, 325–326; the date of the foundation and the precise identity of the founder are not certain; I would go for the earliest of the three possibilities, a commander for Antigonos Monophthalamos (Billows, *Antigonos*, app. 3, no 112).
21. Richard A. Billows, 'Anatolian Dynasts: the Case of the Macedonian Eupolemos in Karia', *Classical Antiquity* 8, (1982), 173–206; Billows, *Kings and Colonists*, 93–94.
22. Memnon, *FGrH* 434 F 11 6.
23. For a rather speculative reconstruction of Mithradates' ancestry, see A. B. Bosworth and P.V. Wheatley, 'The Origin of the Pontic House', *JHS* 118, 1998, 155–164.
24. Memnon, *FGrH* 434 F 11 7; Trogus, *Prologue* 17; Appian, *Mith.*, 9; Strabo 12.41.
25. Justin 24.14.
26. Roger A. Bagnall, *The Administration of the Ptolemaic Possession Outside Egypt*, (Leiden 1976), 113, though he rather pushes the evidence too far at times; see also J. D. Grainger, *Cities of Pamphylia*, (Oxford 2009), ch. 4.
27. Memnon, *FGrH* 434 F 11.9.
28. Justin 17.2.4.
29. Memnon, *FGrH* 434 F 11.8.
30. Ibid, 9.
31. *I. Didyma* 123 = Burstein 25.
32. Memnon, *FGrH* 434, F 11.8.
33. Ibid, 11.9.
34. Justin, 24.4–5; Pausanias 10.19.5–6.
35. G. Nachtergael, *Les Galates en Grèce at les Sotéria de Delphes*, (Brussels 1977).
36. Memnon, *FGrH* 434 F 11.10.
37. Livy 38.16.1–6; H. H. Schmitt, Die *Staatsverträge des Altertums*, vol. 3, (Munich 1969), no 469.
38. Livy 38.16.11–12.
39. *OGIS* 748; Marcel Launey, 'Un episode oublie de l'invasion Galate en Asie Mineure 278/7 av. J.-D.', *Revue des Etudes Grecques* 46, (1944), 217–236.
40. Strabo 13.1.27, quoting Hegesianax, *FGrH* 45 F 3.
41. Allen, *Attalid Kingdom*, 136.
42. *I. Erythrai* 24 and 28.
43. *I. Didyma* 426.
44. *Palatine Anthology* 7.442.
45. Plutarch, *Parallela Minora* 15.
46. *OGIS* 765.
47. J. Keil and A. von Premerstein, *Bericht uber eine Reise in Lydien*, (Vienna 1911), vol 2, 19.
48. Pausanias 10.32.4.
49. Pausanias 10.30.9.
50. *Astronomical Diaries*, – 275.
51. Livy 38.16.11.

52. Allen, *Attalid Kingdom*, 136–139; Francois Chamoux, 'Pergame et les Galates', *Revue de Etudes Grecques* (1988), 492–500.

53. Justin 25.1.2–10 and 2.1–7; Diogenes Laertius 2.141; W. W. Tarn, *Antigonos Gonatas*, (London 1913), 165.

54. Appian, *Syr.*, 65; Lucian, *Zeuxis*, 9–11.

55. Paul Moraux, 'L'establissement des Galates en Asie Mineure', *Istanbuler Mitteilungen* 7, (1957), 56–75; Mitchell, *Anatolia*, 19–20.

56. Worrle, *Chiron* 5, a heavy load of interpretation has been put on this inscription; from the point of view of Galatian raids it must be seen as one more item of evidence; to build a chronological theory on it seems too much.

57. Jones, *Cities*, 42–43; this will be considered in more detail in Chapter 12.

58. R. M. Errington, *A History of Macedonia*, (California 1990), 163–164.

59. *Vita Aratoi*; Diogenes Laertios 7.1.8.

60. Worrle, *Chiron* 5 – see note 56.

61. Porphyry, *FGrH* 160 F 32.5.

62. B. Bar-Kochva, 'On the Sources and Chronology of Antiochos I's battle against the Galatians', *Proceedings of the Cambridge Philosophical Society* 19, (1973), 1–8, written before the publication of the new inscription, concluded that 272 was the better date; but this would involve Antiochos rushing back and forth between Galatian and Egyptian enemies and since he seems to have been the aggressor in the Syrian war, it seems best to have him finish one war before starting another.

63. Pausanias 10.32.4.

64. Mitchell, *Anatolia*, 7–18.

Chapter 11

1. *Astronomical Diaries*, 274.

2. Justin 17.2.9–10.

3. Pausanias 1.7.3; Porphyry, *FGrH* 260 F 32.4; Eusebios, Chronographia 1.40.5.

4. *Astronomical Diaries*, 274.

5. Pausanias 1.7.1; Callimachos 4.185–187; H.P. Laubscher, 'Ein Ptolemaischer Gallierdenkmal', *Antike Welt* 32, (1987), 131–159.

6. *Astronomical Diaries*, 274.

7. Ibid.

8. Ibid, -275.

9. Trogus, *Prologue* 26; A. Kuhrt and S. M. Sherwin-White, 'Aspects of Seleukid Royal Ideology: the Cylinder of Antiochos I from Borsippa', *JHS* 111, 1991, 71–85.

10. Ptolemy's journey is noted on the Pithom Stele, G. Roeder, *Das Agyptische Gottwelt*, (Zurich 1959), Doc. II; also Theokritos Idyll 17.98–101.

11. Polyainos 4.15 (the expedition was Antiochos III's).

12. Refuted by David Lorton, 'The supposed expedition of Ptolemy II to Persia', *Journal of Egyptian Archaeology* 59, (1971), 160–194.

13. J. D. Grainger, *The Syrian Wars*, (Leiden 2010), 84–87.

14. *Astronomical Diaries* 270.

15. Austin 168.

16. Stephanus of Byzantium, sv 'Ankyra' = *FGrH* 740, F 14.

17. Mitchell, *Anatolia*, 19–20.

18. *Astronomical Diaries*, 276.

19. Grayson 11.

20. Grayson 12.
21. Diodoros 19.15.2; Appian, *Syr.*, 53.
22. J. Balty, 'L'Apamène antique et les limites de la Syria secunda', in *La Géographie administrative et politique d'Alexandre a Mahomet*, (Strasbourg n.d.), 41–75.
23. This and the following section are based on my *Cities of Seleukid Syria*, where the more detailed argument is laid out, with plans and full references.
24. Aperghis, *Economy*, ch 4.
25. Houghton, *Seleucid Coins, passim.*
26. B. Bar-Kochva, *The Seleukid Army*, (Cambridge 1979).
27. Austin 164.
28. *OGIS* 220 = *I. Ilion* 34 = Austin 165.
29. *OGIS* 222 = *I. Erythrai* 504 = Austin 169.
30. *OGIS* 223 = *I. Erythrai* 31 = Austin 170.
31. *I. Ilion* 45B = Austin 171.
32. *OGIS* 221 = *I. Ilion* 33 = Austin 164.

Chapter 12
1. Ogden, *Polygamy*, 124–125, being, as he says, 'duly cautious'.
2. Trogus, *Prologue*, 26.
3. Ibid.
4. A. Kuhrt and S. M. Sherwin-White, 'Aspects of Seleukid Royal Ideology: the Cylinder of Antiochos I from Borsippa', *JHS* 111, (1991), 71–85.
5. J. D. Grainger, *Cities of Pamphylia*, (Oxford 2009), 81.
6. Cohen, *Hellenistic Settlements/Asia*, 131–132.
7. *OGIS* 229 = Austin 174.
8. Strabo 12.8.15; Cohen, *Hellenistic Settlements/Asia*, 281–285.
9. Richard A. Billows, *Kings and Colonists, Aspects of Macedonian Imperialism*, (Leiden 1994), discusses in Chapter 6 the Macedonians who settled in Asia, though few can be exactly dated; also Jones, *Cities*, 44–45.
10. Pliny *NH* 5.120; Strabo 13.4.13; Cohen, *Hellenistic Settlements/Asia*, 209–212.
11. *OGIS* 234; Stephanus of Bysantium, 'Alabanda'; Cohen, *Hellenistic Settlements/Asia*, 248–250.
12. Strabo 14.4.46; Jones, *Cities* 44.
13. Strabo 14.2.25; Stratonikeia: Cohen, *Hellenistic Settlements/Asia*, 268–273.
14. Allen, *Attalid Kingdom* 15–16.
15. *OGIS* 748.
16. Jones, *Cities* 42 and note 24; the significance of the coins is that they show that the city must have been named for the Seleukid Stratonike, not the Attalid queen of that name, who was the wife of Eumenes II in the time after 191; Cohen, *Hellenistic Settlements/Asia*, 232–238.
17. Strabo 13.1.33; Jones, *Cities* 42; Cohen, *Hellenistic Settlements/Asia*, 148–151.
18. *OGIS* 219 = Austin 162.
19. Jones, *Cities* 128–129; Cohen, *Hellenistic Settlements/Asia*, 285–290 (Apollonia), 349–350 (Seleukeia).
20. Jones, *Cities*, 129 and note 10; Cohen, *Hellenistic Settlements/Asia*, 278–281
21. Jones, *Cities*, 141; Cohen, *Hellenistic Settlements/Asia*, 348–349.
22. Mitchell, *Anatolia*, 17–18.
23. Jones, *Cities* 128; Cohen, *Hellenistic Settlements/Asia*, 346–348.

24. Pliny *NH* 5.108; Jones, *Cities* 43.
25. Apollonia: Jones, *Cities* 43; Cohen, *Hellenistic Settlements/Asia*, 253–255; Herakleia Salbake is generally ignored; W. M. Ramsay, *Cities and Bishoprics of Phrygia*, (Oxford 1895), 189–191 mentions it briefly.
26. Cohen, *Hellenistic Settlements/Asia*, 305–308.
27. Pliny *NH* 5.105; Ramsay, *Cities and Bishoprics*, ch. 2, with the plan facing p. 35.
28. See the list in Billows, *Kings and Colonists*, 179.
29. Paul Moraux, 'L'etablissement des Galates en Asie Mineure', *Istanbuler Mitteilungen*, 7, (1957), 56–75.
30. Strabo 13.4.2.
31. Ibid.
32. *OGIS* 55 = Austin 270.
33. So Ogden, *Polygamy*, 59–60; the Son's identity has been a longstanding problem.
34. Trogus, *Prologue* 26; Athenaios 593; Welles, *RC* 14; Frontinus 3.2.11; Appian, *Syr.*, 65.

Chapter 13
1. J. D. Grainger, *The Syrian Wars*, (Leiden 2011), Chapter 5.
2. *Astronomical Diaries*, – 261.
3. A. Davesne, 'Le tresor d'Audincik, 1974', in M. Amandry and G. Le Rider (eds), *Tresors et circulation monetaire en Anatolie antique*, (Paris 1994), 37–43.
4. A. Davesne, 'Les Ptolemies en Seléucide: le trésor d'Huseyinli', *Revue Numismatique* (1992), 23–36.
5. A. Davesne, 'Le Deuxième Guerre de Syrie ... et les temoinages numismatiques', in M. Amandry and S. Hurter (eds), *Travaux de numistiques grecques offerts à Georges le Rider*, (London 1999), 123–124.
6. J.-P. Rey-Coquais, *Arados et sa Perée*, (Paris 1974); J. D. Grainger, *Hellenistic Phoenicia*, (Oxford 1991), 55–56.
7. H. Seyrig, 'Arados et sa perée sous les rois seléucides', *Syria* 28, (1951), 206–217.
8. Plutarch, *Moralia* 45B; Athenaios 5.209e and 8.334a; *Lindos Chronicle* 37; Polyainos 5.18.
9. Houghton, *Seleucid Coins*, Antiochos II.
10. Strabo 12.4.2; Memnon, *FGrH* 434 F 14; Pliny *NH* 5.148; Eisebios, *Chronographia* 200; Cohen, *Hellenistic Settlements/Asia* 400–402.
11. *OGIS* 266 = Austin 20; Allen, *Attalid Kingdom*, 22–25; Jones, *Cities*, 47; *Hellenistic Settlements/Asia* 171–172 (Philetairia), 205–206 (Attaleia).
12. Strabo 13.1.67; Allen, *Attalid Kingdom*, 26.
13. In fact the deaths are only approximately dated, but the fact that they all happened about 255 is clearly important.
14. Memnon, *FGrH* 434 F 14.
15. Diodoros 31.19; the date is, needless to say, approximate.
16. G.T. Griffith, *The Mercenaries of the Hellenistic World*, (Cambridge 1935), *passim*; every ruler hired Galatians (or Gauls).
17. Justin 41.4.6–7; Strabo 11.9.2–3.
18. Justin 41.4.6.
19. *Astronomical Diaries*, -255.
20. The date of the marriage is not known, only its ending: Eusebios, *Chronographia* 1.40.5; Justin 28.1.2.
21. Lionel Casson, *Ships and Seamanship in the Ancient World*, (Princeton 1971), 90.

22. Athenaios 5.203c; J. D. Grainger, *Hellenistic and Roman Naval Wars, 336–31 BC*, (Barnsley 2011), Chapter 6.
23. E. Bresciani, 'La spedizione de Tolomeo II in Siria in un ostrakon inedito de Karnak', in W. Maehler and V. M. Strocka (eds), *Das Ptolemäische Agypten, Akten des internationalen Symposion .. 1976 in Berlin*, (Mainz 1978), 31–37 = Burstein 97.
24. C. C. Edgar (ed.), *Zenon Papyri in the University of Michigan Collection*, (Ann Arbor 1931), II.59242 and 59251; Porphyry, *FGrH* 260 F 43; Hieronymos, *In Danielam* 11.6.
25. Athenaios 2.45c; Pliny *NH* 7.33.
26. *OGIS* 225 = Austin 173 = *I. Didyma* II.492 = Welles, *RC* 18–20.
27. Borsippa: A. Kuhrt and S. M. Sherwin White, 'Aspects of Seleucid Royal Ideology: the Cylinder of Antiochos I from Borsippa', *JHS* 111, (1991), 71–86; Hierapolis and Ionian League: Lucian, *de dea Syria*, 18–25; Delos: *Inscriptions de Delos*, (Paris 1926–1979), nos 161, 199, 253, 385 and others; Sardis: W. H. Buckler and D. M. Robinson, *Sardis* VII.1, *Greek and Latin Inscriptions*, (Leiden 1932), no 86.
28. *Astronomical Diaries*, -274, -253.
29. Remarked by Sherwin-White and Kuhrt, *Samarkhand to Sardis*, 25.
30. There is no ancient testimony on this; it seems to be a modern assumption.
31. W. Clarysse, 'A Royal Visit to Memphis and the end of the Second Syrian War', in *Studies in Ptolemaic Memphis*, (Louvain 1980), 85–89.
32. *Astronomical Diaries* –250, -248.
33. M. Guarducci, *Inscriptiones Creticae*, (Rome, 1935–1950), Lyttos 8.
34. Grainger, *Syrian Wars*, 142–144.
35. Houghton, *Seleucid Coins*, Antiochos II; J. Youroukova, 'La Presence des monnaies de bronze des premiers Seléucides en Thrace: leur importance historique', *Studia P. Naster Oblata*, vol 1, (Louvain 1982), 115–126.
36. Justin 26.3.2–6; Polybios 10.22.3; A. Laronde, *Cyrène et la Libye hellenistique*, (Paris 1967), 381–383.
37. Austin 267.
38. *Astronomical Diaries*, – 247; Ogden, *Polygamy*, 129.
39. *Astronomical Diaries*, – 247.

Chapter 14
1. Poison: Appian *Syr.*, 65, Athenaios 595b – e (from the unreliable Phylarchos); natural: Polyainos 8.5 and (by implication) Justin 27.1.1.
2. Porphyry, *FGrH* 260 F 43.
3. Ptolemy III was crowned on the next day, 26 or 27 January: Holbl, *Ptolemaic Empire* 46.
4. A. Laronde, *Cyrène et la Libye hellenistique*, (Paris 1987), 382–415.
5. P. Gurob = Austin 266.
6. Ibid; F. Piejko, 'Episodes from the Third Syrian War in a Greek Papyrus, 246 BC', *Archiv fur Papyrusforschung* 36, (1990), 13–27.
7. *Astronomical Diaries*, -245.
8. Porphyry, *FGrH* 260 F 43; he calls the two men 'rulers of Antioch', which must mean they were members of the city's ruling oligarchy; also Polyainos 8.50.
9. Austin 267; *Astronomical Diaries*, -245.
10. P. Gurob = Austin 266.
11. R. Duryat, *Arados hellenistique, étude historique et monétaire*, (Beirut 2005), 229–232.
12. *OGIS* 54 = Austin 268.
13. Appian, *Syr.*, 65; but the diarist knew nothing of his visit; see J. D. Grainger, *The Syrian Wars*, (Leiden 2010), 161–162.

14. Justin 27.2.2.
15. Ibid, 27.1.9; Jerome, *In Danielam* 11.7.6.
16. Jerome, *In Danielam* 11.7.7–9; Porphyry *FGrH* 260 F 43.
17. Eusebios, *Chronographia* 1.40.6; Justin 28.5.3.
18. Polybios 4.51.4; 8.22.11.
19. *OGIS* 229 = Austin 174.
20. Houghton, *Seleucid Coins*, Seleucus II.
21. Strabo 16.2.14; Duryat, *Arados*.
22. J.-P. Rey-Coquais, 'Inscription grecque découverte à Ras Ibn Hani: stèle des mercenaries lagides sur la cote Syrienne', *Syria* 65, (1978), 313–325 = Austin 273.
23. Strabo 16.2.12; Porphyry, *FGrH* 260 F32.6; Eusebios, *Chronographia* 1.40.6.
24. Athenaios 13.593c; R. S. Bagnall, *The Administration of the Ptolemaic Possessions Outside Egypt*, (Leiden, 1976), 170–171.
25. *I. Didyma* II.493 = Welles, *RC* 22 = *OGIS* 227 = Austin 175.
26. Bagnall, *Administration*, 160–161; P. M. Fraser, *Samothrace*, Inscriptions 39, 40; Polybios 4.35.13.
27. Houghton, *Seleucid Coins*, Seleucus II, Antiochus Hierax.
28. Cohen, *Hellenistic Settlements/Asia*, 157–159.
29. A. Jahne, 'Die "Syrische Frage", Seleukeia Pierien und die Ptolemaeer', *Klio* 56, (1974), 501–519.
30. J. D. Grainger, *Cities of Pamphylia*, (Oxford 2009), 101–103.
31. Justin 27.2.9.
32. Justin 27.2.7; Trogus, *Prologue* 27; Strabo 16.2.14; *OGIS* 214.
33. Polyainos 4.9.6 and 8.61; Justin 27.2.10–11.
34. Ibidem; Athenaios 13.577f – 578a and 593a.
35. O. Morkholm, *Early Hellenistic Coinage*, (Cambridge 1991), 190–191; Houghton, *Seleucid Coins*, Seleucus II; L. Robert, 'Inscription hellenistique d'Iran', *Hellenica* 11/12, (Paris 1960), 85–91.
36. Strabo 11.9.2–3.
37. Frank L. Holt, *Thundering Zeus*, (California 1999), has a fairly convincing reconstruction of events, which is followed here.
38. Justin 41.4.7.
39. *Astronomical Diaries*, -237.

Chapter 15

1. Frank L. Holt, *Thundering Zeus*, (California 1999), 153.
2. Romilla Thapar, *Asoka and the Decline of the Mauryas*, (Oxford 1997), 260.
3. Michael Mitchiner, *The Early Coinage of Central Asia*, (London 1973).
4. M. A. R. Colledge, *The Parthians*, (London 1967), 26, 67.
5. Strabo 11.9.1; Pliny *NH* 6.44; M.-L. Chaumont, 'Etude d'histoire parthe II: capitals et residences des premiers Arsacides', *Syria* 50, (1973), 217–222.
6. Those in Hyrkania were still functioning a generation later: Polybios 10.31.6–11.
7. Allen, *Attalid Kingdom*, 186.
8. Justin 27.2.12.
9. *OGIS* 269–277 = Austin 231; Trogus, *Prologue* 27.
10. Allen, *Attalid Kingdom*, app. 2.
11. Livy 38.16.13.

12. C. Boehringer, 'Antiochos Hierax am Hellespont;, in M. J. Price, A. Barnett and R. Bland (eds), *Essays in Honour of Robert Carson and Kenneth Jenkins*, (London 1993), 37–47; Houghton, *Seleucid Coins*, Antiochus Hierax.

13. Polyainos 4.17.

14. Houghton, *Seleucid Coins*, Antiochus Hierax.

15. Polyainos 4.17.

16. Justin 27.3.9–10; Aelian, *Animal*, 6.44; Pliny *NH* 7.158.

17. Porphyry, *FGrH* 260 F 32.8.

18. Justin 41.5.1.

19. To take only one collection, D. B. Weisberg, *Late Babylonian Texts in the Oriental Institute*, (Malibu 1991), lists five texts dated to the reign of Seleukos II out of 30 which are dated to a particular reign.

20. *Astronomical Diaries*, -273 and -241, for example.

21. Ibid, -234.

22. Eusebios, *Chronographia* 1.40.5; Justin 28.1.4 (with several errors).

23. Strabo 16.2.4–7.

24. *Astronomical Diaries*, -230.

25. Ibid, -229.

26. Polybios 5.40.6–42.3.

27. S. M. Sherwin-White, 'Ritual for a Seleucid King at Babylon', *JHS* 103, 1983, 156–159.

28. Houghton, *Seleucid Coins*, Seleucus III; J.-P. Rey-Coquais, *Arados et sa Peree*, (Paris 1974); the mints did not operate until Seleukos III's reign, but the change dates from 227.

29. Justin 27.3.12.

30. *OGIS* 269–277 = Austin 236.

31. Porphyry *FGrH* 260 F 32.9; Appian, *Syr.*, 68; Polybios 32.71.4 and 5.40.5; for the date of the accession of Antiochos III, cf E. Grzybek, 'Zu einer babylonischen Königsliste aus der hellenistischer Zeit', *Historia* 41, 1992.

Abbreviations

1. Ancient sources and Collections of sources

Appian, *Syr.* – Appian, *The Syrian Wars*.

Appian, *Mith.* – Appian, *The Mithradatic Wars*.

Astronomical Diaries – A. B. Sachs and H. Hunger, *Astronomical Diaries and Related Texts from Babylonia*, vols I – III, Vienna, 1988–2002.

Austin – Michel Austin, *The Hellenistic World from Alexander to the Roman Conquest*, 2nd ed., Cambridge 2006.

Burstein – S. M. Burstein, *The Hellenistic Age from the Battle of Ipsos to the death of Cleopatra VII*, Cambridge 185.

FGrH – F. Jacoby, *Die Fragmente der griechischen Historiker*, Berlin from 1923.

Grayson – A. K. Grayson, *Assyrian and Babylonian Chronicles*, Locust Valley NY, 1975;

Houghton, *Seleucid Coins* – Arthur Houghton and Catherine Lorber, *Seleucid Coins, a Comprehensive Catalogue*, Lancaster PA, 2002.

I. Didyma – A. Rehm, *Milet*, vol. 3, *Die Inschriften*, Berlin 1914.

I. Erythrai – H. Engelmann and R. Merkelbach, *Die Inschriften von Erythrai und Klazomenai*, Bonn 1973.

I. Ilion – P. Frisch, *Die Inschriften von Ilion*, Bonn 1975.

OGIS – W. Dittenberger, ed., *Orientis Graeci Inscriptionem Selectae*, Leipzig, 1903–1905.

Welles, *RC* – C. B. Welles, *Royal Correspondence of the Hellenistic Period*, New Haven 1934.

2. Modern Studies

Allen, Attalid Kingdom – R. E. Allen, *The Attalid Kingdom, a Constitutional History*, Oxford 1983.

Aperghis, Economy – G. G. Aperghis, *The Seleukid Royal Economy*, Cambridge 2004.

Billows, *Antigonos* – Richard A. Billows, *Antigonos the One Eyed*, California, 1990

Cohen, *Hellenistic Settlements/Asia* – G. M. Cohen, The *Hellenistic Settlements in Europe, the Islands and Asia Minor*, California 1995.

Cohen, *Hellenistic Settlements/Syria* – G. M. Cohen, The *Hellenistic Settlements in Syria, the Red Sea and North Africa*, California 2006.

CRAI – *Comptes Rendus de l'Académie des Inscriptions et Belles-Lettres*.

Holbl, Ptolemaic Empire – Gunther Holbl, *A History of the Ptolemaic Empire*, London 2001.

JHS – *Journal of Hellenic Studies*.

Jones, *Cities* – A. H, M. Jones, *Cities of the Eastern Roman Provinces*, 2nd ed., Oxford 1971.

Mitchell, *Anatolia* – Stephen Mitchell, *Anatolia, Land, Men and Gods in Asia Minor*, vol. 1, *The Celts and the Impact of Roman Rule*, Oxford 1993.

Ogden, *Polygamy* – D. Ogden, *Polygamy, Prostitutes, and Death*, London 1999.

Sherwin-White and Kuhrt, *Samarkhand to Sardis* – Susan Sherwin-White and Amelie Kuhrt, *From Samarkhand to Sardis, a New Approach to the Seleucid Empire*, London 1993.

Bibliography

(See also Abbreviations)

Adams, R. McC., *Heartland of Cities* (Chicago 1981).

Adams, R. McC. and H.J. Nissen, *The Uruk Countryside, the Natural Setting of Urban Societies* (Chicago 1972).

Allen, R.E., *The Attalid Kingdom, a Constitutional History* (Oxford 1983).

Atkinson, K. M. T., 'The Seleucids and the Greek Cities of Western Asia Minor,' *Antichthon* 2 (1978), 32–57.

Aymard, A., 'Une ville de la Babylonie Seleucid d'après les contrats cunéiformes', *Revue des Etudes Anciennes* 40 (1938), 5–42;

Badian, E., 'The Struggle for the Succession to Alexander the Great', *Gnomon* 34 (1962).

Bagnall, Roger A., *The Administration of the Ptolemaic Possession Outside Egypt* (Leiden 1976).

Bagnall, A., 'The Origins of Ptolemaic Cleruchs', *Bulletin of the American Society of Papyrologists* 21 (1984), 7–20.

Balty, J., 'L'Apamène antique et les limites de la Syria Secunda', in *La géographie administrative et politique d'Alexandre à Mahomet* (Strasbourg, n.d.), 41–75.

Bar-Kochva, B., 'On the Sources and Chronology of Antiochos I's battle against the Galatians', *Proceedings of the Cambridge Philosophical Society* 199 (NS 19) (1973), 1–8.

Bar-Kochva, B., *The Seleukid Army* (Cambridge 1979).

Beaulieu, Paul-Alain, 'Textes Administratives inedits d'èpoque hellenisiques provenant des archives du Bit Res', *Revue Assyriologie* 32 (1989), 53–81.

Beek, Martín A., *Atlas of Mesopotamia* (trans. D.R. Walsh, ed. H. H. Rowley) (London 1962).

Bernard, P., 'Fouilles de la mission franco-sovietique à l'ancienne Samarkand (Afrasiab), 1989,' (*CRAI* 1990), 356–380.

Bernard, P., 'Fouilles de la mission franco-ouzbeque à l'ancienne Samarkand, 1990–1991', (*CRAI* 1992), 275–311.

Bernard, P. *et al.*, *Fouilles d'Ai Khanoum* (Paris, from 1973).

Bernard, P. and H.-P. Francfort, *Etudes de géographie historique sur la plaine d'Ai Khanoum (Afghanistan)* (Paris 1978).

Bernard, P., 'Herakles, les grottes de Karafto et le sanctuaire du mont Sambulos en Iran', *Studia Iranica* 9 (1980), 301–324.

Bevan, E. R., *The House of Seleucus*, 2 vols (London 1902), (reprinted 1966).

Billows, Richard A., *Kings and Colonists, Aspects of Macedonian Imperialism* (Leiden 1995).

Billows, Richard A., 'Anatolian Dynasts: the Case of the Macedonian Eupolemos in Karia', *Classical Antiquity* 8 (1982), 173–206.

Boehringer, C., 'Antiochos Hierax am Hellespont', in M. J. Price, A. Barnett and R. Bland (eds), *Essays in Honour of Robert Carson and Kenneth Jenkins* (London 1993), 37–47.

Bosworth, A. B. and P.V. Wheatley, 'The Origin of the Pontic House', *JHS* 118 (1998), 155–164.

Bosworth, A. B., *The Legacy of Empire, Politics, Warfare and Propaganda under the Successors* (Oxford 2002).

Bouché-Leclercq, A., *Histoire des Seléucides*, 2 vols (Paris 1913).

Brashear, William M., 'A New Fragment on Seleucid History', *Atti del XVII Congresso Internazionale de Papirologia* (Naples 1984), 345–350.

Breebaart, A. H., 'King Seleucus, Antiochus and Stratonice', *Mnemosyne* 20 (1967), 154–164.

Bresciani, E., 'La spedizione de Tolomeo II in Siria in un ostrakon inedito de Karnak', in W. Maehler and V. M. Strocka (eds), *Das Ptolemäische Agypten, Akten des internationalen Symposion .. 1976 in Berlin* (Mainz 1978), 31–37.

Broderson, K., 'Die Liebeskranke Königssohn und die Seleukidische Herrshaftsauffassung', *Athenaeum* 63 (1985), 459–469.

Cambridge Ancient History, vols VII and VIII, 2nd ed., (Cambridge 1984 and 1989).

Casson, Lionel, *Ships and Seamanship in the Ancient World* (Princeton 1971).

Chamoux, Francois, 'Pergame et les Galates', *Revue de Etudes Grecques* (1988), 492–500.

Chaumont, M.-L., 'Etude d'histoire parthe II: capitals et residences des premiers Arsacides', *Syria* 50 (1973), 217–222.

Clarysse, W., 'A Royal Visit to Memphis and the end of the Second Syrian War', in *Studies in Ptolemaic Memphis* (Louvain 1980), 85–89.

Cohen, G. M., *The Seleucid Colonies, Historia* Einzelschriften 34 (Wiesbaden 1978).

Colledge, M. A. R., *The Parthians* (London 1967).

Cook, J. M., *The Persian Empire* (London 1983).

Cumont, Franz, 'The Population of Syria', *Journal of Roman Studies* 26 (1936), 187–190.

Davesne, A., 'Le trésor d'Audincik, 1974', in M. Amandry and G. Le Rider (eds), *Trésors et circulation monétaire en Anatolie antique* (Paris 1994), 37–43.

Davesne, A., 'Les Ptolemies en Seleucide: le trésor d'Huseyinli', *Revue Numismatique* (1992), 23–36.

Davesne, A., 'Le Deuxieme Guerre de Syrie ... et les temoinages numismatiques', in M. Amandry and S. Hurter (eds), *Travaux de numistiques grecques offerts à Georges le Rider* (London 1999), 123–124.

Devine, A. M., 'Diodoros' Account of the Battle of Gaza', *Acta Classica* 27 (1984), 31–40.

Doty, L. Timothy, 'The archive of the Nana-Iddin Family from Uruk', *Journal of Cuneiform Studies* 30 (1989), 65–91.

Downey, Glanville, *A History of Antioch in Syria* (Princeton NJ 1961).

Durayt, R., *Arados hellenistique, étude historique et monétaire* (Beirut 2005).

Eddy, Samuel K., *The King is Dead, Studies in Near Eastern Resistance to Hellenism, 334–31 BC* (Lincoln, Nebraska 1961).

Engels, Donald W., *Alexander the Great and the Logistics of the Macedonian Army* (California 1978).

Errington, R. M., 'From Babylon to Triparadisos, 323–320 BC', *JHS* 90 (1970), 49–77.

Errington, R. M., *A History of Macedonia* (California 1990).

Fraser, P. M., *Cities of Alexander the Great* (Oxford 1996).

Funck, B., 'Zur Innenpolitik des Seleukos Nikator', *Acta Antiqua* 22 (1974), 505–520.

Goossens, G., *Hierapolis de Syrie* (Louvain 1943).

Grainger, J. D., *Alexander the Great Failure, the Collapse of the Macedonian Empire* (London 2008).

Grainger, J. D., *Seleukos Nikator, Building a Hellenistic Kingdom* (London 1990).

Grainger, J. D., *Cities of Seleukid Syria* (Oxford 1990).

Grainger, J. D., *The Syrian Wars* (Leiden 2010).

Grainger, J. D., *Cities of Pamphylia* (Oxford 2009).

Grainger, J. D., *Hellenistic Phoenicia* (Oxford 1991).

Grainger, J. D., *Hellenistic and Roman Naval Wars, 336–31 BC* (Barnsley 2011).

Green, Peter, *Alexander to Actium* (California 1990).

Griffith, G.T., *Mercenaries of the Hellenistic World* (Cambridge 1935).

Gruen, E.S., 'The Coronation of the Diadochoi', in J. Eadie and J. Ober, *The Craft of the Ancient Historian, Essays in Honor of Chester G. Starr* (Lanham Md, 1985), 253–271.

Grzybek, E., 'Zu einer babylonischen Königsliste aus der hellenistischer Zeit', *Historia* 41 (1992).

Habicht, Christian, *Athens from Alexander to Anthony*, trans. Deborah Lucas Schneider (Cambridge, MA, 1997).

Hadley, R. A., 'The Foundation Date of Seleucia-on-the-Tigris', *Historia* 27 (1978), 228–230.

Hadley, R. A., 'Royal Propaganda of Seleucus I and Lysimachus', *JHS* 94 (1974), 50–65.

Hauben, H., 'A Royal Toast in 302 BC', *Ancient Society* 5 (1974), 105–119.

Hauben, H., 'Philokles, king of the Sidonians and general of the Ptolemies', *Studia Phoenicia* 5 (Leuven 1987), 413–427.

Heinen, H., 'L'expedition de Ptolemée III en Orient et la sedition domestique de 245 av. J.C.', *Archiv für Papyrusforschung*, 36 (1990), 29–37.

Holleaux, Maurice, 'Lysias Philomelou', *Revue des Etudes Anciennes* 17 (1915), 237–243.

Holt, Frank L., *Alexander the Great and Baktria* (London 1989).

Holt, Frank L., *Thundering Zeus* (California 1999).

Holt, Frank L., *Lost World of the Golden King* (California 2012).

Honigmann, Ernst, 'Historische Topographie von Nordsyrien im Alterum,' *Zeitschrift der Deutsche Palasteins Verlag* (1923), 149–193, and 1924, 1–64.

Hopkins, Clark (ed.), *Topography and Archaeology of Seleukeia on the Tigris* (Ann Arbor 1972).

Huss, Werner, 'Ptolemaios der Sohn', *Zeitschrift für Papyrologie und Epigrafik*, 121 (1998), 229–250.

Invernizzi, Antonio, 'Seleuceia on the Tigris, Centre and Periphery in Seleukid Asia' in P. Bilde (ed.) *Centre and Periphery in the Hellenistic World* (Aarhus 1997), 230–250.

Jahne, A., 'Die "Syrische Frage", Seleukeia Pierien und die Ptolemaeer', *Klio* 56 (1974), 501–519.

Jones, A. H. M., *Cities of the Eastern Roman Provinces*, 2nd ed., (Oxford 1971).

Karttunen, Kalus, *India and the Hellenistic World* (Helsinki, 1997).

Kertesz, I., 'Ptolemy I and the Battle of Gaza', *Studia Aegyptica* (1974), 231–241.

Kraeling, C. H. (ed.), *Gerasa, City of the Decapolis* (New Haven 1938).

Kuhrt, Amelie, 'Akhaimenid Babylonia: Sources and Problems', in H. Sancisi-Weerdenburg and A. Kuhrt (eds), *Akhaimenid History* IV (Leiden 1990), 177–194.

Kuhrt, Amelie, 'Berossos' Babyloniaka and Seleukid rule in Babylonia', in Kuhrt and Sherwin-White (eds), *Hellenism in the East* (London 1987).

Kuhrt, A. and S.M. Sherwin-White (eds), *Hellenism in the East, the interaction of Greek and non-Greek civilizations from Syria to Central Asia after Alexander* (London 1987).

Kuhrt, A. and S. M. Sherwin-White, 'Aspects of Seleukid Royal Ideology: the Cylinder of Antiochos I from Borsippa', *Journal of Hellenic Studies* 111 (1991), 71–85.

Laronde, A., *Cyrène et la Libye hellénistique* (Paris 1967).

Laubscher, H.P., 'Ein Ptolemäischer Gallierdenkmal', *Antike Welt* 32 (1987), 131–159.

Launey, Marcel, 'Un episode oublie de l'invasion Galate en Asie Mineure 278/7 av. J.-D.', *Revue des Etudes Grecques* 46 (1944), 217–236.

Launey, M., *Recherches sur les armées hellénistiques* (Paris 1949–1950).

Lorton, David, 'The supposed expedition of Ptolemy II to Persia', *Journal of Egyptian Archaeology* 59 (1971), 160–194.

Lund, Helen S., *Lysimachos, a Study in Hellenistic Kingship* (London 1992).

Ma, John, *Antiochos III and the Cities of Western Asia Minor* (Oxford 1999).

McEvedy, Colin, *Cities of the Classical world*, ed. Douglas Stuart Oles (London 2011).

McEwan, Gilbert, 'Babylonia in the Hellenistic Period', *Klio* 70 (1988), 412–421.

Marfoe, Leon, *Kamid el-Loz, 14, Settlement History of the Biqa up to the Iron Age* (Bonn 1998).

Matheson, Sylvia, *Persia, an Archaeological Guide* (London 1977).

Mehl, A., *Seleukos Nikator und sein Reich* (Louvain 1986).

Mildenberg, Leo, 'A note on the coinage of Hierapolis-Bambyce', 273–283.

Mitchiner, Michael, *The Early Coinage of Central Asia* (London 1973).

Moraux, Paul, 'L'établissement des Galates en Asie Mineure', *Istanbuler Mitteilungen* 7 (1957), 56–75.

Morkholm, O., *Early Hellenistic Coinage* (Cambridge 1991).

Nachtergael, G., *Les Galates en Grece at les Soteria de Delphes* (Brussels 1977).

Oikonomides, Al. N., 'The Death of Ptolemy "the Son" at Ephesos and P. Bouriant 6', *Zeitschrift fur Papyrologie und Epigrafik*, 56 (1984), 148–152.

Olmstead, A. T., 'Cuneiform Texts and Hellenistic Chronology', *Classical Philology* 32 (1932), 1–14.

Peremans, Willy, 'Les Revolutions égyptiennes sous les Lagides', *Das Ptolemäische Agypten*, ed. H. Maehler und V. M. Strocka (Mainz 1978), 39–50.

Piejko, F., 'Decree of the Ionian League in Honor of Antiochus I, ca 267–262 BC', *Phoenix* 45 (1991), 126–147.

Piejko, F., 'Episodes from the Third Syrian War in a Greek Papyrus, 246 BC', *Archiv fur Papyrusforschung* 36 (1990), 13–27.

Raychaudhuri, Hemchandra, *Political History of Ancient India* (Oxford 1996).

Rey-Coquais, J.-P., 'Inscription grecque découverte à Ras Ibn Hani: stèle des mercenaries lagides sur la cote Syrienne', *Syria* 65 (1978), 313–325.

Rey-Coquais, J.-P., *Arados et sa Perée* (Paris 1974).

Rider, Georges le., 'Antiochos II à Mylasa ..., Note Additionelle', *Bulletin de Correspondence Hellenique*, 120 (1996), 773–775.

Robert, L., 'Inscriptions Seléucides de Phrygie et d'Iran', *Hellenica* VII (1949), 5–29.

Robert, L., 'Inscription hellénistique d'Iran', *Hellenica* 11/12 (Paris 1960), 85–91.

Robert, L., 'Encore une inscription grecque d'Iran', (*CRAI* 1967), 281–296.

Robert, L., 'Pline VI, 49. Demodamas de Milet et la reine Apame', *Bulletin de Correspondence Hellenique* 108 (1984), 468–474.

Roeder, G., *Das Agyptische Gottwelt* (Zurich 1959).

Rostovtzeff, M. M., 'Seleucid Babylonia: bullae and seals of clay with Greek inscriptions', *Yale Classical Studies* 3 (1932), 1–114.

Sachs, A. J. and D. J. Wiseman, 'A Babylonian King List of the Hellenistic period', *Iraq* 16 (1954), 202–211.

Sarkisian, G. Kh., 'New Cuneiform Texts from Uruk of the Seleukid period in the Staatsliche Museen zu Berlin', *Staatsliche Muzeen, Forschungen under Berichte* (1974), 15–58.

Sauvaget, J., *Alep*, 2 vols (Paris 1941).

Schmitt, H. H., Die *Staatsvertrage des Altertums*, vol 3 (Munich 1969).

Schober, L., *Untersuchungen zur Geschichte Babyloniens und der Oberen Satrapien zem 323–303 v. Chr.* (Frankfurt 1981), 128–129.

Scullard, H. H., *The Elephant in the Greek and Roman World* (London 1974).

Seibert, J., *Historiche Beitrage zu den dynastischen Verbundungen in hellenistischer Zeit* (Wiesbaden 1967).

Seyrig, H., 'Le monnayage de Hierapolis de Syrie à l'epoque d'Alexandre', *Revue Numismatique* 11 (1972), 11–12.

Seyrig, H., 'Arados et sa perée sous les rois seléucides', *Syria* 28 (1951), 206–217.

Seyrig, H., 'Seleucus I et la fondation de la monarchie syrienne', *Syria* 47 (1970), 290–311.

Shear, T. L., *Kallias of Sphettos and the Revolt of Athens in 286 BC* (Princeton 1978).

Sherwin-White, S. M., 'Seleucid Babylonia: a case study for the installation and development of Greek rule', in Kuhrt and Sherwin-White, *Hellenism in the East*, 1–31.

Sherwin-White, S. M., 'Ritual for a Seleucid King at Babylon', *Journal of Hellenic Studies* 103 (1983), 156–159.

Simpson, R. Hope, 'Antigonos, Polyperchon and the Macedonian Regency', *Historia* 6 (1957), 371–373.

Spek, R. J. van der, 'The Babylonian Temple during the Macedonian and Parthian Domination', *Biblioteca Orientalia* 42 (1985), 542–562.

Stern, Ephraim, *The Material Culture of the Land of the Bible in the Persian Period, 358–332 BC* (Warminster 1982).

Tarn, W. W., 'Two Notes on Seleucid History', *JHS*, 60 (1940), 84–94.

Tarn, W. W., *Antigonos Gonatas* (London 1913).

Tarn, W. W., 'The First Syrian War', *JHS* 44 (1934), 155–162.

Tarn, W. W. and G. T. Griffith, *Hellenistic Civilisation*, 3rd ed. (London 1952).

Tarn, W. W., *Hellenistic Military and Naval Developments* (Cambridge 1930).

Tcherikower, V., *Die Hellenistiche Stadtegrundungen vom Alexander dem Grossen bis auf der Romerzeit* (Leipzig 1927).

Thapar, Romilla, *Asoka and the Decline of the Mauryas* (Oxford 1997).

Verbrugghe, Gerald P. and John M. Withersham, *Berossos and Manetho* (Ann Arbor 1996).

Viesse, A. E., *Les 'Revoltes Eguyptienes'* (Louvain 2006).

Waggoner, N. M., 'The Early Alexander Coinage at Seleuceia on the Tigris', *American Numismatic Society Museum Notes* 15 (1969), 21–30.

Wallenfels, R., 'Apkallu Sealings from Hellenistic Uruk', *Baghdader Mitteilungen*, 24 (1993), 309–333.

Wheatley, P., 'Ptolemy Soter's Annexation of Syria 320 B.C.', *Classical Quarterly* 45 (1995), 433–440.

Wheatley, P., 'Antigonos Monophthalamos in Babylonia, 310–308 BC', *Journal of Near Eastern Studies* 61 (2002), 39–47.

Wheatley, P., 'The Besieger in Syria 314–312 B.C. Historiographical and Chronological Notes', in P. Wheatley and R. Hannah (eds), *Alexander and his Successors: Essays from the Antipodes* (Claremont, 2009), 323–333.

Wilhelm, Adolf, 'Kleinasiatische Dynasten', *Neue Beitrage zur greichische Inschriften* (Vienna 1911), 48–63.

Will, E., *Histoire politique du monde hellenistique*, 2 vols, 2nd ed., (Nancy 1979–1982).

Winnicki, Jan K., 'Der zweite Syrische kreig, in lichte des demotischen Karnak ostrakans und der greichischen papyri des Zenon archivs', *Journal of Juristic Papyrology*, 21 (1991), 87–104.

Winnicki, Jan K., 'Militäroperationen von Ptolemaios I und Seleukos in Syrien in den Jahren 312–311 v. Chr', *Ancient Society* 20 (1989), 55–92 and 22, (1991), 147–227.

Worrle, M., 'Antiochos I, Akhaios der Altere und die Galater', *Chiron*, 5 (1975), 59–87.

Youroukova, J., 'La Presence des monnaies de bronze des premiers Seléucides en Thrace: leur importance historique', *Studia P. Naster Oblata*, vol 1 (Louvain 1982), 115–126.

Index